C O
ILLUSTRATED

BIRDS
OF EASTERN AFRICA

HarperCollins*Publishers* Ltd
77-85 Fulham Palace Road
London W6 8JB

To my family and the people I love

First published 1995

3 5 7 9 10 8 6 4

97 99 00 98

ISBN 0 00 219937 8

Produced by HarperCollins Hong Kong

COLLINS
ILLUSTRATED CHECKLIST

BIRDS
OF EASTERN AFRICA

Written and illustrated by
BER van PERLO

HarperCollins*Publishers*

ACKNOWLEDGEMENTS

A book like this can only be produced with the help of many people. Therefore I would like to thank my friends Peter de Leeuw and Dick ten Bosch for their support and encouragement. I am also very grateful to Fleur Ng'weno and Yvonne Malcolm-Coe who guide the Wednesday morning bird walks from the National Museum in Nairobi; to Dr Leon Bennun, Patrick Gichuki and James Wachira for access to and help with the skin collection of the National Museums of Kenya; to Dr René Dekker for his advice and for allowing me access to the collection at the National Museum of Natural History in Leiden, the Netherlands (where I also met Dr Chris Smeenk who kindly lent me his slides of Kenyan raptors); to Dr M. Louette and Alain Reygel who made it possible for me to work in the Musée Royal de l'Afrique Centrale in Tervuren, Belgium; to Peter Colston for providing access to the collection of the Zoological Museum in Tring, United Kingdom and Dr Cees Roselaar (Institute for Systematics and Population Biology, Zoological Museum, Amsterdam) for his help and advice.

My special thanks go to my brother Cees van Perlo and to Ans Bloo for their generous help in preparing the distribution maps and the text.

PREFACE

This book was originally conceived in 1982 when I made my first trip to Kenya. While there I discovered that though there were several field guides available, I could not find one that contained all the birds I saw. Even the fine volumes of Mackworth-Praed & Grant – apart from being too bulky to carry around in the field – do not show all the species of eastern Africa. I decided therefore to make my own bird guide using Mackworth-Praed & Grant as an initial checklist.

At first I did not think about publishing the work, but encouraged by friends and family I presented the first version to Collins in 1989, and felt proud that they were willing to publish it once I had painted the coloured pencil plates in gouache.

The purpose of this book is to help the user to identify in the field all the birds that occur within the region covered, that is Kenya, Tanzania, Uganda, Ethiopia, Somalia and Socotra Island. Every species have been illustrated in order that they can all be identified. For easy field use the size of the book has been kept as small as possible by condensing the text and giving only the most relevant data.

Needless to say, as an amateur ornithologist (and artist), I do not pretend to participate in any scientific dispute.

Ber van Perlo
Wijchen
The Netherlands

CONTENTS

INTRODUCTION

SOURCES OF INFORMATION

During many visits to Kenya, and after living there for more than a year, I have seen the Kenyan landscapes and a great number of bird species – but of course not all of them. Therefore I have had to use other sources for this guide, the foremost of which have been the skin collections of Nairobi, Leiden, Tervuren and Tring. Also very important have been the written and recorded references listed at the end of the book.

AREA AND SPECIES COVERED

The area covered consists of Kenya, Tanzania, Uganda, Ethiopia, Somalia and Socotra Island. Data collection was finished by the latter half of 1992. All species mentioned by Short (1990) are depicted, as are the birds in the checklists of Ethiopia (Urban, 1971) and Somalia (Ash, 1983). The records of new species mentioned in *Scopus* (as recently as the July 1992 issue) are also included, as are some species (especially seabirds) whose presence in the area is not yet confirmed. Therefore this book should be comprehensive until 1993 for Kenya, Uganda and Tanzania and in the main will also be so for Ethiopia, Somalia, Djibouti and Socotra Island (Socotra Island, though no longer part of Africa, is included because it is so in Mackworth-Praed & Grant). The writer regrets that the new independent status of Eritrea could not be taken into account; it is treated as part of Ethiopia (though see Endemism, p. 13).

NOMENCLATURE

Sequence and names of species change constantly. This happens for instance when scientists lump species together or split one, so that a species may change to a race (the term used in this book for its shortness, instead of the currently more widely used term subspecies) or the other way around. To form some sort of foundation for this book, a system for sequence and names has been derived from the literature listed in the bibliography.
For the non-passerines (plates 1–55) the SEQUENCE follows the first three volumes of *The Birds of Africa*. For the passerines (plates 56–96) the family order of Voous (1977) has been applied and the genera and species sequence of Hall & Moreau (1970).
SCIENTIFIC NAMES and the related systematic level are based on the first four volumes of *The Birds of Africa*, Short (1990), Hall & Moreau (1970) and Johnsson (1993) (in that order).
ENGLISH NAMES are successively taken from Short (1990), the first four volumes of *The Birds of Africa*, Hall & Moreau (1970) and Johnsson (1993). In a few cases names and systematic status have been adapted to recent publications in *Scopus*, *Le Gerfaut* and *The Ibis*. Where I deviate from this approach a note (without discussion) is made under the species concerned. In some cases I have applied other combinations and sequences of species for the purposes of layout.

IDENTIFICATION

Identification of a bird is based upon how it looks (appearance) together with what it does (habits), where we see it (habitat), the chance or probability that we see it there (occurrence) and the sounds it makes (voice).

Appearance

Each species is illustrated as an adult male in breeding plumage. Other plumages are added when different, in which case the female is shown behind the male, in a more horizontal position. The symbols and the abbreviations used in the text and on the plates are as follows:

SYMBOL	EXPLANATION
♂	male
♀	female
imm	immature
br	breeding plumage
n-br	non-breeding (or winter) plumage

Note that for many (but not all) weaver species, sunbirds and whydahs, the males (and sometimes even the females) have a breeding and a non-breeding plumage. These are not shown because the non-breeding plumage of the (in some cases much) larger male closely resembles the normal female plumage, albeit often with one or more feathers of the breeding plumage shining through. The male non-breeding plumage of many other species (especially of northern migrants) are often not as deeply coloured as the full breeding dress and might resemble more or less that of the normal female plumage.

Every bird that has not attained full adult plumage, including juveniles and sub-adults, is called an IMMATURE in this book. If there is more than one plumage for immatures, the one most likely to be seen in the field is depicted.

Different RACES are only illustrated when they are recognisable as such. Some species have several similar looking races, as well as one or more that is more distinct. Only the distinct races are marked (as a, b, c etc.) on the plates and mentioned in the text.

A COLOUR FORM is a variation of the normal plumage. These forms are represented on the plates where at least 5–15% of the total population of a species is coloured differently in some way.

In the text opposite the plates (and sometimes running on to the next or previous page) information is given about size, main characteristics and differences with related species.

The **SIZE** is given in centimetres.

- For most species, size is the total length between the tip of bill and end of tail (L)
- For seabirds the size is given as wingspan (W)
- For a few tall birds the size is height (H)
- Because measuring birds is difficult, size data in literature are not uniform. For this reason sizes above 15 cm are given in multiples of 5 cm. This enables the user to compare the size of a bird he/she wants to identify with other birds.

Full descriptions of feathering and bare parts are not given because the plates contain sufficient information on these areas. Only when these are the most essential features or when they are not visible on the plate are they mentioned. Information about differences (or resemblances) with other species is restricted, especially when similar species are separated geographically or altitudinally.

Habits

Information about habits – though an important identification tool – has been given sparsely in order to keep the book at an optimal size.

An interesting habit of many bird species is that they lay eggs in the nests of other species, which consequently raise the hatchlings as their own young. This 'parasitism' is not only found with the Eurasian Cuckoo (and other cuckoo species) but also, for instance, with the group of indigobirds and whydahs. On plates 92, 93 and 94 the members of this group are illustrated near the species that they parasitise.

Habitat

Habitat can be defined as the home area of a free-living creature where it can find food, shelter and – in breeding condition – the circumstances in which to reproduce. A habitat can be described as a combination of climate, altitude, earth surface-form, soil type, humidity, vegetation and human influence.

Information about **ALTITUDE** has been given in multiples of 250 metres. Altitudes where the species may also be seen, though less frequently, have been put between brackets.

SYMBOL	EXPLANATION
<	Lower than
>	Higher than

- Areas above 1500 metres are called THE HIGHLANDS (but do not necessarily look mountainous).

- At about 3000 metres the AFRO-ALPINE ZONE starts (usually looking very rugged and mountainous indeed).

- FOREST is the habitat in which the canopy of tall trees is continuous and completely closed. Normally forests are confined to areas with higher rainfall and therefore have a rather moist atmosphere.

- WOODLAND is any other habitat in which trees dominate, usually in areas with lower rainfall. Woodland is (and looks) drier than forest.

- A WOODED habitat is a place with some trees, but where bush, scrub and grass tend to be more dominant.

- MIOMBO is a form of woodland where thornless *Brachystegia* and *Julbernardia* trees are dominant (Britton).

- CULTIVATION in this book is an area of small-holder plots.

Occurrence

Range, season and status determine the occurrence or possibility of seeing a species in a certain area. This information can be found on the DISTRIBUTION maps (after the plates).
The shaded areas are the known RANGE of the species.
The presence of most MIGRANTS depends on the northern or tropical seasons, but beware that individual birds may stay behind when the main body of the species returns for instance to its breeding grounds in Europe.

TEXT KEY	MAP KEY	EXPLANATION
NM (northern migrant)	Vertical arrows in the top left corner	Migrants from Europe and western Asia
AM (African migrant)	Horizontal arrows	Migrants coming from other parts of Africa
OM (other migrant)	Horizontal arrow in the Indian Ocean	Migrants from outside these areas
(NM), (AM) and (OM)	Interrupted arrows	Many species are partly migratory (local populations can be supplemented by non-local birds at certain times of the year)

The status of a species can be described as common, frequent, uncommon, rare or vagrant. The chances of seeing a particular bird refer to the likelihood of it being seen in its habitat and range. A species is rare when its range is very restricted or its total population very small. A vagrant lives in other parts of the world, reaches our area only by accident and hence has been seen there less than five times. Information about status on the maps and on the plates is given as follows:

STATUS	CHANCE OF SEEING SPECIES	MAPS	PLATES
Common	60–100%	Dark shading	Green number
Frequent	10–60%	Mid-grey shading	Blue number
Uncommon	Very small	Pale grey shading	Red number
Rare or vagrant	Negligible	Small cross	Red number

Always check plates **and** maps, because a green, blue or red number on the plates is given if a species is common, frequent or uncommon **in its own distribution area** (or the main part of it), so that for instance a bird that lives only in Somalia and is common there has a green number on the plate even though it does not occur in the other countries.

Because of insufficient information on species occurrence there, Djibouti is generally not indicated on the distribution maps.

Voice

Information about song and call is generally restricted to those groups of birds that have a hidden lifestyle (those that live in forests and swamps and those that are active at night), those that are difficult to identify from appearance only (nightjars, swifts, larks, pipits and cisticolas) and those that are well known for their vocal abilities (thrushes and warblers). Voice information for some other groups has been included because sound examples for most of the group members could be collected (swallows, small hornbills). In the vocalisations no distinction has been made between calls and songs. The most striking sound has been given as a transcription in italics between quotation marks. Attention has been paid to pitch, loudness, sound quality, length and structure.

10

General pitch has been given on a rough subjective scale:

DESCRIPTION	EXPLANATION
Extremely low (shortened to extra low)	As low as you can imagine (e.g. Eurasian Bittern)
Very low	(e.g. Feral Dove)
Low	Pitch of an average man's voice (e.g. Corncrake)
Mid-high	Pitch of an average woman's voice (e.g. Blue-eared Starling)
High	(e.g. Common Bulbul)
Very high	(e.g. Mousebird)
Extremely high (shortened to extra high)	So high that the sound is just within human hearing range (ear-reach) (e.g. Variable Sunbird)

LOUDNESS is generally indicated by general terms such as soft, loud and crescendo. Louder parts of the calls are put in capitals.

SOUND QUALITY has been described in terms like shrieking, magpie-like, liquid etc. Often songs and calls are compared to those of other birds like reed warblers (for example the well-known Eurasian Reed Warbler *Acrocephalus scirpaceus*, 68.7) or to the miauling of a domestic cat.

LENGTH: if a transcription ends on '-' the call or song goes on with at least three similar notes, syllables or phrases.

STRUCTURE: changes in pitch are often indicated by â, ê, î, ô or û for parts of the song that are higher and *a*, *e*, *i*, *o*, or *u* for parts that are lower. The way in which notes follow each other is described in terms like accelerated, staccato and unstructured, and by the way the parts of a transcription are connected. For instance, in '*treet treet treet*' each syllable is well separated, '*treet-treet-treet*' sounds as one 'word' and '*treettreettreet*' is almost a trill.

A **strophe** is a recognisable complete part of a bird's repertoire that can be dissected into successive phrases, syllables and notes. Strophes can, however, be as short as one note.

A special feature of the song and/or call of many bird species is that it is given in **duet**. This means that two birds (normally a female and a male) produce sounds that might follow each other so closely or are interwoven so harmoniously that the resulting song or call sounds as though it is from a single bird.

Endemism

This is a fascinating phenomenon. An endemic is a species that occurs only in an area with well-defined boundaries like a continent, a country or an island.

The endemic birds of the countries covered by this book are marked E at the end of the relevant text entry, followed by the name of the country to which they belong (in brackets). Since the independence of Eritrea in 1993, 17 of the 30 endemics of Ethiopia have lost this status because now they occur in both countries; these are indicated by square brackets, [E]. Of the remaining 13 there is one (59.8) that so far (1995) has only been sighted in Ethiopia and the status of which is thus still uncertain.

PARTS OF A BIRD

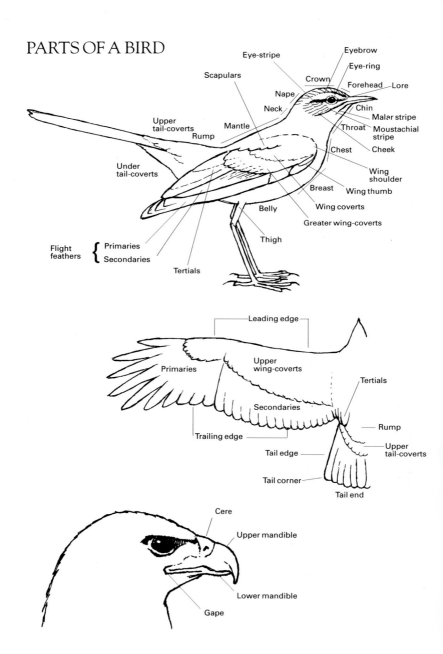

Eye-stripe
Eyebrow
Eye-ring
Scapulars
Crown
Forehead Lore
Nape
Chin
Neck
Malar stripe
Upper tail-coverts
Mantle
Throat Moustachial stripe
Rump
Chest Cheek
Under tail-coverts
Wing shoulder
Breast Wing thumb
Wing coverts
Belly
Greater wing-coverts
Thigh
Flight feathers { Primaries
Secondaries
Tertials

Leading edge
Primaries
Upper wing-coverts
Secondaries
Tertials
Trailing edge
Rump
Tail edge
Upper tail-coverts
Tail corner
Tail end

Cere
Upper mandible
Lower mandible
Gape

12

Plate 1

1

SECRETARYBIRD *Sagittarius serpentarius* H 125 cm.
Habitat: <3000 m. Dry, open, bushed and wooded, natural and
cultivated areas.

1

2 OSTRICH *Struthio camelus* H 250 cm. Race *molibdophanus* (a)
from C Kenya northwards, race *massaicus* (b) from C Kenya
southwards. Habitat: <2000 m. Dry, open plains and semi-desert.

a

b

♀

2

Plate 2

1 **BLACK-BROWED ALBATROSS** *Diomedea melanophrys* W 225 cm. Habitat: open sea; occasionally at harbours and creeks.

2 **SHY ALBATROSS** *Diomedea cauta* W 255 cm. Imm (not shown) also with white, black-edged under-wing. Habitat: open sea.

3 **SOUTHERN GIANT PETREL** *Macronectes giganteus* W 195 cm. White (a) and normal (b) forms shown. Habitat: open sea, seashore and harbours.

4 **PINTADO PETREL** *Daption capense* W 85 cm. Habitat: open sea.

5 **THIN-BILLED PRION** *Pachyptila belcheri* W 55 cm. Rather pale. Note distinct white eyebrow. Habitat: open sea.

6 **DOVE PRION** *Pachyptila desolata* W 60 cm. Note grey, almost complete, chest-band. Habitat: open sea.

7 **BROAD-BILLED PRION** *Pachyptila vittata* W 60 cm. Note all-white chest and throat. Habitat: open sea.

8 **JOUANIN'S PETREL** *Bulweria fallax* W 80 cm. Note slim appearance and lengthened middle tail-feathers. Habitat: open sea.

imm

1

2

a

b

3

5

4

6

7

8

Plate 3

1 **MASCARENE PETREL** *Pterodroma aterrima* W 90 cm. (Species not mentioned for Africa by Brown et al.) Note dark, stout bill and uniformly dark underparts. Habitat: open sea.

2 **KERGUELEN PETREL** *Pterodroma brevirostris* W 90 cm. Under-wing all dark but strongly reflecting. Habitat: open sea.

3 **HERALD PETREL** *Pterodroma arminjouiana* W 95 cm. (Species not mentioned for Africa by Brown et al.) Pale (a) and dark (b) forms shown. Note stout bill and pale, almost double, wing-patch. Habitat: open sea.

4 **SOFT-PLUMAGED PETREL** *Pterodroma mollis* W 90 cm. Note rather pied appearance. Habitat: open sea.

5 **WEDGE-TAILED SHEARWATER** *Puffinus pacificus* W 100 cm. Pale (a) and dark (b) forms shown. Note slender bill and long pointed tail. Habitat: open sea.

6 **WHITE-CHINNED PETREL** *Procellaria aequinoctialis* W 140 cm. Habitat: open sea.

7 **SOOTY SHEARWATER** *Puffinus griseus* W 100 cm. Note large pale wing-patch. Habitat: open sea.

8 **FLESH-FOOTED SHEARWATER** *Puffinus carneipes* W 105 cm. Note flesh-coloured bill and feet. Habitat: open sea.

9 **AUDUBON'S SHEARWATER** *Puffinus lherminieri* W 70 cm. Note small size and slender bill. Habitat: open sea.

Plate 4

1 **WILSON'S STORM-PETREL** *Oceanites oceanicus* L 17 cm. Note square tail and protruding feet. Habitat: normally open sea.

2 **WHITE-FACED STORM-PETREL** *Pelagodroma marina* L 20 cm. Note yellow webs of protruding feet. Habitat: open sea.

3 **BLACK-BELLIED STORM-PETREL** *Fregetta tropica* L 20 cm. Note black line down belly (difficult to see). Habitat: open sea.

4 **WHITE-BELLIED STORM-PETREL** *Fregetta grallaria* L 20 cm. An all-black form also exists. Note white belly without black line. Habitat: open sea.

5 **MATSUDAIRA'S STORM-PETREL** *Oceanodroma matsudairae* L 25 cm. No white primary shafts. Habitat: open sea.

6 **SWINHOE'S STORM-PETREL** *Oceanodroma monorhis* L 20 cm. Note white flight-feather shafts. Habitat: open sea.

7 **LEACH'S STORM-PETREL** *Oceanodroma leucorhoa* L 20 cm. Note forked tail. Feet not protruding. Habitat: shallow parts of the sea.

8 **RED-BILLED TROPICBIRD** *Phaethon aethereus* W 105 cm. Note dense back-barring and amount of black at wing tip of imm. Habitat: open sea.

9 **RED-TAILED TROPICBIRD** *Phaethon rubricauda* W 105 cm. Note blackish bill and amount of black at wing tip of imm. Habitat: open sea.

10 **WHITE-TAILED TROPICBIRD** *Phaethon lepturus* W 90 cm. Habitat: open sea.

11 **LITTLE GREBE** *Tachybaptus ruficollis* L 20 cm. Note cream-yellow patch at gape. Habitat: <3000(&>) m. Quiet rivers, lakes, dams, ponds and pools.

12 **BLACK-NECKED GREBE** *Podiceps nigricollis* L 28 cm. Note long slender neck and upcurved bill. Habitat: rift valley lakes; also on sewage ponds and even at sea.

13 **GREAT CRESTED GREBE** *Podiceps cristatus* L 50 cm. Habitat: 1500-3000(&>) m. Freshwater and alkaline lakes with cool water.

4

imm

8

imm

9

10

imm

11   n-br

12   n-br

13   n-br

Plate 5

1 **CAPE GANNET** *Sula capensis*   W 165 cm. Note whitish head of imm. Habitat: open sea. AM

2 **BROWN BOOBY** *Sula leucogaster*   W 140 cm. Adult with brown (not white) chest and neck. Habitat: open sea. (Might breed on Latham Island.) OM

3 **RED-FOOTED BOOBY** *Sula sula*   W 150 cm. White (a) and brown (b) forms shown. Imm has red feet, while adult has partly white tail. Habitat: open sea. OM

4 **MASKED BOOBY** *Sula dactylatra*   W 150 cm. Note white collar of imm. Adult has dark eye and white (not partly yellow) head. Habitat: open sea. (Breeds on Latham Island.)

5 **GREAT CORMORANT** *Phalacrocorax carbo*   L 90 cm. N-br plumage without white thighs. Habitat: large lakes and rivers with open banks and shores; also in lagoons, estuaries, marshes and inundations.

6 **LONG-TAILED CORMORANT** *Phalacrocorax africanus*   L 85 cm. Prefers perching on trees over water, not on the ground. Habitat: mainly rivers, lakes, marshes and inundations with fringing vegetation and trees; also in estuaries and mangroves.

7 **SOCOTRA CORMORANT** *Phalacrocorax nigrogularis*   L 80 cm. White cheek tufts missing when n-br. Habitat: mainly at sea and seashore.

Plate 6

1 **LESSER FRIGATEBIRD** *Fregata ariel* W 185 cm. The ♀ and imm very variable. Note form of demarcation between black and white on belly and in wing pit. Habitat: open sea.

2 **GREATER FRIGATEBIRD** *Fregata minor* W 220 cm. The ♀ and imm very variable. Note extent of white on head and black cap of ♀. Imm has little or no white in wing pit. Habitat: open sea. (Less rare than other frigatebirds.) OM

3 **CHRISTMAS ISLAND FRIGATEBIRD** *Fregata andrewsi* W 220 cm. The ♀ and imm very variable. Note form of demarcation between black and white on belly and in armpit. Habitat: open sea.

4 **GREAT WHITE PELICAN** *Pelecanus onocrotalus* W 315 cm, L 155 cm. Very large. More white than Pink-backed Pelican. Habitat: rift valley lakes.

5 **PINK-BACKED PELICAN** *Pelecanus rufescens* L 125 cm. Greyer and smaller than Great White Pelican. Habitat: mainly larger lakes but also rivers, marshes and inundations.

6 **AFRICAN DARTER** *Anhinga rufa* L 80 cm. Perches in trees with wings held half open. Habitat: mainly along fresh water bodies with fringing vegetation; sometimes in mangroves.

6

Plate 7

1   **WESTERN REEF-EGRET** *Egretta gularis* L 60 cm. White (a) and dark (b) forms shown. Note heavy, yellow, slightly decurved bill, extension of yellow on legs and, in dark form, extension of white on throat. Habitat: coral flats and other coastal areas; rarely at lakes.

2   **LITTLE EGRET** *Egretta garzetta* L 65 cm. White (a) and dark (b) forms shown. Note slender black bill and, in dark form, grey (not white) chin. Habitat: shallow fresh water areas; also mangrove creeks and coastal pools.

3   **MADAGASCAR EGRET** *Egretta dimorpha* L 70 cm. White (a) and dark (b) forms shown. Note rather heavy, black, slightly decurved bill, extension of yellow on legs and, in dark morph, white chin (not throat). Habitat: coastal areas.

4   **GREAT WHITE EGRET** *Egretta alba* L 95 cm. Gape extends behind eye. Habitat: lake margins, river banks, inundations and coastal areas including seashore.

5   **YELLOW-BILLED EGRET** *Egretta intermedia* L 70 cm. Note bicoloured legs and rather short bill. Habitat: lake and swamp margins, river banks, inundations and coastal areas.

6   **BLACK HERON** *Egretta ardesiaca* L 65 cm. Note characteristic shape of head and bill. Unfolds wings repeatedly (like a fast-opening umbrella) to shut off glare when fishing (a). Habitat: prefers coastal areas; also at lake margins, river edges, marshes and inundations.

7   **CATTLE EGRET** *Bubulcus ibis* L 55 cm. Goes to roost in low-flying V-formation. Habitat: grassland near cattle or game. (AM)

8   **GREEN-BACKED HERON** *Butorides striatus* L 40 cm. Often in horizontal stance with outstretched neck. Habitat: water with dense fringing vegetation; also on open coral flats.

9   **COMMON BITTERN** *Botaurus stellaris* L 65 cm. Habitat: papyrus, reed beds, rice fields and tall grass near water's edge. Voice: extra low, pushed-out, booming '*uhtHoo uhtHoo*' ('*uh*' not always audible). (NM)

10   **LITTLE BITTERN** *Ixobrychus minutus* L 35 cm. Note white wing coverts. Habitat: marshes, wet grassland and mangroves. Voice: mid-high, regular, dull '*woh woh woh*'. (NM)

11   **DWARF BITTERN** *Ixobrychus sturmii* L 25 cm. Note all-dark wings and yellow feet. Habitat: thick reedy cover with some trees and shrub in or near marshes, inundations, mangroves, lakes and streams. Voice: mid-high, dull, barking '*wohwohwoh*'. (AM)

12   **RUFOUS-BELLIED HERON** *Ardeola rufiventis* L 40 cm. Often in horizontal stance. Habitat: swamps, inundations and reedy edges of lakes and swamps. Voice: rasping '*graaak*' and other grunts.

13   **MADAGASCAR SQUACCO HERON** *Ardeola idae* L 45 cm. N-br plumage darker-mantled and more heavily streaked than Squacco Heron. Br plumage probably not seen outside Madagascar. Habitat: wooded marshes and mangroves. AM

14   **SQUACCO HERON** *Ardeola ralloides* L 45 cm. The sudden sight of white wings on takeoff is spectacular. Habitat: mangroves, marshes, lakes and slow streams with fringing vegetation.

15   **WHITE-BACKED NIGHT-HERON** *Gorsachius leuconotus* L 55 cm. Active when dark. Habitat: dense forest undergrowth near slow streams and lakes, fringing vegetation of rivers and streams, and mangroves. Voice: very low, crow-like '*cra cra cra cra*'.

16   **BLACK-CROWNED NIGHT-HERON** *Nycticorax nycticorax* L 55 cm. Active when dark. Often gregarious. Habitat: lakes and rivers with bordering trees, bush, mangroves, papyrus or reed beds. Voice: mid-high, pushed out, short, barking '*wha*'. (NM)

Plate 8

1 **GOLIATH HERON** *Ardea goliath* L 140 cm, H 150 cm. Habitat: shallow water of lakes, rivers, creeks, marches and mangroves.

2 **GREY HERON** *Ardea cinerea* L 100 cm. Note yellowish leg colour. Habitat: open or reedy margins and nearby areas of lakes, rivers, marshes and estuaries. (NM)

3 **BLACK-HEADED HERON** *Ardea melanocephala* L 95 cm. Normally feeds far away from water. Note black colour of imm legs. Habitat: grassy areas, forest clearings, near lakes, rivers, marshes, estuaries and coastal areas.

4 **PURPLE HERON** *Ardea purpurea* L 90 cm. Skulking. Note general slim appearance. Habitat: papyrus and reed beds along lakes, rivers, dams, ponds and in mangroves; occasionally on coastal mud flats.

5 **WHITE STORK** *Ciconia ciconia* L 100 cm. Gregarious. Note white tail. Habitat: >1500 m. Any open habitat with large insects, mice, moles, frogs and other amphibians. NM

6 **BLACK STORK** *Ciconia nigra* L 95 cm. Rarely are more than 3 or 4 seen together. Note form of white triangle in wing pit with widening black at leading edge. With white (not black) upper tail-coverts. Habitat: tall grass, reeds and herbage near streams and other small areas of water, but also in open dry grassland. AM NM

7 **ABDIM'S STORK** *Ciconia abdimii* L 75 cm. Very gregarious. Note form of white triangle in wing pit with narrow black leading edge. Has black upper tail-coverts. Habitat: open grassland and farmland, often near settlement. AM

8 **WOOLLY-NECKED STORK** *Ciconia episcopus* L 85 cm. Gregarious at dusk. Habitat: <3000 m. Open shore of sea, rivers, streams and dams; also in grassland.

9 **HAMERKOP** *Scopus umbretta* L 55 cm. Builds very large nests, which are however often taken over by owls, kestrels, geese, ducks, pigeons, monitor lizards or snakes. Habitat: muddy margins of lakes, rivers, streams, dams, ponds and creeks.

10 **MARABOU** *Leptoptilos crumeniferus* W 260 cm, L 150 cm. Very large. Flies with retracted head and neck (unlike other storks). Habitat: dry areas including towns where it can feed on fish, small and young animals, carrion and refuse.

11 **YELLOW-BILLED STORK** *Mycteria ibis* L 95 cm. Note black tail (often difficult to see in flight) and pinkish colouring. Habitat: any habitat with fish; prefers larger water bodies.

12 **AFRICAN OPEN-BILLED STORK** *Anastomus lamelligerus* L 95 cm. Very gregarious. Feeds on molluscs with its specially adapted bill. Habitat: <1500 (&>) m. Shallow water. (AM)

13 **SADDLE-BILLED STORK** *Ephippiorhynchus senegalensis* L 145 cm. The ♀ has yellow eye. Habitat: any shallow water and swampy areas.

Plate 9

1 **WATTLED IBIS** *Bostrychia carunculata* L 80 cm. Feeds in groups. Habitat: grassland, farmland, marshes and open forests; roosts at cliffs. [E] (Ethiopia)

2 **OLIVE IBIS** *Bostrychia olivacea* L 70 cm. Difficult to see in its forest habitat. Habitat: >1000 m in Usambaras (Tanzania), >2000 m elsewhere. Open places in forests. Voice: mid-high '*wa waa waa wâ-waa*'.

3 **HADADA** *Bostrychia hagedash* L 75 cm. Calling noisily in flight. Note short legs. Habitat: <3000 m. Wooded streams, moist grassland, marshes, mangroves, cultivated areas, lawns and parks. Voice: shouts its name '*haa-daadaa*'.

4 **SPOT-BREASTED IBIS** *Bostrychia rara* L 45 cm. Habitat: forest streams and wooded swamps.

5 **WALDRAPP** *Geronticus eremita* L 80 cm. Birds in Ethiopia used to migrate from Turkey. It is unclear whether this species can still be seen in Ethiopia, as the breeding colony from where the birds came to winter in Ethiopia is now deserted. Habitat: rocky mountain sides and valleys, alpine grassland.

6 **SACRED IBIS** *Threskiornis aethiopica* L 75 cm. Habitat: wetlands, grassland, farmland, sewage ponds, lagoons and estuaries.

7 **GLOSSY IBIS** *Plegadis falcinellus* L 60 cm. Note slim, long-legged appearance. Habitat: swamps, inundations, lake margins and lagoons. (AM) (NM)

8 **LESSER FLAMINGO** *Phoeniconaias minor* L 100 cm. Habitat: alkaline lakes; occasionally estuaries. (AM)

9 **GREATER FLAMINGO** *Phoenicopterus ruber* L 140 cm. Habitat: mainly alkaline rift valley lakes; also estuaries and lagoons. (AM) (NM)

10 **SHOEBILL** *Balaeniceps rex* L 150 cm. Habitat: large swamps.

11 **AFRICAN SPOONBILL** *Platalea alba* L 90 cm. Habitat: shallow parts of larger (inland) water bodies and estuaries.

12 **EURASIAN SPOONBILL** *Platalea leucorodia* L 90 cm. Habitat: shallow parts of larger water bodies. (NM)

Plate 10

1 FULVOUS WHISTLING-DUCK *Dendrocygna bicolor* L 50 cm. Habitat: lakes and dams with some floating vegetation; also in swampy areas. Voice: high '*tuWêêh*' ('*tu*' very short).

2 WHITE-FACED WHISTLING-DUCK *Dendrocygna viduata* L 45 cm. More gregarious than Fulvous Whistling-Duck. Habitat: rivers, dams, inundations, coastal areas with some floating vegetation and swamps. Voice: extra high, sweeping, fast, fluted '*wêêtweet-weet*'.

3 EGYPTIAN GOOSE *Alopochen aegyptiacus* L 70 cm. Habitat: <4000 m. Habitat: rivers, streams, lakes, dams and ponds; normally not in coastal areas.

4 RUDDY SHELDUCK *Tadorna ferruginea* L 65 cm. Habitat: <4000 m. Dry areas with small water bodies or streams. (Breeds in Bale Mountains, Ethiopia.) (NM)

5 SPUR-WINGED GOOSE *Plectropterus gambensis* L 100 cm (♂), 75 cm (♀). Habitat: <3000 m. Large water bodies and wetlands.

6 BLUE-WINGED GOOSE *Cyanochen cyanopterus* L 70 cm. Often rests with neck between fluffed-out mantle feathers. Habitat: >1750 m. Marshes, wet grassland and alpine moorland. [E] (Ethiopia)

7 KNOB-BILLED DUCK *Sarkidiornis melanotos* L 75 cm (♂), 60 cm (♀). Habitat: <3000 m. Wetlands, often near or surrounded by woodland.

8 WHITE-BACKED DUCK *Thalassornis leuconotus* L 40 cm. Habitat: <3000 m. Secluded parts of lakes, dams and pools with some floating and fringing vegetation. Voice: extra high, sweeping '*witleêt*' ('*wit*' short).

9 AFRICAN PYGMY GOOSE *Nettapus auritus* L 30 cm. Habitat: <1750 (&>) m. Quiet, clear water with some floating and emergent vegetation. Voice: extra high, short, fluted '*tuctucwêêt-tuctucwêêtweetweet*'.

10 SOUTHERN POCHARD *Netta erythrophthalma* L 50 cm. Habitat: clear lakes with reedy margins. Voice: mid-high rasping Mallard-like '*rrrrha-rrrrha*'. (AM)

11 MACCOA DUCK *Oxyura maccoa* L 50 cm. Note shape and stance of tail. Habitat: <3000 m. Fresh (sometimes alkaline) shallow lakes with emergent vegetation. Voice: very low, dry, drawn-out, rattling '*purrrrrrr*'.

12 HARTLAUB'S DUCK *Pteronetta hartlaubii* L 50 cm. Habitat: well-wooded streams especially in forests. Voice: low, hurried, Mallard-like mumbling '*ruprupruprup-ruprup-*' (♂) and mid-high, loud, Mallard-like gaggling (♀).

13 TUFTED DUCK *Aythya fuligula* L 45 cm. Note yellow eye and, in ♀, white ring between bill and head. Habitat: open water of lakes, dams and rivers. Voice: very high, very liquid, very fast '*nâpjapjaak*' and high, sharp '*cratchcratchcratch*'. NM

14 FERRUGINOUS DUCK *Aythya nyroca* L 40 cm. Note white under tail-coverts; ♀ is less brilliant chestnut. Habitat: lakes, often between floating vegetation. Voice: Mallard-like but more rolling. NM

15 COMMON POCHARD *Aythya ferina* L 50 cm. The ♀ is the only darkish brown duck without (or hardly) any white on head. Habitat: lakes, dams and open water in marshes. Voice: as Mallard but more growling '*graaa graaa graaa*'. Also a very high, liquid squeaking. AM

Plate 11

1 **EURASIAN WIGEON** *Anas penelope* L 50 cm. Note bill shape and bent neck of ♀. Habitat: shallow, sheltered, open (parts of) lakes and dams mainly in the highlands. In Ethiopia also common in brackish and saline water near Red Sea. Voice: high, sweet, gliding-down, short whistle '*fiiuuw*'. NM

2 **GADWALL** *Anas strepera* L 55 cm. Bill more slender than Mallard. Habitat: <2500(&>) m. Wetlands with some open water. Voice: as Mallard. NM

3 **COMMON TEAL** *Anas crecca* L 40 cm. Note small size and in ♀ hazel (not red) eye. Voice: very high, short, cricket-like '*crick crick*'. NM

4 **CAPE TEAL** *Anas capensis* L 45 cm. Note red eye and bill. Habitat: mainly alkaline and brackish lakes. Voice: low, frog-like, soft muttering.

5 **MALLARD** *Anas platyrhynchos* L 60 cm. Habitat: wetlands, especially sheltered open water with submerged floating or fringing vegetation. Voice: well-known duck gaggling. NM

6 **YELLOW-BILLED DUCK** *Anas undulata* L 55 cm. Habitat: 1500 m. Lakes, dams, rivers, estuaries, pools and sewage ponds. Voice: as Mallard.

7 **AFRICAN BLACK DUCK** *Anas sparsa* L 55 cm. Habitat: 1500-4250 m. Montane, well-wooded streams; at highest levels in open pools and streams. Voice: mid-high, loud, Mallard-like '*crick crick crick*'.

8 **NORTHERN PINTAIL** *Anas acuta* L 60 cm. Note slender profile of ♀ accentuated by lengthened tail. Habitat: dams, ponds, estuaries and other fresh and brackish wetlands. Voice: high, liquid, short whistles '*friu-friu friu*'. NM

9 **RED-BILLED TEAL** *Anas erythrorhynchos* L 45 cm. Habitat: open shallow fresh lakes, dams and inundations with submerged, floating and fringing vegetation. Voice: high, Mallard-like '*pjehpjeh-pjèèh-pjèèh*'.

10 **HOTTENTOT TEAL** *Anas hottentota* L 35 cm. Habitat: shallow waters with fringing reed beds and papyrus. Also on large open lakes and dams. Voice: very high, dry chuckle '*tekêhkehkehkehkeh te-tɛkkêhteh*'.

11 **GARGANEY** *Anas querquedula* L 40 cm. Note rather distinct face markings of ♀. Habitat: mainly sheltered shallow parts of fresh lakes, dams and estuaries. Voice: low, dry, short rattles '*crrcrrc*'. NM

12 **NORTHERN SHOVELER** *Anas clypeata* L 50 cm. Habitat: <3000 m. Shallow fresh lakes, pools, inundation and marshes. Voice: mid-high rattling '*rataptap*' and '*keekerreck*'. NM

13 **CAPE SHOVELER** *Anas smithii* L 50 cm. Habitat: inundations, sewage ponds and other (often alkaline) water bodies. Voice: Mallard-like '*wêêk-wuhwuhwuh*'.

Plate 12

1 **OSPREY** *Pandion haliaetus* L 60 cm. Head of imm with less contrast. Habitat: coastal waters, estuaries, lakes and rivers. (AM) (NM)

2 **AFRICAN CUCKOO-HAWK** *Aviceda cuculoides* L 40 cm. Flies from tree to tree in light kite-like fashion. Habitat: <3000 m. Forest edges, woodland, bushland and scrubland.

3 **WESTERN HONEY-BUZZARD** *Pernis apivorus* L 55 cm. Many colour forms, only two shown. Note small protruding head and typical tail pattern in which some bars seem to be missing, but this is not always distinctive. Habitat: forest edges and open woodland. NM

4 **BAT-HAWK** *Macheiramphus alcinus* L 45 cm. Falcon-like but with lighter wing beat. Hunts only at dusk, mainly catching small bats. Habitat: <2000 m. Forest edges, woodland, lake and seashores near large roosts (caves) of bats. Also in towns. Voice: extra high, sharp '*wiiiu-wiiiu-*' slightly rising in pitch and volume.

5 **BLACK-SHOULDERED KITE** *Elanus caeruleus* L 30 cm. Habitat: <3000 m. Open, wooded and bushed areas including cultivations, plantations, parks and suburban gardens.

6 **SCISSOR-TAILED KITE** *Chelictinia rioccourii* L 30 cm. Habitat: semi-desert and open, bushed and wooded habitats with some grass cover. (AM)

7 **BLACK KITE** *Milvus migrans* L 55 cm. African race *parasitus* (a) throughout. Note yellow bill and dark head of adult. NM race *m. migrans* (b) throughout. Note black tip to bill, pale head and brown (not rufous) trousers. NE African race *aegyptius* (c) southwards to C Kenya. Note yellow bill, pale head, rufous middle tail-feathers and rufous trousers. Habitat: roadsides, suburban gardens and refuse sites.
Voice: very high, quavering, slow trill '*pihurrrrrrrrr*'. ('*pih*' extra high, lashing, short). (NM)

12

Plate 13

1 **AFRICAN FISH-EAGLE** *Haliaeetus vocifer* L 75 cm. Habitat: large lakes, rivers, inundations, mangroves and seashore. Voice: free, triumphant, Herring Gull-like *'waaak waaa waaa kaa-ka-ka-'* often in an unsynchronised duet with its partner.

2 **PALM-NUT VULTURE** *Gypohierax angolensis* L 70 cm. Habitat: <1500 m. Open forests and plantations with oil palms, the fruits of which it eats.

3 **LAMMERGEIER** *Gypaetus barbatus* L 100 cm. Habitat: 1500(&<)-5000 m. Open country near cliffs, gorges and steep slopes.

4 **EGYPTIAN VULTURE** *Neophron percnopterus* L 65 cm. Habitat: <2000(&>) m. Arid or dry, open and wooded country near cliffs. Often near cattle enclosures. In Ethiopia and Somalia often in towns and villages.

5 **HOODED VULTURE** *Necrosyrtes monachus* L 70 cm. Habitat: <3000 m. Wooded, bushed and open country.

6 **CONGO SERPENT EAGLE** *Dryotriorchis spectabilis* L 60 cm. Note large eyes. Habitat: <1500 m. Mid- and ground strata of dense forests.

7 **AFRICAN HARRIER-HAWK** *Polyboroides typus* L 65 cm. Habitat: <3000 m. Forest edges, moist wooded habitats and suburban gardens.

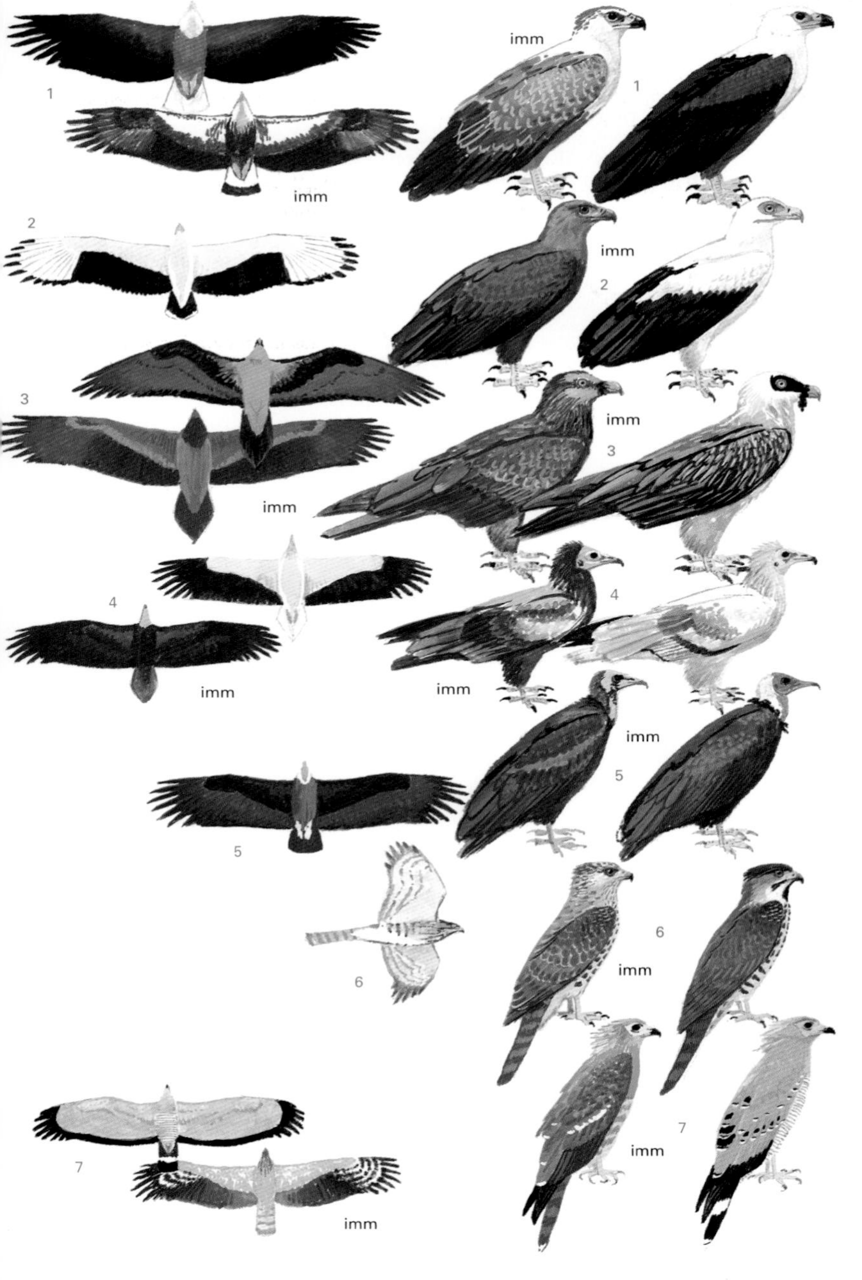
1
imm
imm
1
2
imm
2
3
imm
imm
3
4
imm
4
imm
imm
5
5
6
6
imm
7
imm
7
imm

Plate 14

1 **BATELEUR** *Terathopius ecaudatus* L 60 cm. Habitat: <3000 (&>) m. Hunts over dry open plains and bushed and wooded country.

2 **BROWN SNAKE-EAGLE** *Circaetus cinereus* L 70 cm. Rarely hovers. Note upright stance when perched on tree top. Habitat: <2000 m. Dense bush, scrub and woodland with baobab. Voice: very high piercing yelps '*tjark tjark tjark*'.

3 **SOUTHERN BANDED SNAKE-EAGLE** *Circaetus fasciolatus* L 60 cm. Normally skulks in dense foliage. Note yellow cere and gape and tail pattern. Light brown chest more or less sharply demarcated from darker belly barring. Habitat: <1500 m. Coastal forests. Voice: low cackle '*cuckcuckcuckcurrunk*'.

4 **BANDED SNAKE-EAGLE** *Circaetus cinerascens* L 60 cm. Normally perches in dead or poor-leaved trees. Note yellow cere and gape, and tail pattern. No contrast between breast colouring and belly barring. Habitat: <2000 m. Riverine woodland and forest patches in more open country. Voice: mid-high, toy trumpet-like '*uRuh uckuruuh*'.

5 **SHORT-TOED SNAKE-EAGLE** *Circaetus gallicus* L 65 cm. NM race *g. gallicus* (a) rare vagrant in Uganda and Kenya, N African race *beaudouini* (b) vagrant in NW Uganda and NW Kenya, African race *pectoralis* (c) (Black-chested Snake-Eagle) throughout. May hover; perches conspicuously. Note grey gape and cere and whitish or pale buff (not yellow) legs. Habitat: <3500 m. Dry, stony and lightly wooded plains and hillsides, often near water. Voice: very high or low, short, almost human whistle '*fiu fiu fiu*'.

1
imm
♀
♂
imm
1
imm
2
2
imm
3
3
imm
4
4
5a
imm
imm
5a
5b
imm
5b
5c
imm
imm
5c

Plate 15

1 **AFRICAN WHITE-BACKED VULTURE** *Gyps africanus* L 90 cm. White of adult's lower back not always very visible. Under-wing pattern more contrasting than in other vultures and griffons. Habitat: <3000 m. Open, bushed and wooded habitats.

2 **RUEPPELL'S GRIFFON** *Gyps rueppellii* L 90 cm. Habitat: open, bushed and wooded habitats. Generally in more arid areas than White-backed Vulture.

3 **EUROPEAN GRIFFON** *Gyps fulvus* L 100 cm. Note slightly buff colouring of both adult and imm but this not very visible in flight. Habitat: mountains and surrounding country. NM

4 **CINEREOUS VULTURE** *Aegypius monachus* L 110 cm. Habitat: open, mountainous areas. NM

5 **LAPPET-FACED VULTURE** *Aegypius tracheliotus* L 100 cm. Habitat: <3000 m. Open, mountainous, bushed and wooded areas.

6 **WHITE-HEADED VULTURE** *Aegypius occipitalis* L 80 cm. Habitat: <3000 m. Open semi-desert and bushed and wooded grassy areas.

Plate 16

1 **PALLID HARRIER** *Circus macrourus*   L 45 cm. The ♀ and imm very difficult to distinguish from Montagu's Harrier, though ♀ has less contrast in under-wing, darker upper-wing and more contrast in face than Montagu's. Pale primaries of ♀ under-wing more contrasting to darker secondaries than shown. Imm's black cheek is less distinctly demarcated from throat and neck than Montagu's. Habitat: <4000 m. Dry, open, natural and cultivated plains. NM

2 **MONTAGU'S HARRIER** *Circus pygargus*   L 45 cm. See Pallid Harrier. The ♀ underwing as shown, in imm pale borderline around dark cheek not as distinctly demarkated from neck sides as shown. Habitat: <4000 m. Open grass plains, occasionally in more wet areas.

3 **AFRICAN MARSH-HARRIER** *Circus ranivorus*   L 50 cm. Note barred tail and slim profile. Browner and with less contrast than Eurasian Marsh-Harrier. Habitat: <3000 m. Larger swamps; also grass- and farmland. NM

4 **EURASIAN MARSH-HARRIER** *Circus aeruginosus*   L 50 cm. Heavy build. Note pale head of ♂. Habitat: marshes, reed beds and tall grass. NM

5 **GABAR GOSHAWK** *Micronisus gabar*   L 35 cm. Normal (a) and dark (b) forms shown. Note pale grey breast, red cere and legs, black eye (except imm), white edges of secondaries and white upper tail-coverts. Habitat: <2000 m. Woodland, open bush and scrubland, suburban gardens and villages. Voice: very high, sharp, fluting '*weeh wick-wick*' often continued with rapid '*-wicwicwicwicwicwicwic-*'.

6 **DARK CHANTING GOSHAWK** *Melierax metabates*   L 50 cm. Note fine barring of underparts and barred upper tail-coverts. Folded wing looks even-coloured. Habitat: <3000 m. Open bush and woodland. Voice: high, loud, fluting '*wiooh wiooh wiooh wiorooh-wiorooh-wioh wioh wioh*' (each '*wioh*' sharply descending).

7 **EASTERN CHANTING GOSHAWK** *Melierax canorus*   L 50 cm. Note white upper tail-coverts. Folded wing rather contrasting white and grey. Habitat: <3000 m. Often in more open, drier habitats than Dark Chanting Goshawk. Voice: mid-high, resounding, rapid '*wuut-wuut-wuutwuutwuutwutwutwut-*' (accelerated and in crescendo) and mid-high, descending, bouncing, rapid '*wuuh - wicwicwickerrrrrrr*'.

Plate 17

1 **BLACK GOSHAWK** *Accipiter melanoleucus* L 45 cm (♂), 55 cm (♀). Normal (a) and dark (b) adults may be paired. Habitat: <3000 m. Forests, wood- and bushland, suburban gardens and parks.

2 **EURASIAN SPARROWHAWK** *Accipiter nisus* L 30 cm (♂), 40 cm (♀). Note white eyebrow, yellow eye, barred under wing-coverts and barred tail (without white) of ♂. The ♀ has white eyebrow and blacker (less chestnut-brown) barring of underparts than Levant Sparrowhawk. Habitat: <3000 m. Woodland and nearby open country.

3 **LEVANT SPARROWHAWK** *Accipiter brevipes* L 35 cm (♂), 40 cm (♀). Note dark, almost black, wing tips. Very similar to Shikra but larger and paler. Compare also under wing-coverts. Habitat: dry, wooded grass- and farmland.

4 **CHESTNUT-FLANKED SPARROWHAWK** *Accipiter castanilius* L 30 cm (♂), 35 cm(♀). Rather like African Goshawk but flanks unbarred chestnut and under-wing barred black-on-white. Also resembles Rufous-chested Sparrowhawk but that species has no bars below, has white eyebrows, but no white in tail. Habitat: dense forests.

5 **AFRICAN GOSHAWK** *Accipiter tachiro* L 35 cm (♂), 45 cm (♀). Note clear white tail-barring. Habitat: <3000 m. In and near forests, miombo and other woodland, mangroves and suburban gardens.

6 **LONG-TAILED HAWK** *Urotriorchis macrourus* L 60 cm. Habitat: <1500 m. Forest canopies.

7 **RUFOUS-CHESTED SPARROWHAWK** *Accipiter rufiventris* L 30 cm (♂), 35 cm (♀). Habitat: 1500-3000 m. Dense forests, woodland, plantations and nearby open country.

8 **OVAMPO SPARROWHAWK** *Accipiter ovampensis* L 30 cm (♂), 35 cm (♀). Normal adult (a) and dark adult (b) forms shown. Also normal imm (c) and rufous imm (d) forms shown. Note red cere (adult) and white stripes on tail shafts (difficult to see). Dark form less distinctly barred in wing and tail than dark Gabar Goshawk(16.5). Habitat: <2000 m. Open wood- and bushland.

9 **SHIKRA** *Accipiter badius* L 30 cm (♂), 35 cm (♀). Barring not visible on closed tail. Note very fine barring of underparts. Habitat: <3000 m. Woodland with tall-grassed areas and suburban gardens.

10 **RED-THIGHED SPARROWHAWK** *Accipiter erythropus* L 25 cm (♂), 30 cm (♀). Upperparts almost all black, with a few white feathers in scapulars. Note narrow white band over upper tail-coverts. Habitat: 500-1000 m. Dense forests.

11 **AFRICAN LITTLE SPARROWHAWK** *Accipiter minullus* L 25 cm (♂), 30 cm (♀). Habitat: <3000 m. Wood- and bushland; less in forests than Red-thighed Sparrowhawk.

Plate 18

1 **GRASSHOPPER-BUZZARD** *Butastur rufipennis* L 35 cm (♂), 40 cm (♀). Habitat: more or less wooded areas. AM

2 **LIZARD-BUZZARD** *Kaupifalco monogrammicus* L 30 cm. Note thick-set upright stance, dark eye and black median throat streak. Single white tail-band diagnostic. Habitat: <3000 m. Forest edges, woodland, cultivated areas and farmland.

3 **COMMON BUZZARD** *Buteo buteo* L 50 cm (♂), 55 cm (♀). Very variable (see flight patterns). Usually with pale band across breast. Often with chestnut-brown tail. Habitat: open forests and bushed grassland mainly in some well-established migration routes east and west of Lake Victoria and the rift valley west of Uganda. Voice: loud, explosive, rapidly descending '*miau*'. NM

4 **MOUNTAIN BUZZARD** *Buteo oreophilus* L 40 cm (♂), 45 cm (♀). No conspicuous white area between breast and belly. Generally dark brown, normally without any chestnut. Habitat: 1500-4000 m. In (and around) forests and woodland. Voice: very high, blown, slightly descending '*pifuuh*' ('*pi-*' very short and sharp).

5 **LONG-LEGGED BUZZARD** *Buteo rufinus* L 55 cm (♂), 65 cm (♀). Very variable (see flight patterns). Dark (a) form in E Africa more frequent than normal (b) form, which is rather buff and rusty red, with tail very pale and unmarked. Habitat: semi-desert and other open areas. Voice: loud, explosive, descending '*iau*'. NM

6 **RED-NECKED BUZZARD** *Buteo auguralis* L 40 cm (♂), 45 cm (♀). Note white (dark-spotted) belly of adult contrasting with dark breast. Habitat: open woodland. AM

7 **AUGUR BUZZARD** *Buteo rufofuscus* L 50 cm (♂), 55 cm (♀). Normal (a) and dark (b) forms shown. Note short tail of adult. Habitat: hilly open country, woodland, cultivated and suburban areas.

18

Plate 19

1 LESSER SPOTTED EAGLE *Aquila pomarina* L 60-70 cm. Under wing-coverts normally slightly paler than flight feathers. Upper wing-coverts slightly paler than those of Greater Spotted Eagle. Tight trousers of perched birds noticeable. Soars with 'drooping' wing tips. Rather straight rear wing-edge. Short, only slightly wedge-shaped, tail. Rump of imm with white 'U' shape. Habitat: open miombo and other woodland. NM

2 GREATER SPOTTED EAGLE *Aquila clanga* L 65-75 cm. Flight feathers less dark than under wing-coverts. Pale upper wing-patches (on primaries) larger than those of Lesser Spotted Eagle. 'Drooping' wing tips like Lesser Spotted Eagle. Habitat: dry, lightly wooded plains, often near water. NM

3 TAWNY (& STEPPE) EAGLE *Aquila rapax* L 65-80 cm. Pale and dark forms shown of *A. rapax nom.* (Tawny Eagle) and dark form of *orientalis* (a) (Steppe Eagle). Gape of Steppe Eagle extends behind eye. Heavy bill, loose trousers and short legs diagnostic. White patches on upper wing more contrasting than on spotted eagles. Steppe Eagle may have tawny nape but never as much as Imperial Eagle (20.1). Rather curved rear wing-edge. Soars with level or slightly upturned wing tips. Habitat: <3000 (&>)m. Dry, open, bushed and wooded country. Steppe Eagle not normally found further south than N Tanzania and uncommon in Uganda. (NM)

Plate 20

1 **IMPERIAL EAGLE** *Aquila heliaca* L 80 cm (♂), 85 cm (♀). Under wing-coverts of imm even-coloured, without white band. Rump of imm greyer than imm Tawny Eagle. Habitat: hilly, open, bushed and wooded country. NM

2 **WAHLBERG'S EAGLE** *Aquila wahlbergi* L 55 cm (♂), 60 cm (♀). Narrow tail gives flight silhouette distinct cross-form. Only eagle with (faint) tail barring. Pale form (a) rare. Habitat: <2000(&>)m. Wood-, bush-, scrub-, grass- and farmland. AM

3 **VERREAUX'S EAGLE** *Aquila verreauxi* L 80 cm (♂), 90 cm (♀). Note short inner secondaries. Habitat: <3500 m. Bushed and wooded mountain sides with cliffs and rocky ravines.

4 **GOLDEN EAGLE** *Aquila chrysaetos* L 80 cm (♂), 90 cm (♀). (Not illustrated and no map provided.) Not unlike Imperial Eagle but adult without white in mantle and scapulars, also slimmer and with relatively short secondaries. Immature very distinctive, overall dark with striking white basal half of flight and tail feathers. Habitat: Bale Mountains (>3500 m) in Ethiopia. (*Alauda* 61:200-201)

Plate 21

1 **LONG-CRESTED EAGLE** *Lophaetus occipitalis* L 50 cm (♂), 55 cm (♀). Habitat: <3000 m.
Forest edges, swampy bushed grassland, cultivation and suburban gardens.

2 **CASSIN'S HAWK-EAGLE** *Spizaetus africanus* L 55 cm (♂), 60 cm (♀). Note dark under wing-coverts.
Longer-tailed than Ayres's Hawk-Eagle. Habitat: 1500-2500 m. Forest canopies.

3 **BOOTED EAGLE** *Hieraaetus pennatus* L 50 cm (♂), 60 cm (♀). Pale (a) and dark (b) forms shown.
Note small size (as Common Buzzard). Characteristic mantle- and upper-wing pattern.
Habitat: <4000 m. Forests, dry woodland, open or slightly bushed and wooded hilly country and desert.
Voice: extra high, staccato '*dzipdzipdzipdzipdzip*' and very high, sweeping, staccato '*djip-djip-djip-djip-*'. NM

4 **AYRES'S HAWK-EAGLE** *Hieraaetus dubius* L 50 cm (♂), 55 cm (♀). White forehead of adult
diagnostic. Note barred under wing-coverts. Habitat: <3000 m. Canopy of forests and woodland.
Voice: very high, pressed-out '*fuwêêh fuwêêh fuwêêh*' ('*fu-*' short).

5 **AFRICAN HAWK-EAGLE** *Hieraaetus spilogaster* L 65 cm (♂), 80 cm (♀). Note oval wings.
Habitat: <1500(&>) m. Open wood- and bushland often near streams and rocky hillsides.
Voice: Fish-Eagle-like, slightly rising '*KleeeKleeekleeekleekleeklee*'.

6 **MARTIAL EAGLE** *Polemaetus bellicosus* L 80 cm (♂), 95 cm (♀). Habitat: <3000 m. Semi-desert and
more or less wooded and bushed areas.

7 **CROWNED EAGLE** *Stephanoaetus coronatus* L 80 cm (♂), 100 cm (♀). Note yellow (not pale grey)
feet and gape of imm. Habitat: <3000 m. Forests, miombo and other woodland. Voice: very high, excited
'*puwêepuwêepuwêe-*' undulating in pitch and volume, synchronised with up-and-down flight.

21

Plate 22

1 **AFRICAN PYGMY FALCON** *Polihierax semitorquatus* L 20 cm (♂), 25 cm (♀). Smallest African raptor. Roosts and breeds in nests of buffalo-weavers or sparrow-weavers. Note rather shrike-like stance on top of shrubs or trees. Habitat: <1750 m. More or less bushed areas and semi-desert with some trees of nesting weavers.

2 **LESSER KESTREL** *Falco naumanni* L 30 cm. Note pale under-wing of ♀. Gregarious; often together with other falcon and kestrel species. Hovers less than Common Kestrel. Habitat: open, bushed and wooded areas, short grassland and farmland. NM

3 **COMMON KESTREL** *Falco tinnunculus* L 35 cm. Hovers but also hunts from perch. Habitat: <4500 m. Open or lightly wooded country, often near cliffs and buildings. (NM)

4 **WHITE-EYED KESTREL** *Falco rupicoloides* L 35 cm. Note barred grey tail. Pale eye only visible at close range. Habitat: <2000 m. Dry, open country with scattered trees.

5 **FOX-KESTREL** *Falco alopex* L 40 cm. Under-wing all-rufous except flight feathers. Habitat: mountains and semi-desert with rocky hills.

6 **GREY KESTREL** *Falco ardosiaceus* L 35 cm. Note unbarred tail. Under-wing lightly barred. When perched, wing tips shorter than tail (unlike Sooty Falcon, 23.2). Hunts at dusk from perch or in low flight over ground (unlike Sooty Falcon). Habitat: <2000 m. More or less wooded grassland, often near water.

7 **DICKINSON'S KESTREL** *Falco dickinsoni* L 30 cm. Rather like Grey Kestrel but wing darker than mantle and tail barred. Habitat: open woodland (including miombo), plantations, edges of inundations. Often near palms.

8 **RED-NECKED FALCON** *Falco chicquera* L 35 cm. Hunts in swift flight. Habitat: <1500 m. Open, tall-grassed or swampy habitats with palms.

9 **EASTERN RED-FOOTED FALCON** *Falco amurensis* L 30 cm. Roosts in groups. Migrates from Asia, needs several days to cross Indian Ocean. Habitat: open country. OM

10 **RED-FOOTED FALCON** *Falco vespertinus* L 30 cm. Flight kestrel-like but without hovering and poising. May roost in large groups in high trees, even in towns. Habitat: dry, open and bushed grassland. NM

Plate 23

1   **ELEONORA'S FALCON** *Falco eleonorae* L 35 cm. Normal (a) and dark (b) forms shown. Looks slim and very long winged. Under wing-coverts darker than flight feathers. Habitat: a large group winters in Ruaha National Park, Tanzania. NM

2   **SOOTY FALCON** *Falco concolor* L 30 cm. Normal (a) and dark (b) forms shown. Note white chin of normal form. Habitat: moist, more or less wooded grassland. (AM) (NM)

3   **NORTHERN HOBBY** *Falco subbuteo* L 35 cm. Rufous confined to under tail-coverts, lower belly and thighs. Habitat: forest edges, miombo and more or less wooded natural and cultivated areas. NM

4   **AFRICAN HOBBY** *Falco cuvieri* L 30 cm. Habitat: <3000 m. Forest edges, but also in rural areas densely covered with plots and huts.

5   **LANNER** *Falco biarmicus* L 40 (♂), 45 cm (♀). Differs from Saker by being greyer with buff-rufous crown and tail barring. Longer tailed than Peregrine. Habitat: <3250(&>) m. Open country, often near cliffs or buildings.

6   **SAKER** *Falco cherrug* L 45 cm (♂), 60 cm (♀). Note pale (not buff-rufous) crown. Habitat: marshes and lake margins with nearby trees. NM

7   **PEREGRINE** *Falco peregrinus* L 35 cm (♂), 50 cm (♀). (Not all races depicted.) African race *minor* (a) (uncommon) throughout, palaearctic race *calidus* (b) (rare) mainly along coast. Note short tail, stout build and pale grey upper tail-coverts. Habitat: open country, coasts and city centres. Often near cliffs or high buildings. (NM)

8   **BARBARY FALCON** *Falco pelegrinoides* L 35 cm (♂), 55 cm (♀). (Species level as by Short.) Note rufous in face and general pale appearance. Habitat: desert and semi-desert. NM

9   **TAITA FALCON** *Falco fasciinucha* L 30 cm. Note light grey upper tail-coverts, short tail, rufous in face and slightly rufous under wing-coverts. Habitat: mountainous, dry, open country, normally near cliffs.

Plate 24

1 **RING-NECKED FRANCOLIN** *Francolinus streptophorus* L 25 cm. Note white-and-black barred collar and breast. Habitat: 500-2000 m. Grassy, sparsely bushed and wooded hillsides.

2 **RED-WINGED FRANCOLIN** *Francolinus levaillantii* L 30 cm. Note red in wing, spotted black marking on face mask and throat, and large long bill. Habitat: 1750-3000 m. Stony, sloping, grass- and farmland; woodland with scrub, tall grass and reedy spots.

3 **SHELLEY'S FRANCOLIN** *Francolinus shelleyi* L 30 cm. Note red in wing, large bill, finely barred underparts and black mantle blotching. Habitat: 500-3000 m. Stony, more or less wooded and bushed habitats, often with rocky outcrops.

4 **MOORLAND FRANCOLIN** *Francolinus psilolaemus* L 30 cm. Note red in wing and barring, scaling and spotting of underparts. Habitat: 2250(&<)-4000 m. Montane heath, grass- and moorland.

5 **SMITH'S FRANCOLIN** *Francolinus levaillantoides* L 35 cm. Note red in wing and black and rufous striping of underparts. Habitat: 2000-2500 m. Rocky, grassy, more or less wooded and bushed mountain slopes.

6 **CRESTED FRANCOLIN** *Francolinus sephaena* L 30 cm. Note reflecting triangular mottles on neck, throat and upper breast, and white eyebrow. Often walks with cocked tail. Habitat: <1500(&>)m. Dry, bushed and shrubbed areas with some grass cover, often near forest and water.

7 **SCALY FRANCOLIN** *Francolinus squamatus* L 30 cm. Rather plain. Habitat: 750-3000 m. Tall grassy and shrubby forest glades and forest edges.

8 **FOREST FRANCOLIN** *Francolinus lathami* L 20 cm. Habitat: 500-1500 m. Dense forests.

9 **NAHAN'S FRANCOLIN** *Francolinus nahani* L 20 cm. Habitat: 1000-1500 m. Dense forests.

10 **HILDEBRANDT'S FRANCOLIN** *Francolinus hildebrandti* L 35 cm. Note upright stance. No bare skin around eye. Habitat: 2000-2500 m. Rocky hillsides with rough grass and patches of dense scrub.

11 **HEUGLIN'S FRANCOLIN** *Francolinus icterorhynchus* L 30 cm. Note yellowish pink bare skin behind eye, orange bill and unmarked belly-centre. Habitat: 500-1500 m. Open and bushed grass- and farmland.

12 **CLAPPERTON'S FRANCOLIN** *Francolinus clappertoni* L 35 cm. Note bare red eye area, rufous crown and nape, scaly mantle and wings and pale buff wing-patch. Habitat: <2500 m. Rocky hillsides and dry, lightly wooded and bushed habitats.

13 **HARWOOD'S FRANCOLIN** *Francolinus harwoodi* L 30 cm. Note bare red eye area and double-scaled breast and flanks. Habitat: tall reed beds with some trees along streams and adjoining (cultivated) areas. E (Ethiopia)

14 **HANDSOME FRANCOLIN** *Francolinus nobilis* L 35 cm. Habitat: 2000-2500 m. Dense forest undergrowth, bamboo, giant heath and moorland.

15 **JACKSON'S FRANCOLIN** *Francolinus jacksoni* L 35 cm. Note upright stance. Habitat: 2250-3000 m. Dense undergrowth of forests, bamboo, moorland and giant heath. E (Kenya)

16 **CHESTNUT-NAPED FRANCOLIN** *Francolinus castaneicollis* L 35 cm. Note white black-edged striping and white throat. Habitat: 1000-4000(&>) m. Tall grass in forest glades and dense undergrowth of forest edges.

17 **DJIBOUTI FRANCOLIN** *Francolinus ochropectus* L 35 cm. Occurs only in Djibouti. Habitat: dense vegetation of dry watercourses. E (Djibouti)

18 **ERCKEL'S FRANCOLIN** *Francolinus erckelii* L 30 cm. Note dark face. Habitat: 2000-3500 m. Steep forest glades with scrub, tall grass and herbage.

19 **COQUI FRANCOLIN** *Francolinus coqui* L 25 cm.(Not all races depicted.) Southern race *c. coqui* (a) in Tanzania. The ♂ of this race has extensive barring of underparts and plain orange-buff head, while ♀ has orange-buff breast. Other races (b) have more marked head and unbarred breast and belly. Habitat: more or less wooded and bushed areas.

20 **RED-NECKED SPURFOWL** *Francolinus afer* L 35 cm. (Not all races depicted.) Race *melanogaster* (a) in E Tanzania, race *leucoparaeus* (b) in E Kenya, race *cranchii* (c) in SW Uganda and W Tanzania. Note red legs. Habitat: <1500 m. Forest patches and other bushed and wooded natural and cultivated areas with long grass.

21 **GREY-BREASTED SPURFOWL** *Francolinus rufopictus* L 35 cm. Combines grey-brown legs and orange-pink bare throat. Habitat: grassy areas with scattered trees; dense undergrowth along streams. E (Tanzania)

22 **YELLOW-NECKED SPURFOWL** *Francolinus leucoscepus* L 35 cm. Habitat: <2500 m. Forest edges and other wooded and bushed, natural and cultivated areas.

Plate 25

1 **WHITE-SPOTTED FLUFFTAIL** *Sarothrura pulchra* L 15 cm. Habitat: 500-2000 m. Swampy forests and surrounding areas with tree cover. Voice: mid-high, fluting, rapid, slightly speeded-up '*poo-poo-poo-poo-poo-poo-poo-poo*' and very high, fast '*tutitititititititi*'.

2 **BUFF-SPOTTED FLUFFTAIL** *Sarothrura elegans* L 17 cm. Habitat: <3000 m. Forests, bamboo, dense bush, scrubland, plantations, cultivation and gardens with dense undercover. Voice: low, hollow, ominous, level '*hoooooo-*' (4 sec) with slight tremolo, and extra low, hollow, rolling '*rururururururu-*'.

3 **RED-CHESTED FLUFFTAIL** *Sarothrura rufa* L 15 cm. Habitat: <3000 m. Marshy reed beds and papyrus swamp. Also in thick herbage and tall grass near rivers and ponds. Voice: high, piping, slow '*hooo hooo hooo -*' (each '*hooo*' gliding up slightly) sometimes in duet with very high contra-song '*piu -*' with each '*hooo*'. Also a call like alarm cry of Blacktailed Godwit.

4 **CHESTNUT-HEADED FLUFFTAIL** *Sarothrura lugens* L 15 cm. Habitat: tall wet grassland, dense shrubbery at forest edges and miombo. Voice: mid-high, hollow '*oooeh oooeh oooeh -*' (2 x '*oooeh*' per 3 sec '*-eh*' slightly falling off). Also long series of slowly speeding-up '*oooh oooh -*' rising in pitch and volume and trailing off at the end.

5 **BOEHM'S FLUFFTAIL** *Sarothrura boehmi* L 15 cm. Habitat: short wet grassland, inundations and river margins. Voice: mid-high, level, rhythmic hooting '*ooh ooh ooh ooh -*'. (AM)

6 **STRIPED FLUFFTAIL** *Sarothrura affinis* L 15 cm. Habitat: 1500-3250 m. Dry grassland. In Kenya, also in moorland. Voice: mid-high, thin, hollow trilling '*oooo oooo oooo -*' (25 per min) each '*oooo*' crescendoing and then slightly trailing off.

7 **WHITE-WINGED FLUFFTAIL** *Sarothrura ayresii* L 15 cm. White wing-panel only visible in flight. Habitat: marshes, reed beds and rough wet grass. Voice: low rapid '*ooh-ooh-ooh-ooh-ooh-*' often combined in duet, each '*ooh*' slightly swept up. (AM)

8 **COMMON QUAIL** *Coturnix coturnix* L 20 cm. Note plain underparts of ♀. Habitat: 1000(&>)-3000 m. Dry areas with grass or crops of varied height. Voice: extra high, liquid, staccato, rapid '*Gét-me-then, Gét-me-then -*'. (AM)

9 **BLUE QUAIL** *Coturnix chinesis* L 20 cm. The ♀ darker and more blotched underneath than other ♀ quails. Habitat: <2000 m. Moist open grassland near swamps. Voice: rather low, descending, rasping '*wêhwehweh -*'. (AM)

10 **HARLEQUIN QUAIL** *Coturnix delegorguei* L 15 cm. Habitat: <1250(&>) m. Slightly bushed grass- and farmland. Voice: extra high, irregular, rather sharp '*wheet wheet-wheet wheet -*'. (AM)

11 **STONE PARTRIDGE** *Ptilopachus petrosus* L 25 cm. Note bantam-like posture. Habitat: rocky hillsides with dense scrub, tall grass cover and more or less bush.

12 **QUAIL-PLOVER** *Ortyxelos meiffrenii* L 12 cm. Habitat: 1000(&>)-2000 m. Normally in dry habitats with some grass cover and more or less bush.

13 **COMMON BUTTON-QUAIL** *Turnix sylvatica* L 14 cm. Flies with slower wing beats than true quails. Note bright yellow eye. Habitat: <1500 (&>) m. Tall grass- and farmland. Voice: strange, very low, hollow, shivering slightly, cresendoing '*wohoohoohoohoohoohoo*'.

14 **BLACK-RUMPED BUTTON-QUAIL** *Turnix hottentota* L 14 cm. Slower wing beat than true quails. Black rump visible in flight. Habitat: 1000-2000 m. Short, partly bare grassland and inundations. Voice: strange, very low, hollow, pumping, regular '*whoo-whoo-whoo-whoo-whoo-*'.

15 **ARABIAN CHUKAR** *Alectoris melanocephalus* L 35 cm. (Species mentioned by Urban; not seen in Africa since 1890.) Habitat: desert with hardly any grass cover.

16 **SAND PARTRIDGE** *Ammoperdix heyi* L 25 cm. Note rufous tail corners. Habitat: <750 m. Arid, hilly and rocky country with some shrub and grass.

17 **VULTURINE GUINEAFOWL** *Acryllium vulturinum* L 60 cm. Habitat: <2000 m. Dry, bushed and wooded areas, including forest edges.

18 **CRESTED GUINEAFOWL** *Guttera pucherani* L 50 cm. (Not all races depicted.) Race *edouardi* (a) in Somalia, E Kenya, NE and SW Tanzania, race *p. pucherani* (b) in Uganda, W Kenya and SW Tanzania. Habitat: <2000 m. Dense undergrowth of forests and woodland. Voice: high, sharp, repeated '*druu-wêê druu-wêê*' ('*wêê*' lashing and high) and low, dry, speeding-up cackles and rattles like '*tetrût-tetrût-trrrreh*'.

19 **HELMETED GUINEAFOWL** *Numida meleagris* L 55 cm. Habitat: <2250 m. Dry, natural and cultivated areas with more or less tree cover, shrub and bush.

20 **UDZUNGWA PARTRIDGE** *Xenoperdix udzungwensis* L 30 cm. (New species, discovered in 1991; English name provisional.) Habitat: 1250-2000 m. Forest interiors. Map (not provided) as for Rufous-winged Sunbird (80.17). E (Tanzania)

25

Plate 26

1 NKULENGU RAIL *Himantornis haematopus* L 45 cm. Habitat: 500-750 m. Undergrowth along forest streams. Voice: low, rhythmic '*bôôm tuckêh-heh bôôm tuckêh-heh*' (actually an inseparable duet).

2 GREY-THROATED RAIL *Canirallus oculeus* L 30 cm. Habitat: undergrowth along forest streams.

3 AFRICAN CRAKE *Crex egregia* L 25 cm. Habitat: <2000 m. Moist grassland, inundations and swamps. Voice: mid-high, loud, cackling '*ceck-ceck-ceckceckceck-*'. (AM)

4 CORNCRAKE *Crex crex* L 30 cm. Habitat: <3000 m. Grass plains and areas near marshes and rivers. Voice: low, dry, double rattle '*crexcrex crexcrex -*'. NM

5 ROUGET'S RAIL *Rougetius rougetii* L 30 cm. Habitat: <1750 m. Tall grass, reeds and shrubbery near streams and ponds. [E] (Ethiopia)

6 AFRICAN WATER-RAIL *Rallus caerulescens* L 30 cm. Habitat: <3000 m. Reed beds of marshes, lake margins and stream banks. Voice: very high, fluting, slackened and slightly lowered piping trill.

7 BAILLON'S CRAKE *Porzana pusilla* L 20 cm. Note very dark appearance. Habitat: reed beds and tall grass of swamps and margins of lakes, streams and ponds. Voice: low, dry rattle normally slackened at the end. (NM)

8 LITTLE CRAKE *Porzana parva* L 20 cm. May walk over floating vegetation. Note red bill-base. Habitat: swamps and other places with reeds and tall grass. Voice: low, falling off '*wrurrrr*'. NM

9 STRIPED CRAKE *Aenigmatolimnas marginalis* L 20 cm. Note pale rufous under tail-coverts. Habitat: dense vegetation in shallow water of marshes, inundations and other wet habitats. Voice: mid-high, dry, very fast near-trill '*trrrrrr-*' (like a fast sewing machine). AM

10 SPOTTED CRAKE *Porzana porzana* L 25 cm. Habitat: <2500 m. Dense reeds and herbage in shallow parts of marshes, inundations and ponds. Voice: very high, sweeping '*wheet wheet wheet -*'. NM

11 BLACK CRAKE *Amaurornis flavirostris* L 20 cm. Habitat: <3000 m. Reed beds, papyrus and shrubbery at lake margins, dams, ponds and streams.

12 COMMON MOORHEN *Gallinula chloropus* L 35 cm. Imm has white under tail-coverts but no red at bill. Habitat: 1000(&<)-3000 m. Fresh lakes, dams, ponds, quiet streams and marshes with fringing and some floating vegetation. Voice: high, sharp, tinking '*beckbeckbeck*'.

13 LESSER MOORHEN *Gallinula angulata* L 25 cm. Habitat: <2000 m. Dams, ponds, swamps and inundations with fringing and floating vegetation. Voice: very high '*peek peek peek*'. AM

14 PURPLE SWAMPHEN *Porphyrio porphyrio* L 45 cm. Habitat: <2500(&>) m. Large swamps and shallow lakes with reeds, papyrus and floating vegetation.

15 ALLEN'S GALLINULE *Porphyrio alleni* L 25 cm. Habitat: marshes and inundations with tall grass and other vegetation.

16 RED-KNOBBED COOT *Fulica cristata* L 40 cm. Note bluish-white bill colour. N-br bird has blunt demarcation between black face and bluish-white upper mandible. Neck held up more straight than Eurasian Coot. No white trailing edge of wings in flight. Habitat: <3000 m. Fresh lakes, dams and ponds with tall fringing vegetation.

17 EURASIAN COOT *Fulica atra* L 40 cm. Note pinkish-white bill colour. Black face-feathering points into pinkish-white upper mandible. Neck held more bent than Red-knobbed Coot. Note white trailing edge. Habitat: fresh, brackish and salt lakes with some floating and emerged vegetation. NM

18 AFRICAN FINFOOT *Podica senegalensis* L 50 cm. Swims with 'pumping' head. Habitat: <2000 m. Quiet rivers, streams and pools with overhanging trees and shrubs. Also in mangroves and along papyrus. Voice: mid-high, dry, very short rattles '*crrut crrut-crrut crrut -*'.

26

Plate 27

1 **WATTLED CRANE** *Bugeranus carunculatus* L 125 cm. Habitat: shallow water of wet, wide-open habitats.

2 **COMMON CRANE** *Grus grus* L 115 cm. Habitat: open areas, away from trees and shrub. NM

3 **BLACK CROWNED-CRANE** *Balearica pavonina* L 100 cm. Note colouring of cheeks. Habitat: 3000 m. Breeds in marshes but feeds in natural and cultivated areas with tall grass.

4 **GREY CROWNED-CRANE** *Balearica regulorum* L 105 cm. Note cheek colouring. Habitat: 750-1500(&>)m. Roosts and nests in or near wet places but feeds in open and wooded grass- and farmland.

5 **DEMOISELLE CRANE** *Anthropoides virgo* L 95 cm. Habitat: <2000 m. Dry, lightly wooded, short-grassed plains, marshes, open farmland, lake edges and river banks. NM

6 **BLACK-BELLIED BUSTARD** *Eupodotis melanogaster* L 60 cm. Generally blonder brown (especially tail) than Hartlaub's Bustard and mainly grey (not mainly black) face markings. Habitat: <2500 m. Tall grassland with some trees and lightly wooded farmland.

7 **DENHAM'S BUSTARD** *Neotis denhami* L 75 cm. Habitat: 500-3000 m. Open plains, also in more or less wooded habitats.

8 **HEUGLIN'S BUSTARD** *Neotis heuglini* L 75 cm. The ♀ has grey (not rufous) neck. Habitat: desert and semi-desert with some occasional grass cover.

9 **HARTLAUB'S BUSTARD** *Eupodotis hartlaubii* L 60 cm. Note dark grey tail, grey-brown appearance and black (not mainly grey) face mask. The ♀ neck greyer than ♀ Black-bellied Bustard. Habitat: <1750 m. Arid and dry open plains with scarce shrub and some acacias.

10 **BUFF-CRESTED BUSTARD** *Eupodotis ruficrista* L 55 cm. The ♂ has distinct crest, no black behind eye and no white along black of neck. Black-bellied ♀ has no grey or black in face. Habitat: <1500 m. Dry, open, tall grassland, often with some shrub and trees.

11 **ARABIAN BUSTARD** *Ardeotis arabs* L 90 cm. No black in wing. Habitat: semi-desert and other dry open areas with some grass cover, trees and thickets.

12 **WHITE-BELLIED BUSTARD** *Eupodotis senegalensis* L 60 cm. Note light grey hind neck of ♀. Habitat: <2000 m. Lightly bushed parts, often near streams, in open natural and cultivated areas, often with only sparse grass cover.

13 **LITTLE BROWN BUSTARD** *Eupodotis humilis* L 45 cm. Both ♂ and ♀ rather plain except some black markings on nape and throat of ♂. Upperparts less distinctly striped and blotched than other bustards. Habitat: dry, open bush.

14 **KORI BUSTARD** *Ardeotis kori* L 100 cm. Habitat: <2000 m. Dry, open plains with some trees and bush.

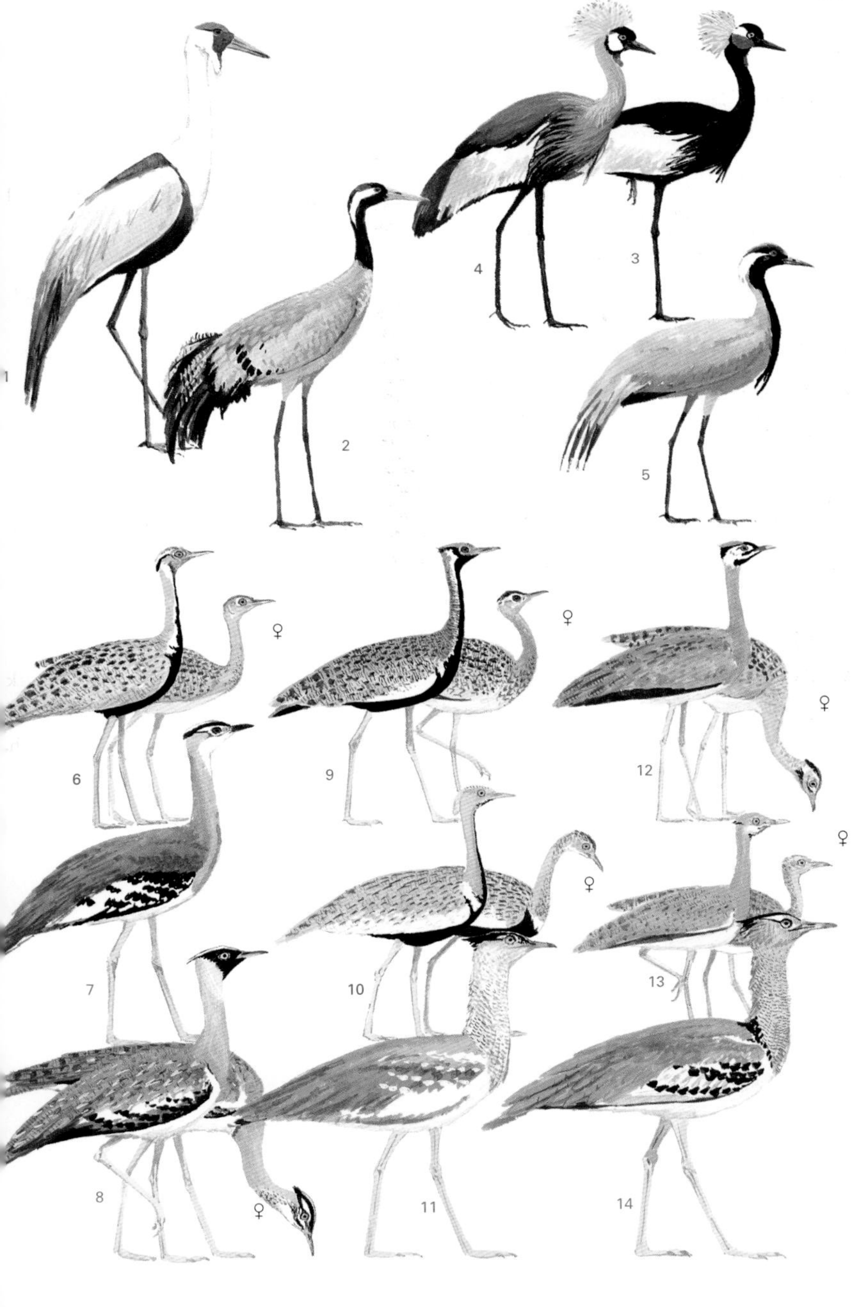
1
2
3
4
5
6
♀
7
8
♀
9
♀
10
♀
11
12
♀
13
♀
14

27

Plate 28

1 **LESSER JACANA** *Microparra capensis*   L 15 cm. Habitat: 1750-3000 m. Swamps, lakes, ponds and slow streams with floating vegetation. Voice: very high, descending, fast, bouncing '*diditidititititi*'. (Note that map 28.1 on p.223 is incorrect: Lesser Jacana is always uncommon.)

2 **AFRICAN JACANA** *Actophilornis africana*   L 30 cm. Habitat: <3000 m. Swamps, lakes, ponds and slow rivers with floating vegetation. Voice: mid-high, drawn-out '*weh*' and high yelping often descending '*wetwetwetwet-wetwet-wetwet-*'.

3 **PAINTED-SNIPE** *Rostratula benghalensis*   L 25 cm. Habitat: muddy places in fringing vegetation of lakes, dams, ponds and slow rivers. AM

4 **CRAB-PLOVER** *Dromas ardeola*   L 40 cm. Habitat: open seashore. (AM)

5 **EURASIAN OYSTERCATCHER** *Haematopus ostralegus*   L 40 cm. Habitat: open sandy and rocky shores mainly at sea. NM

6 **COMMON STILT** *Himantopus himantopus*   L 40 cm. Habitat: shallow rift valley lakes, estuaries and inundations. (NM)

7 **EURASIAN AVOCET** *Recurvirostra avosetta*   L 45 cm. Habitat: mainly bare edges of rift valley lakes. Also at seashores, lagoons and creeks. (AM) (NM)

8 **STONE-CURLEW** *Burhinus oedicnemus*   L 45 cm. Note pattern of folded wing without grey. Habitat: sandy lake and river banks. NM

9 **SENEGAL THICKNEE** *Burhinus senegalensis*   L 40 cm. Note pattern of folded wing. Very similar to Water Thicknee but wing coverts almost white in a pattern of parallel black, white, pale grey, white and black strips. Bill extensively yellow. Habitat: sandy lake and river banks.

10 **WATER THICKNEE** *Burhinus vermiculatus*   L 40 cm. Note pattern of folded wing. Wing coverts mainly grey with only a narrow strip of white along upper black line. Bill almost all black. Habitat: river banks, lake shores, estuaries and mangroves.

11 **SPOTTED THICKNEE** *Burhinus capensis*   L 45 cm. Rests by day in shade under bush. Habitat: <2000 m. Open, dry, rocky riverbeds and other arid, more or less wooded, natural and cultivated areas. NM

28

1

2 imm

3 ♂ ♀

4

5 n-br

6 ♂ ♀

7

8 9 10 11

Plate 29

1 **EGYPTIAN-PLOVER** *Pluvianus aegyptius* L 20 cm. Habitat: mainly along sandy river banks; also at lake shores. Often near settlement.

2 **BURCHELL'S COURSER** *Cursorius rufus* L 20 cm. (Species allocation as by Hayman.) Note demarcation between darker forebelly and pale hindbelly. Less thickset than Cream-coloured Courser. Habitat: arid areas with more or less grass cover.

3 **CREAM-COLOURED COURSER** *Cursorius cursor* L 25 cm. Note gradual paling of underparts to under tail-coverts. Larger and more thickset than Burchell's Courser. Habitat: desert, semi-desert and open and bushed grass- and farmland. (AM)

4 **TEMMINCK'S COURSER** *Cursorius temminckii* L 20 cm. Habitat: <3000 m. Dry, more or less bushed habitats, bare fields and burnt ground. Voice: high, hooting, unhurried '*hac hac hac zhunk*' ('*zhunk*' lower and inhaled).

5 **TWO-BANDED COURSER** *Cursorius africanus* L 20 cm. Nocturnal. Habitat: <2000 m. Arid and dry habitats with scarce grass and occasionally some scrub. Voice: extra high, piercing, almost level, rapid '*fifififififi-fi-fi*'; also mid-high dry rattles.

6 **THREE-BANDED COURSER** *Cursorius cinctus* L 25 cm. Nocturnal. Habitat: dry, more or less wooded and bushed habitats including open miombo. Voice: high, excited, staccato yelps '*wew-wew-wew-wew-wew-*'.

7 **VIOLET-TIPPED COURSER** *Cursorius chalcopterus* L 30 cm. Nocturnal. Beautiful purple tips of flight feathers not visible in folded wing. Habitat: more or less wooded and bushed habitats. Voice: strange peacock-like '*roh miâû-eh*' ('*roh*' low and short '*miâû*' gliding up).

8 **COMMON PRATINCOLE** *Glareola pratincola* L 25 cm. Dark rufous under wing-coverts often seemingly black in flight, but narrow white trailing edge of secondaries diagnostic. Wings not longer than tail. Habitat: open areas near lakes, rivers and seashore. (NM)

9 **BLACK-WINGED PRATINCOLE** *Glareola nordmanni* L 25 cm. No white trailing edge of secondaries. Tail in perched bird shorter than wings. Habitat: open sandy areas with some grass near lakes, rivers and occasionally the sea. NM

10 **MADAGASCAR PRATINCOLE** *Glareola ocularis* L 25 cm. Habitat: open sandy sea- and lake shores and muddy river banks; also in sand dunes. AM

11 **ROCK PRATINCOLE** *Glareola nuchalis* L 20 cm. Habitat: rocky river and lake shores; also on sandy and muddy beaches.

29

Plate 30

1 **LITTLE RINGED PLOVER** *Charadrius dubius* L 15 cm. Note yellow eye-ring. No white wing-bar in flight. Habitat: shores of rift valley lakes. Occasionally along seashores, rivers and short grass away from water. NM

2 **RINGED PLOVER** *Charadrius hiaticula* L 20 cm. Note partly yellow bill, orange legs and white wing-bar in flight. Habitat: mainly seashore. Occasionally also on open lake and river banks or away from water. NM

3 **KITTLITZ'S PLOVER** *Charadrius pecuarius* L 15 cm. Note brownish (not grey or buff and grey) upperparts. No black or dark chest-collar or breast-patches. Habitat: <2500 m. Dry, short grass near lakes and dams. Also at sandy and muddy edges of lakes and streams.

4 **THREE-BANDED PLOVER** *Charadrius tricollaris* L 20 cm. Note white forehead. White wing-bar in flight. Habitat: <3000 m. Edges of ponds, streams and sewage ponds. Rarely at salt water.

5 **FORBES'S PLOVER** *Charadrius forbesi* L 20 cm. Note dark forehead. No wing-bar. Habitat: open, more or less grassy habitats away from water. Sometimes in muddy places near water. Breeds between rocks. AM

6 **KENTISH PLOVER** *Charadrius alexandrinus* L 15 cm. Only br ♂ has rufous-buff crown. Less grey than White-fronted Plover. White collar closed in neck. Habitat: open shores of sea and alkaline rift valley lakes. Occasionally along rivers. (AM)

7 **WHITE-FRONTED PLOVER** *Charadrius marginatus* L 20 cm. No black on breast or chest. White hindcollar incomplete. Habitat: sandy and rocky seashores. Also at lake and river banks.

8 **CHESTNUT-BANDED PLOVER** *Charadrius pallidus* L 15 cm. Habitat: brackish and alkaline lakes.

9 **LESSER SANDPLOVER** *Charadrius mongolus* L 20 cm. Bill size as other plovers. Some have no white spots in front of eye. N-br plumage with rather scaled and uneven-coloured upperparts. Habitat: open seashore and other open sandy and muddy coastal habitats. Occasionally at lakes. Voice: short '*keelip*', sharper than Greater Sandplover. NM

10 **GREATER SANDPLOVER** *Charadrius leschenaultii* L 25 cm. Note oversized bill. Race *columbinus* (not shown) however has bill like Lesser Sandplover, but all races have distinct white spots before eye in br plumage. Habitat: as Lesser Sandplover. Voice: call more trilling than Lesser Sandplover. NM

11 **CASPIAN PLOVER** *Charadrius asiaticus* L 20 cm. Note complete pale brown breast-band in n-br plumage. Habitat: prefers dry places even in coastal areas; short grass, burnt ground and sand dunes. NM

12 **GREY PLOVER** *Pluvialis squatarola* L 30 cm. Note black wing pits, visible in flight. Habitat: mainly coastal saltwater habitats. Occasionally at shores of large lakes. NM

13 **PACIFIC GOLDEN PLOVER** *Pluvialis fulva* L 25 cm. Note pale grey wing pits, visible in flight. Habitat: mainly fresh water habitats in coastal regions; rarely at large rift valley lakes. NM

30

n-br
1

n-br
2

2

1

2

n-br
3

n-br

4

5

n-br

♀
6

n-br

♀
7

♀
8

n-br
9

♀

n-br

10

♀

n-br

11

♀

12

13

12

13

n-br
12

n-br
13

Plate 31

1 **AFRICAN WATTLED LAPWING** *Vanellus senegallus* L 35 cm. Habitat: <2250 m. Bare, muddy, sandy and short-grassed ground near marshes and lake, pond and river shores.

2 **WHITE-HEADED LAPWING** *Vanellus albiceps* L 30 cm. Habitat: sandy river banks often in forested areas.

3 **SPOT-BREASTED LAPWING** *Vanellus melanocephalus* L 35 cm. Habitat: 1750-4250 m. Montane grass- and moorland, often near cattle. E (Ethiopia)

4 **BLACKSMITH LAPWING** *Vanellus armatus* L 30 cm. Habitat: dry muddy and marshy shores of lakes, dams, ponds, lagoons and swamps. Voice: extra high, metallic '*tingctingc -*' (hence the species' name).

5 **BLACK-HEADED LAPWING** *Vanellus tectus* L 25 cm. Habitat: semi-desert with some grass cover. Sometimes far from water.

6 **SPUR-WINGED LAPWING** *Vanellus spinosus* L 25 cm. Habitat: <1000 m. Bare, sandy, muddy and grassy lake shores and river banks; rarely at the seashore.

7 **BROWN-CHESTED LAPWING** *Vanellus superciliosus* L 25 cm. Habitat: dry, short grassland and bare fields; also at bare river and lake shores. AM

8 **SENEGAL LAPWING** *Vanellus lugubris* L 25 cm. Note pattern of open wing and white forehead. Not in highlands. Habitat: <1500 m. Dry, open and bushed grass- and farmland.

9 **BLACK-WINGED LAPWING** *Vanellus melanopterus* L 25 cm. Note pattern of open wing. White forehead not sharply demarcated. Habitat: 1500-3000 m. Grassland and burnt ground.

10 **CROWNED LAPWING** *Vanellus coronatus* L 30 cm. Habitat: <3000 m. Dry habitats with a few trees and some shrub and grass cover.

11 **SOCIABLE LAPWING** *Vanellus gregarius* L 30 cm. Habitat: dry, open habitats; also at river edges and other more wet places. NM

12 **LONG-TOED LAPWING** *Vanellus crassirostris* L 30 cm. Race *leucoptera* (a) from Southern Africa not (yet) seen in E Africa, but birds intermediate with normal E African race *c. crassirotris* (b) reported from S Tanzania. Habitat: <2250 m. Floating vegetation at lake shores and calm river banks. Also in large swamps and inundations.

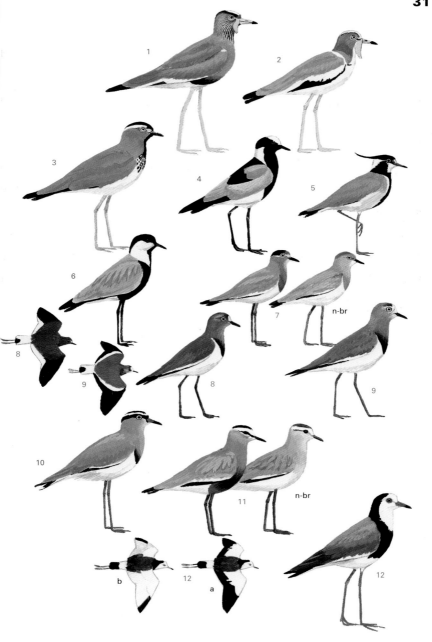

31

Plate 32

1 **SANDERLING** *Calidris alba* L 20 cm. Note dark shoulder of n-br plumage. Habitat: at the actual water's edge of the sea and large lakes. NM

2 **RED KNOT** *Calidris canutus* L 25 cm. Note size and stocky appearance. Habitat: seashore and other coastal habitats. NM

3 **RUFOUS-NECKED STINT** *Calidris ruficollis* L 14 cm. N-br plumage very much like Little Stint but greyer and more tapered because of longer tail and wings. Note patches at chest sides. Habitat: normally at seashore.

4 **LITTLE STINT** *Calidris minuta* L 14 cm. N-br plumage rusty grey (not pure grey as Rufous-necked Stint). Note patches at chest sides. Habitat: normally at freshwater bodies, only occasionally at the actual seashore. NM

5 **TEMMINCK'S STINT** *Calidris temminckii* L 13 cm. Note yellow-green legs, white outer tail-feathers and grey chest in n-br plumage. Habitat: marsh pools and muddy lake edges. Uncommon at the coast. NM

6 **LONG-TOED STINT** *Calidris subminuta* L 13 cm. Note yellow legs, grey chest and mottled upperparts in n-br plumage. Wing-bar very narrow. Habitat: muddy lake edges. Rarely at sea. NM

7 **PECTORAL SANDPIPER** *Calidris melanotos* L 20 cm. Note yellow legs, green bill, long neck and grey chest. No wing-bar. Habitat: marsh, wet grassland and muddy water edges. Rarely at the coast. OM

8 **DUNLIN** *Calidris alpina* L 20 cm. Note long slightly decurved bill, faint eyebrow, short legs and grey chest (in n-br plumage). Habitat: normally in coastal areas, but also at lake and dam edges. NM

9 **CURLEW SANDPIPER** *Calidris ferruginea* L 20 cm. Note long, slender, slightly decurved bill; narrow chest streaking (in n-br plumage); long legs and white upper tail-coverts. Habitat: prefers coastal areas, but also at muddy fresh and alkaline lake edges, dams and inundations. NM

10 **BROAD-BILLED SANDPIPER** *Limicola falcinellus* L 15 cm. Note streaking of neck, chest and faint streaking of mantle in n-br plumage, short greenish legs, white outer tail-feathers and kinked bill. Habitat: muddy and sandy seashore and lake shores. NM

11 **BUFF-BREASTED SANDPIPER** *Tryngites subruficollis* L 20 cm. Looks as if smoking a (black) cigarette. Habitat: marshes and short grassland. NM

12 **RUFF** *Philomachus pugnax* L 30 cm (♂), 20 cm (♀). (The many br plumages of ♂ not depicted.) Note white ring around bill base (as if smoking a cigar) and white ovals to tail sides. Habitat: river banks and edges of lakes, dams and inundations. NM

32

Plate 33

1 **BLACK-TAILED GODWIT** *Limosa limosa* L 40 cm. Habitat: wetlands and lake shores. Also in coastal areas but rarely at the seashore itself. NM

2 **BAR-TAILED GODWIT** *Limosa lapponica* L 40 cm. Habitat: sea and lake shores. NM

3 **ASIATIC DOWITCHER** *Limnodromus semipalmatus* L 35 cm. Long, all-black bill in br and n-br plumage. Note barred white rump and upper tail-coverts. Habitat: shallow water and muddy water edges. NM

4 **EURASIAN CURLEW** *Numenius arquata* L 55 cm. Habitat: sea and lake shores, estuaries, sand dunes, river banks and grassland. NM

5 **WHIMBREL** *Numenius phaeopus* L 45 cm. Note striped head. Habitat: mainly seashore and other coastal areas. Rarely inland. NM

6 **AFRICAN SNIPE** *Gallinago nigripennis* L 25 cm. When flushed at 5-10 m, rises steeply and explosively calling '*tsjuk*' and zigzags (but less so than Common Snipe) away at low level before dropping into cover within 100-200 m. Note long bill, fine neck striping, dark upperparts (black between buff lines), black flank barring, narrow white edges of dark upper wing-coverts, wide white trailing edge of secondaries and extensive white tail sides. Habitat: 1500-3000(&>) m. Moorland, marshes, grassy lake shores and inundations.

7 **GREAT SNIPE** *Gallinago media* L 30 cm. When flushed at 5-10 m shoots away at shallow angle silently or with soft '*itch-itch*', flies in straight line and disappears abruptly into cover within 30-50 m. Note rather wide neck striping, bold flank barring extending to under tail-coverts, white wing-bars (even visible in folded wing), mantle stripes less strong, faint white trailing edge of secondaries and white tail sides. Habitat: swamps and lake edges.

8 **COMMON SNIPE** *Gallinago gallinago* L 25 cm. When flushed at 10-15 m rises steeply and explosively, calls '*tseek*' 1-2 times while zigzagging away before dropping into cover within 200-300 m. Note fine neck striping, brown (not black) flank barring, pale belly, white trailing edge to secondaries, long pointed wings and little white to tail corners. Habitat: marshes, grassy lake and dam shores and inundations. NM

9 **PINTAIL SNIPE** *Gallinago stenura* L 25 cm. When flushed, shoots away with low, sharp '*tsit*' but drops into cover after only a short distance. Note rather short green bill, fine neck striping, pale eyebrow wider before eye (not evenly wide over eye), tawny wing coverts (contrasting with more rufous mantle) and tail not protruding beyond wing tips. No white trailing edge to secondaries. Pin-shaped tail feathers difficult to see in the field. Habitat: inundations and grassy areas. NM

10 **JACK SNIPE** *Lymnocryptes minimus* L 20 cm. Difficult to flush, but if it is, it rises silently and flies straight away over only 50-100 m before dropping into cover again. Note short bill, short legs, unbarred flanks and all-dark tail. No pale stripe over top of crown. Habitat: swamps, short-grassed lake shores and inundations. NM

33

Plate 34

1 **REDSHANK** *Tringa totanus* L 30 cm. Note red basal half of bill, orange-red legs and wide white trailing edge of wing. Habitat: estuaries, lagoons, creeks, lake shores, river banks, streams, pools and sewage ponds. NM

2 **SPOTTED REDSHANK** *Tringa erythropus* L 30 cm. Note unstriped chest and pale colouring in n-br plumage. Colours of bill and legs diagnostic. Habitat: muddy and marshy pools and river banks. NM

3 **MARSH SANDPIPER** *Tringa stagnatilis* L 25 cm. Note fine needle-like bill, long olive-green legs, slim build and, in n-br plumage, plain upperparts. Habitat: muddy and marshy lake shores, river banks, streams and pools. NM

4 **GREENSHANK** *Tringa nebularia* L 30 cm. Note black upcurving bill and green legs. Habitat: muddy lake shores and river banks, pools and coral flats. NM

5 **GREEN SANDPIPER** *Tringa ochropus* L 20 cm. Note dark, almost black and white appearance, especially in flight, straight cut-off white rump and barred tail, and narrow white eye-ring. No white behind eye. Habitat: sheltered pools, streams, creeks and sewage ponds. NM

6 **WOOD SANDPIPER** *Tringa glareola* L 20 cm. Note small size, green bill and legs, long white eyebrow and white rump pointing into mantle. Habitat: secluded areas of marshes, inundations, pools, creeks, ponds and even sewage basins. NM

7 **TEREK SANDPIPER** *Xenus cinereus* L 25 cm. Note yellow-based upcurved bill, dark shoulder, dark line in mantle (forming a 'V' on back), grey (not white) rump and middle tail-feathers. Habitat: seashore and muddy lake, creek and river edges. NM

8 **RUDDY TURNSTONE** *Arenaria interpres* L 25 cm. Habitat: rocky sea- and lake shores. NM

9 **COMMON SANDPIPER** *Actitis hypoleucos* L 20 cm. Note white wedge between (folded) wing and sharply demarcated patches at chest sides. Habitat: short grass near and at edges of lakes, ponds, streams, seashore, creeks and estuaries. NM

10 **RED-NECKED PHALAROPE** *Phalaropus lobatus* L 20 cm. Note very thin, needle-like bill and slender build. Habitat: open sea and large lakes. Occasionally at pools and sewage ponds. NM

11 **GREY PHALAROPE** *Phalaropus fulicarius* L 20 cm. Note short, stout bill and bulky build. Habitat: normally at open sea, but in E Africa so far only seen at large lakes. NM

34

Plate 35

1 SOOTY GULL *Larus hemprichii* L 45 cm. Habitat: coastal areas but occasionally at Lake Turkana. (AM

2 WHITE-EYED GULL *Larus leucophthalmus* L 40 cm. Habitat: seashore and Lake Turkana. (AM)

3 GREAT BLACK-HEADED GULL *Larus ichthyaetus* L 70 cm. Habitat: sea- and lake shores. NM

4 MEDITERRANEAN GULL *Larus melanocephalus* L 40 cm. No black on wing tip (or black only on outer web of first primary). Subadults however have more black at wing tips. Habitat: seashore and Lake Turkana. NM

5 LITTLE GULL *Larus minutus* L 25 cm. Note black under-wing. Imm flying birds with inverted 'W' on upperparts. Habitat: in E Africa thus far only seen at Lake Turkana, but elsewhere normally in coastal habitats. NM

6 SABINE'S GULL *Larus sabini* L 35 cm. Note characteristic wing pattern. Habitat: normally at open sea.

7 GREY-HEADED GULL *Larus cirrocephalus* L 40 cm. Note pale eye and extensive black on wing tips. Habitat: mainly at lakes, rarely at the seashore.

8 BLACK-HEADED GULL *Larus ridibundus* L 40 cm. White on neck runs up to nape and down on throat, confining black to front side of head. Habitat: mainly in coastal areas but hardly at the actual seashore. Inland at large lakes; also at ponds, rivers, farmland and refuse dumps. NM

9 SLENDER-BILLED GULL *Larus genei* L 45 cm. Shape of head, with forward-placed bill, may be best identification feature. Habitat: coastal areas. NM

10 KELP GULL *Larus dominicanus* L 60 cm. Eye normally dark. Note rather short wings. Habitat: seashore and other areas near the coast, including refuse dumps.

11 LESSER BLACK-BACKED GULL *Larus fuscus* L 55 cm. Note pale eye and long wings. Habitat: mainly at lakes, less at the seashore. NM

12 HERRING GULL *Larus argentatus* L 60 cm. Note leg colour. Habitat: seashore, Lake Turkana and Lake Victoria. NM

35

Plate 36

1 **POMARINE SKUA** *Stercorarius pomarinus* L 55 cm (excluding tail streamers). Black form not depicted. Lengthened blunt twisted tail feathers diagnostic, but these are often missing in worn plumage. Black of under-wing 'drips' over flanks. In n-br plumage head and breast densely barred brown. Imm very similar to imm Arctic and Long-tailed Skua but grey on the head of Pomarine is more uniform with rest of body. Also it has grey-white under wing-coverts of primaries, so forming another whitish patch separated from the white parts of the primaries by a dark band. Habitat: seashore and Lake Turkana. NM

2 **ARCTIC SKUA** *Stercorarius parasiticus* L 45 cm (excluding tail streamers). Pale (a) and dark (b) forms shown. Note pointed tail feathers and faint chest-band. N-br plumage as imm plumage but under wing-coverts plain brown, not barred. Imm often with pale rusty neck. Habitat: seashore and Lake Turkana. NM

3 **LONG-TAILED SKUA** *Stercorarius longicaudus* L 35 cm (excluding tail steamers). No chest-band and pale buff throat in br plumage. N-br plumage as imm plumage but belly paler and under wing-coverts unbarred. A dark form exists but is very rare. Imm very much like imm Arctic Skua but neck less rusty and middle tail-feathers slightly lengthened. Habitat: Lake Turkana and seashore. NM

4 **GREAT SKUA** *Catharacta skua* L 60 cm. Note mottled and striped underparts. Imm (not shown) has rufous (not pale brown) underparts. Habitat: normally at sea. NM

5 **SOUTH POLAR SKUA** *Catharacta maccormicki* L 55 cm. Pale (a) and dark (b) forms shown. Underparts not striped or mottled except some striping on imm throat. Habitat: seashore. AM

6 **BLACK TERN** *Chlidonias niger* L 25 cm. N-br and imm plumages very difficult to separate from other chlidonias terns but rump and tail uniformly grey with rest of body. Imm mantle (not shown) slightly darker than wings. Does not plunge-dive but snatches food from water surface. Habitat: rift valley lakes but also occasionally at the seacoast of Somalia. Voice: very high, more or less grating and piercing shrieks. NM

7 **WHITE-WINGED BLACK TERN** *Chlidonias leucopterus* L 25 cm. Note white rump of n-br and imm plumage. Habitat: lakes, but can be seen feeding on insects far from water; does not plunge-dive but snatches food from water surface. Voice: extra high, fluting and siffling shrieks. NM

8 **WHISKERED TERN** *Chlidonias hybridus* L 25 cm. Note grey rump. Slightly larger, longer-winged and with deeper wing-beat than Black Tern; also plunge-dives. Imm mantle darker than Black Tern and rump grey (not white as imm White-winged Tern). Habitat: lakes, occasionally at sea. Voice: rather low, grating rattles. (NM)

9 **LESSER NODDY** *Anous tenuirostris* L 30 cm. Forecrown white, merging gradually to black chin. Habitat: mainly open sea. AM

10 **COMMON NODDY** *Anous stolidus* L 40 cm. Forehead sharply demarcated from black chin. Habitat: mainly out at sea. Breeds on islands near the E African coast. (AM)

11 **AFRICAN SKIMMER** *Rhynchops flavirostris* L 40 cm. Skims (a) mainly at dusk. Habitat:<2000 m. Creeks, rivers and lakes.

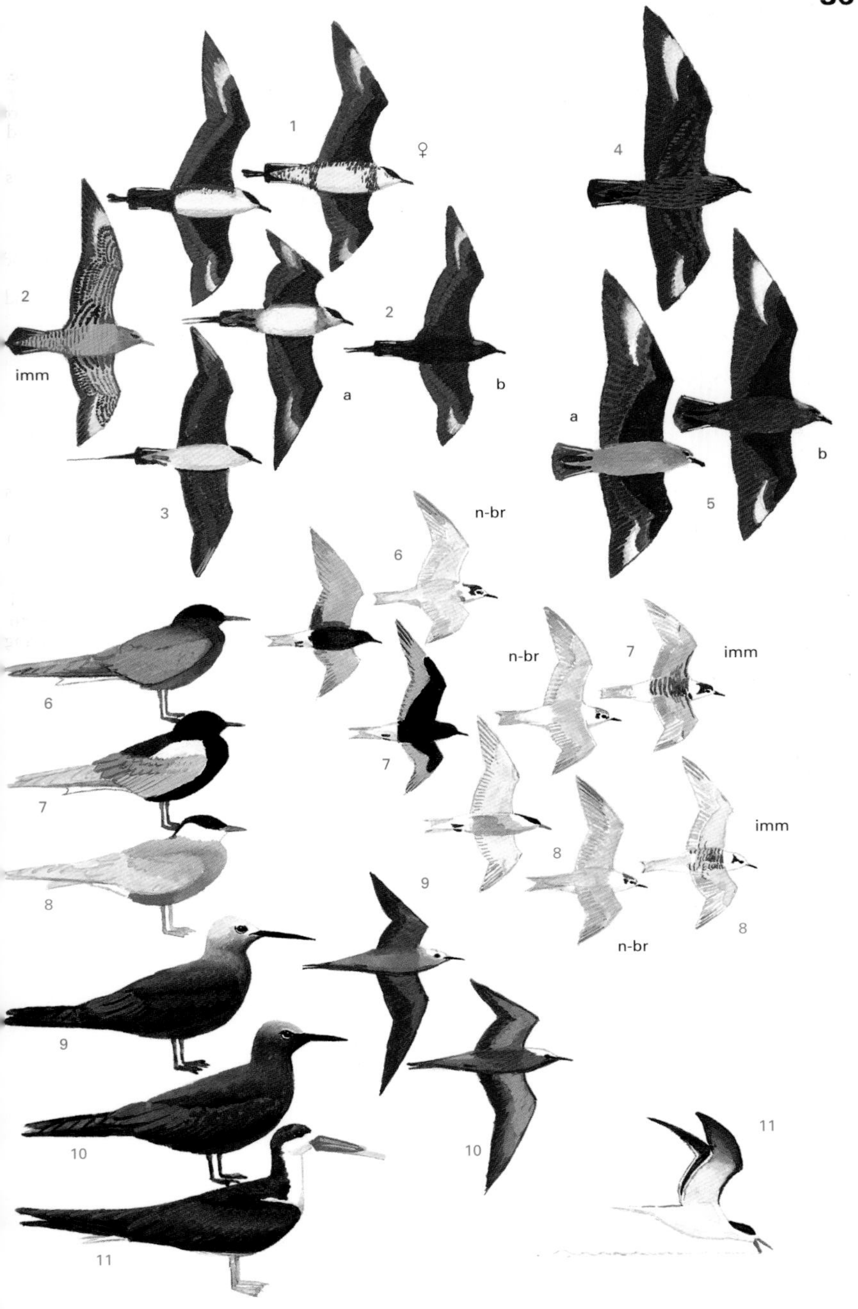
1
♀
2
imm
2
a
b
3
4
a
b
5
n-br
6
6
n-br
7
imm
7
7
9
8
imm
8
9
8
n-br
10
9
10
11
10
11

36

Plate 37

1 CASPIAN TERN *Sterna caspia* L 55 cm. Note bill colour. Habitat: mainly at the seashore and Lake Turkana. Rarely at other lakes. Voice: mid-high, raucous, swept-up '*rhaeeeh rhaeeeh*'. (AM) (NM)

2 SWIFT TERN *Sterna bergii* L 50 cm. Note yellowish bill colour. Habitat: seashore and coastal areas. AM

3 CRESTED TERN *Sterna bengalensis* L 40 cm. Note orange bill colour. Habitat: seashore and other coastal habitats. AM

4 SANDWICH TERN *Sterna sandvicensis* L 45 cm. Note yellow bill-tip, white rump and tail. Habitat: offshore, but also in coastal areas. NM

5 BLACK-NAPED TERN *Sterna sumatrana* L 30 cm. Note almost white plumage, all-black bill and feet. Habitat: seashore. Voice: very high, grating, almost reed warbler-like shrieks '*trip trip trick trick*'.

6 ROSEATE TERN *Sterna dougallii* L 40 cm. Note rosy wash on breast in br plumage. Always very light upperparts with white rump and tail. Tail projects beyond folded wings. Only first three primaries darker grey. Habitat: seashore. Voice: '*uWEETWEEH*' (very high pressed out '*-WEEH*' is slightly higher). (NM)

7 COMMON TERN *Sterna hirundo* L 40 cm. Note black-tipped red bill in br plumage. In n-br plumage, rump almost uniformly grey with rest of upperparts. Dark grey of wing tips spread over more than first four primaries. Habitat: seashore. Rarely at rift valley lakes. Voice: '*KEE-er*' ('*KEE*' very high and sharp). NM

8 WHITE-CHEEKED TERN *Sterna repressa* L 35 cm. Br plumage rather dark brown except cheek. In n-br plumage, rump uniform with mantle and whole of upperparts rather contrasting with white underparts. Habitat: seashore.

9 ARCTIC TERN *Sterna paradisaea* L 40 cm. In br plumage bill all-red and underparts uniformly light grey with upperparts. Tail longer than folded wings. In n-br plumage rump and tail white. Habitat: more offshore than inshore. May however wander inland. Voice: '*eAAAhr*', low and drawn down. NM

10 BRIDLED TERN *Sterna anaethetus* L 40 cm. Eyebrow extends behind eye. Mantle gradually becoming darker. Imm has white underparts as chin. Habitat: seashore.

11 SOOTY TERN *Sterna fuscata* L 45 cm. White confined to forehead. Imm has dark underparts but pale brown under tail-coverts. Habitat: seashore.

12 LITTLE TERN *Sterna albifrons* L 25 cm. Note small size, short-necked profile, yellowish feet (also in n-br plumage), and white forehead to just behind eye in br plumage. Habitat: seashore and Lake Turkana. Occasionally at other lakes. (AM) (NM)

13 SAUNDERS'S TERN *Sterna saundersi* L 25 cm. Note dark feet. Wing tip more extensively black than that of Little Tern. White forehead stops before eye. Habitat: seashore. OM

14 GULL-BILLED TERN *Gelochelidon nilotica* L 40 cm. Note characteristic headshape with black heavy bill and often upright long-necked stance. Habitat: sea and lake shores. NM

1
n-br
2
n-br
1
2
3
3
n-br
4
n-br
4
5
5
6
n-br
6
n-br
7
7
8
n-br
8
9
9
n-br
imm
10
10
11
11
imm
12
12
n-br
13
13
n-br
14
14
n-br

37

Plate 38

1 **WESTERN BRONZE-NAPED PIGEON** *Columba iriditorques* L 30 cm. Note pale tips of outer tail-feathers, and green and violet neck. Habitat: <1500 m. Forest canopies. Voice: mid-high '*oohooroo*', high '*oo-hooroo*' and high '*oohoo-oohoo-oohoo*' (each '*oohoo*' gliding down).

2 **EASTERN BRONZE-NAPED PIGEON** *Columba delegorguei* L 35 cm. Note green nape and white hind-collar of ♂. The ♀ has buff-chestnut (not grey) head. Habitat: 1500-3000(&>) m. Forest canopies. Voice: high, slowly rising, then accelerated, descending '*hoo-coo hoo côô coo-coo-coocoocoocoo*'.

3 **OLIVE PIGEON** *Columba arquatrix* L 40 cm. Note yellow bill and feet and spotted wing and chest. Nape blue-grey (not white-grey). Habitat: 1500-3000(&>) m. Forest canopies and tall plantations. Voice: strange, low, hollow, almost rattling '*coocoocoocoocoocoocoocoo*'.

4 **WHITE-NAPED PIGEON** *Columba albinucha* L 40 cm. Note white-grey nape and unspotted wings. Bill and feet red. Habitat: 1250(&<)-2000 m. Canopies and mid-strata of forests, especially in palms.

5 **AFEP PIGEON** *Columba unicincta* L 35 cm. Habitat: <1750 m. Forest canopies. Voice: low '*oohoo oohoo oohoo -*' (each '*oohoo*' slightly gliding down).

6 **SOMALI STOCK PIGEON** *Columba oliviae* L 40 cm. Note pale colouring and purple crown. Habitat: cliffs and rocky hillsides, with scarce grass and some shrubs, near the seashore. E (Somalia)

7 **SPECKLED PIGEON** *Columba guinea* L 40 cm. Habitat: 500-3000 m. Areas near cliffs, and buildings including towns and villages. Voice: mid-high, slowly rising, rapid '*coocoocoocoocoo -*' and high '*roohoo*'.

8 **WHITE-COLLARED PIGEON** *Columba albitorques* L 40 cm. Has white wing-patch in opened wing. Habitat: 1750-4000 m. Towns, villages and other settlements; woodland, grass- and farmland. [E] (Ethiopia)

9 **ROCK PIGEON** *Columba livia* L 35 cm. True wild Rock Dove of N Ethiopia has pale, sometimes white, rump. Elsewhere many colour forms of Feral Pigeon descendant from the Rock Pigeon are found in cities and towns (not depicted). Habitat: in N Ethiopia wild Rock Doves live around escarpments, rocky gorges and sea cliffs. Voice: very low, descending, fast '*woocoohôoroo*' and drawn-up '*woohoohoo*'.

10 **CHESTNUT-BELLIED SANDGROUSE** *Pterocles exustus* L 30 cm. Unmarked breast of ♀ sharply demarcated from striped and spotted chest. Habitat: <1500 m. Bare semi-desert, dry, open and shrubbed areas with more or less grass cover. (Comes to water within 1-3 hours after sunrise.)

11 **SPOTTED SANDGROUSE** *Pterocles senegallus* L 30 cm. Orange chin and unmarked belly of ♀ merge gradually in mottled throat. Mottling generally not very accentuated. Habitat: desert plains with isolated patches of dense vegetation. (Comes to water within 1-2 hours after sunrise.)

12 **BLACK-FACED SANDGROUSE** *Pterocles decoratus* L 30 cm. Note white underparts and black-mottled belly. Habitat: <1750 m. Open spots like roadsides in dry, open, flat or hilly areas with some grass and scrub; also in dry bushland. (Comes to water within an hour after sunrise.)

13 **LICHTENSTEIN'S SANDGROUSE** *Pterocles lichtensteinii* L 30 cm. Note uniformly barred appearance of ♀. Habitat: arid, hilly, rocky, lightly wooded areas with some scrub. (Drinks just before sunrise or just after sunset but not in large flocks.)

14 **FOUR-BANDED SANDGROUSE** *Pterocles quadricinctus* L 30 cm. Note unmarked chin, throat and chest of ♀. Habitat: open and bushed areas with some grass cover. Also in scrubbed coastal dunes. (Drinks at sunset; otherwise mainly nocturnal.)

15 **YELLOW-THROATED SANDGROUSE** *Pterocles gutturalis* L 35 cm. Note lengthwise striping of ♀ changing to barring on belly. Also white eyebrow and unmarked chin and throat. Habitat: 750-2000 m. Sparsely wooded grass- and farmland. (Drinks within 1-3 hrs after sunrise.)

38

Plate 39

1 **AFRICAN GREEN PIGEON** *Treron calva* L 30 cm. Habitat: <2250 m. Forest edges, cultivation and suburban gardens. Voice: combination of mid-high, short, fast rattles and very high screams.

2 **PEMBA GREEN PIGEON** *Treron pembaensis* L 30 cm. The only green pigeon on Pemba. Habitat: open forests, cultivation, parks and gardens. E (Tanzania)

3 **BRUCE'S GREEN PIGEON** *Treron waalia* L 30 cm. Habitat: dry, wooded grassland, towns, villages and other places with fruiting figs. Voice: starts like creaking door and continues like the yelping of a small dog wanting to be let out.

4 **NAMAQUA DOVE** *Oena capensis* L 25 cm. Note black-and-white banded rump and rufous wings. Habitat: <1750 m. Semi-desert and dry, more or less bushed, habitats. Voice: high, hollow, slurred '*wucwhǫ-OOǫ-*' ('*wuc-*' very short).

5 **TAMBOURINE DOVE** *Turtur tympanistria* L 25 cm. Habitat: <2500 m. Forests, scrub- and woodland, suburban gardens and plantations. Voice: mid-high, hollow, slightly descending '*oo oo-oo oo oo oo-oo oo-oo-oo-coocoocoocoocoocoo*' almost speeded up to a trill at the end.

6 **BLUE-SPOTTED WOOD DOVE** *Turtur afer* L 20 cm. Note red-based yellow bill. Habitat: <2000 m. Forests and bushland, cultivation, mangroves and plantations. Voice: high, slowly descending '*oo oo-oo oo oo-oo-oocoocoocoocoocoo*'.

7 **BLACK-BILLED WOOD DOVE** *Turtur abyssinicus* L 20 cm. Note black bill. Habitat: woodland, dry scrubland, thickets, wooded swamp edges and cultivation. Voice: high, slowly descending '*oo ooooh oovoovoo oovoovoo oocoovoovoovoo*'.

8 **EMERALD-SPOTTED WOOD DOVE** *Turtur chalcospilos* L 20 cm. Note black-tipped red bill. Habitat: <1750 m. More or less wooded and bushed, natural and cultivated areas. Voice: high, slowly descending '*oovoo oo-voo voovoo oovoovoocoocoocoo*'.

9 **BLUE-HEADED WOOD DOVE** *Turtur brehmeri* L 25 cm. Habitat: forest floors and ground strata. Voice: mid-high, starting very slowly, gradually descending '*pioe pioe pioe pioe pioe-pioe poopoopoopoopoo*' (ending in a near-trill).

10 **LEMON DOVE** *Columba larvata* L 25 cm. (Ethiopian race *bronzina*, resembling *l.larvata*, not depicted.) Race *l.larvata* (a) in Kenya and Tanzania, race *jacksoni* (b) in W Uganda. Note plain, unmarked wings. Habitat: 1500 (♂<)-3000 m. Undergrowth and floor of dense forests, parks and suburban gardens. Voice: high, hollow '*woop woop - *' (2 x '*woop*' per 3 sec).

11 **RED-EYED DOVE** *Streptopelia semitorquata* L 30 cm. Tail with grey (not white) corners and dark bar when spread in flight. Rather dark upperparts. Red eye looks dark in the field. Habitat: <3000 m. Forest edges, woodland and suburban gardens. Voice: high, hurried '*coocoocoo coo-coo*'.

12 **AFRICAN MOURNING DOVE** *Streptopelia decipiens* L 30 cm. Note red ring around pale eye. Habitat: <1500 m. Dry wooded habitats with some grass, often near streams. Also in gardens. Voice: high, short '*wooh*' followed by low rattle '*durrrrr*' and '*wooCôôwoo*'.

13 **COLLARED DOVE** *Streptopelia decaocto* L 35 cm. Note large size, pale pinkish-grey colouring, narrow neck-collar, grey rump and dark eye. Habitat: towns and villages (Europe) and plantations (Egypt). Voice: mid-high, rapid '*cooCooo coo*' and a low, harsh, miauling shriek.

14 **AFRICAN COLLARED DOVE** *Streptopelia roseogrisea* L 30 cm. Note very pale greyish-pink appearance. Large white tail corners. Habitat: open and bushed semi-desert with more or less grass cover. Voice: mid-high, unhurried, gliding '*cook-crrrooOôooh*'. (NM)

15 **WHITE-WINGED TURTLE-DOVE** *Streptopelia reichenowi* L 25 cm. Habitat: dry woodland especially with palms, often near streams.

16 **VINACEOUS DOVE** *Streptopelia vinacea* L 25 cm. Note pinkish colouring. Outer tail-feathers white with dark brown base. Belly and under tail-coverts not white. More intensive pink than Ring-necked Dove. Habitat: <1250 m. Dry, more or less wooded and bushed natural and cultivated habitats. Voice: very high, almost rattling, hollow, fast '*ruruRûru-*' and high, fast '*wêêwêêwee-wêêwêêru-*'.

17 **RING-NECKED DOVE** *Streptopelia capicola* L 25 cm. Note white belly and under tail-coverts. Habitat: <2000 m. Forest edges, open woodland and other areas with some trees and bush. Voice: very high, unhurried '*wickwrrrrick-wǫck*'.

18 **WESTERN TURTLE-DOVE** *Streptopelia turtur* L 30 cm. Note black in tail. Habitat: more or less open, leafy woodland. Voice: high '*tûrtur grurrrr*'. NM

19 **DUSKY TURTLE-DOVE** *Streptopelia lugens* L 30 cm. Note rufous-edged tertials. Colouring not much darker than Red-eyed Dove with which it often shares habitat. Habitat: 1750-3250 m. Bamboo, forest edges, cultivations, suburban gardens and other areas. Voice: low, crooning '*cooCooooorr-coorrcoorr*'.

▶

39

20 LAUGHING DOVE *Streptopelia senegalensis* L 25 cm. Note speckled chest-patches. Habitat: parks and gardens, cultivation near settlement and dry, more or less bushed grassland. Voice: very high, descending, fast 'cucCôocoocoo -'.

Plate 40

1 GREY PARROT *Psittacus erithacus* L 30 cm. Habitat: forests and nearby small-scale cultivation.

2 GREY-HEADED LOVEBIRD *Agapornis cana* L 14 cm. (Introduced on Zanzibar, but not seen there since 1920.)

3 FISCHER'S LOVEBIRD *Agapornis fischeri* L 14 cm. Habitat: 1000-2000 m. Birds in Kenya feral. Wooded areas with acacias and baobabs. Crossbred *fischeri* x *personata* (a) from Naivasha, also found in Nairobi, Dar es Salaam and other places. (Note that rump colour should be blue rather than pinkish-purple.)

4 YELLOW-COLLARED LOVEBIRD *Agapornis personata* L 15 cm. Birds outside Tanzania feral with a possible exception in Kenya. Habitat: 1000-2000 m. Bushland with scattered baobab and other trees. E? (Tanzania)

5 BLACK-COLLARED LOVEBIRD *Agapornis swinderniana* L 13 cm. Note blue rump. Habitat: 500-1250 m. Forests and connected well-wooded streams.

6 BLACK-WINGED LOVEBIRD *Agapornis taranta* L 15 cm. Note black primaries. Habitat: 1250-3250 m. Conifer forests and other more or less wooded habitats. [E] (Ethiopia)

7 LILIAN'S LOVEBIRD *Agapornis lilianae* L 14 cm. Note green rump and tail. Habitat: 500-1250(&>) m. More or less wooded country.

8 RED-HEADED LOVEBIRD *Agapornis pullaria* L 13 cm. Note green rump and partly red tail. Habitat: 750-1250 m. Forests and moist wooded grassland.

9 BROWN-NECKED PARROT *Poicephalus robustus* L 35 cm. Note pale yellowish bill. Habitat: <2250(&>) m. Woodland with baobab.

10 RED-FRONTED PARROT *Poicephalus gulielmi* L 30 cm. Note red forehead and wing shoulder. Habitat: 1750-3250 m. Coniferous forests.

11 BROWN PARROT *Poicephalus meyeri* L 25 cm. Note yellow crown and wing shoulder. Habitat: <2250 m. More or less wooded grassland and scrubland with scattered trees, especially baobab.

12 AFRICAN ORANGE-BELLIED PARROT *Poicephalus rufiventris* L 25 cm. The ♀ as ♂ Brown Parrot but with red eye and without yellow. Habitat: <1250 m. Dry bushland with some trees, especially baobab.

13 BROWN-HEADED PARROT *Poicephalus cryptoxanthus* L 25 cm. Note bicoloured bill, yellow line around shoulder and green back. Habitat: <1250 m. Wood- and bushland, palm plantations and mangroves.

14 YELLOW-FRONTED PARROT *Poicephalus flavifrons* L 25 cm. Habitat: 1750-4000 m. Forests. E (Ethiopia)

15 ROSE-RINGED PARAKEET *Psittacula krameri* L 35 cm. Wild in N Uganda, N Ethiopia and N Somalia; elsewhere introduced. Habitat: <2000 m. More or less wooded, natural and cultivated areas, including parks and gardens, and marshes with some trees.

40

Plate 41

1 **EASTERN GREY PLANTAIN-EATER** *Crinifer zonurus* L 50 cm. Note yellow bill. Habitat: <1500(&>) m. Open woodland, cultivated areas and suburban gardens.

2 **BARE-FACED GO-AWAY BIRD** *Corythaixoides personata* L 50 cm. Habitat: <1500(&>) m. More or less wooded, natural and cultivated areas.

3 **GREY GO-AWAY BIRD** *Corythaixoides concolor* L 50 cm. Habitat: open wood- and bushland, parks and gardens. Voice: mid-high, miauling, gliding down '*mûèèèeh*'.

4 **WHITE-BELLIED GO-AWAY BIRD** *Corythaixoides leucogaster* L 50 cm. (Scientific name as by Short.) Habitat: <1500(&>) m. Dry, wooded and bushed habitats. Voice: mid-high, bleating bark '*wèèeeh weh -*'.

5 **GREAT BLUE TURACO** *Corythaeola cristata* L 75 cm. Habitat: 500-2500 m. Forest canopies and forest patches.

6 **ROSS'S TURACO** *Musophaga rossae* L 50 cm. Habitat: 500-2500 m. Canopy of forest remains, miombo, other woodland and gardens; often near streams. Voice: high, short, slowed-down cackling '*rututut-Tut-TUT*'.

7 **GREEN TURACO** *Tauraco persa* L 40 cm. (Not all races depicted.) Race *schalowi* (a) in SW Kenya and W Tanzania, race *livingstonii* (b) in N, NW, C and SE Tanzania. All races combine purple tail and pointed crest. Habitat: <2500 m. Mid-strata and canopy of rather dense forests and woodland. Voice: high, barking '*wah-wah-Wraah-Wraah-Wraah-Wraah*'.

8 **BLACK-BILLED TURACO** *Tauraco schuetti* L 40 cm. Combines black bill, emerald-green tail and neat round crest. Habitat: 500-1000 m. Forest canopies. Voice: mid-high, persistent '*wah-wah wah-wah*' (like small dogs barking).

9 **FISCHER'S TURACO** *Tauraco fischeri* L 40 cm. Habitat: <1500 m. Woodland, cultivation and gardens. Voice: high, speeded-up, loud, barking '*woo woo Wah-Wah-WAHWAHWAH WAHWAH*'.

10 **WHITE-CRESTED TURACO** *Tauraco leucolophus* L 40 cm. Habitat: 1000-2250 m. Leafy canopy at forest edges. Also in wood-, bush- and scrubland.

11 **HARTLAUB'S TURACO** *Tauraco hartlaubi* L 40 cm. Habitat: 1500-3000 m. Forests, parks and suburban gardens.

12 **WHITE-CHEEKED TURACO** *Tauraco leucotis* L 40 cm. Note dark crest. White neck-patch not always present (not in race that lives in same area as Ruspoli's Turaco, for instance). Habitat: forests and connected well-wooded streams.

13 **RUSPOLI'S TURACO** *Tauraco ruspolii* L 40 cm. No white in face except dirty white crest. Habitat: conifer forests with dense undergrowth and surrounding wooded areas. E (Ethiopia)

14 **RWENZORI TURACO** *Musophaga johnstoni* L 40 cm. Race *johnstoni* (a) north of race *kivuensis* (b) both in SW Uganda. Note high, green, purple-pointed bill. Habitat: 2000-3500 m. Forests and bamboo.

15 **PURPLE-CRESTED TURACO** *Musophaga porphyreolopha* L 40 cm. Note black bill. Habitat: <1500 m. Well-wooded streams, forests, woodland, dense bushland, plantations and gardens.

41

Plate 42

1 BLACK-AND-WHITE CUCKOO *Oxylophus jacobinus* L 35 cm. Normal (a) and black (b) forms shown. Black form smaller with proportionally shorter tail than black form of Levaillant's Cuckoo. Habitat: <3000 m. Dry grassland with scattered trees and bush. Voice: very high, piping *'piu piu piu piu -'* and a high, sustained chatter. (AM)

2 LEVAILLANT'S CUCKOO *Oxylophus levaillantii* L 35 cm. Normal (a) and black (b) forms shown. Black form proportionally longer-tailed than Black-and-white Cuckoo. Habitat: <2000 m. Forest edges, wooded swamps, dense moist bushland and gardens. Voice: very high, piping *'piu piu piu piu piu -'* (each *'piu'* gliding down). (AM)

3 GREAT SPOTTED CUCKOO *Clamator glandarius* L 40 cm. Habitat: <3000 m. Dry, more or less wooded and bushed, natural and cultivated habitats. Voice: high, chattering, rattling *'krekweh'* and highe *'rrrrrruuu'*. (AM) (NM)

4 THICK-BILLED CUCKOO *Pachycoccyx audeberti* L 35 cm. Habitat: <1250 m. Miombo. Also other woodland and gallery forests.

5 DUSKY LONG-TAILED CUCKOO *Cercococcyx mechowi* L 35 cm. Note dark, unbarred mantle and rufous barring of outer-primary webs. Imm like Barred Long-tailed Cuckoo but barring more distinct, especially on wing. Habitat: 750-1750 m. Forest mid-strata and undergrowth, often near streams. Voice: very high, repeated, slightly climbing, sweeping *'pu-wee-Wir'* and other whistles.

6 OLIVE LONG-TAILED CUCKOO *Cercococcyx olivinus* L 35 cm. Primaries and outer tail-feathers barred pale buff (not tawny). Habitat: 750-2000 m. Forests and connected well-wooded streams. Voice: mid-high, fluting *'fûwuwu-fûwuwu-fûwuwu-'* and high, lazy *'it-will-rain'*.

7 BARRED LONG-TAILED CUCKOO *Cercococcyx montanus* L 35 cm. Note barred tawny rufous tail and unbarred crown. Habitat: 1500-3000 m. Forest edges and coastal thickets. Voice: high, repeated song of 3 connected parts *'fiiju-fiiju-pii-pûu-pii-pûu- -weetweet-wuh'* (*'fiiju'* gliding down *'pii-pûu'* repeated 3-5 times and *'weetweet-wuh'* very high).

8 YELLOWBILL *Ceuthmochares aureus* L 35 cm. Habitat: <2000 m. Dense undergrowth of forest edges and connected well-wooded streams. Voice: mid-high, scolding *'Kah-Kah-Káh-Kah-Kah'* and extra high, speeded-up trill.

9 SENEGAL COUCAL *Centropus senegalensis* L 40 cm. Note black rump. Mantle and wings chestnut-brown. Habitat: rather dry bush- and scrubland, edges of forests and swamps. Also in tall reedbeds. Voice: mid-high, rather barking *'kah kah kah kah -'* and low, piping, hollow, speeded up, rather fast *'poopoopoopupupupupupupup'* (water bottle song).

10 BLACK COUCAL *Centropus grillii* L 40 cm. In n-br plumage no distinct eyebrow. Habitat: marshes and inundations with bush and shrub patches. Voice: mid-high, harsh rattle *'kraa kraa kraakaakaa-kaa'*.

11 WHITE-BROWED COUCAL *Centropus superciliosus* L 40 cm. (Not all races depicted.) Race *burchellii* (a) in SE Tanzania, with finely barred rump. Note pale eyebrow in other races. Habitat: normally in grassy and reedy places within more or less bushed areas. Occasionally in arid areas. Voice: mid-high, hollow, descending and rising *'uhuhuhuhuhuhuhurrrrruhuhuhuh'* (accelerated to trill in the middle).

12 BLUE-HEADED COUCAL *Centropus monachus* L 45 cm. Note blue sheen on head and neck. Upper tail-coverts unbarred. Throat lightest area of underparts. Mantle browner than wings. Habitat: 500-2000 m. Reed beds, papyrus, tall grass, herbage and shrubbery at river banks or in forest clearings. Voice: mid-high, hollow, piping *'poo-poo-poo-poopoopoo'*.

13 COPPERY-TAILED COUCAL *Centropus cupreicaudus* L 45 cm. No blue sheen on crown and neck. Upper tail-coverts faintly barred buff. Under tail-coverts palest area of underparts. Habitat: reed beds, papyrus and nearby tall grass and shrubbery.

14 EURASIAN CUCKOO *Cuculus canorus* L 35 cm. The ♀ occurs in normal form and a rufous (a) form, ♂ only in normal form, as depicted. Habitat: <1750 m. More or less wooded and bushed habitats. Voice: *'Cûccooh'*. (NM)

15 AFRICAN CUCKOO *Cuculus gularis* L 35 cm. Bill more yellow than other cuckoos and white barring of outer tail-feathers wider. Habitat: <3000 m. Hilly, dry, more or less wooded and bushed habitats. Voice: mid-high *'coo-curi coo-curi -'* (*'curi'* short and falling away). AM

16 RED-CHESTED CUCKOO *Cuculus solitarius* L 30 cm. Often heard but seldom seen. Chin grey not rufous. Habitat: <3000 m. Well-wooded streams, forest belts, suburban gardens and cultivation. Voice: very high, loud, fluting *'IT-will-rain IT-will-rain -'* (no *'cuccooh'* sound!). (AM)

17 BLACK CUCKOO *Cuculus clamosus* L 30 cm. Race *c. clamosus* (a) throughout, race *gabonensis* (b) in W Uganda, W Ethiopia and (uncommon) in W Kenya. Note rufous (not pale grey) chin. Tail not barred. Habitat: <2000 m. Canopy at forest edges, woodland, bush- and scrubland and gardens. Voice: high, loud, fluted *'fuu fuu fûuu'* and other high whistles. AM

▶

18 LESSER CUCKOO *Cuculus poliocephalus* L 25 cm. Only distinguishable from other cuckoos by smaller size and distinctive voice. Habitat: forest edges and dense undergrowth in wood- and bushland. Voice: very high, descending, yelping, rapid '*djipdjipdjipdjip*'. AM NM

19 MADAGASCAR LESSER CUCKOO *Cuculus rochii* L 30 cm. Only distinguishable by voice. Habitat: forests, woodland and bushed areas. Voice: very high, liquid yelping '*whôop whôopwhôop-whop*'.

20 KLAAS'S CUCKOO *Chrysococcyx klaas* L 15 cm. Note white stripe behind eye and plain emerald-green upperparts of ♂. The ♀ has barred chin; belly centre and under tail-coverts only partly barred. Habitat: <3000 m. Forest patches, miombo, parks and gardens. Voice: very high, up-and-down, fluting, plaintive '*it's not trúe dear*'.

21 DIEDERIK CUCKOO *Chrysococcyx caprius* L 20 cm. Note white belly and under tail-coverts of ♀. Habitat: <2000 m. Forests and other more or less wooded and bushed areas including cultivation and gardens. Occasionally in papyrus swamp. Voice: extra high, fast '*it-will-NEVer-rain*'. (AM)

22 YELLOW-THROATED GREEN CUCKOO *Chrysococcyx flavigularis* L 20 cm. Note unbarred upperparts of ♀. Outer tail-feathers mainly white. Outer tail-feathers mainly white. Habitat: 500-1250 m. Forest canopies. Voice: very high, fluting, slightly falling-off '*fee-wee-peepeepeepeepee*'.

23 AFRICAN EMERALD CUCKOO *Chrysococcyx cupreus* L 25 cm. Note regular green and white barring of ♀ underparts. Outer tail-feathers mainly white. Habitat: <2000 m. Glades and edges of dense forests, wood- and bushland, cultivation and suburban gardens. Voice: very high, mellow, liquid, affirmative fluting *tedooh tjuh-dêh*', also rendered as '*helloh judy*' ('*helloh*' gliding, '*judy*' staccato).

Plate 43

1 AFRICAN GRASS OWL *Tyto capensis* L 35 cm. Note slim, high-legged build. No dark wrist mark underneath wing, unlike African Marsh-Owl (43.15). Hunts at night away from settlement. Habitat: <3250 m. Wet grass- and moorland. Voice: high shriek '*wèèèh*' and low, rasping, Mallard-like '*kwer kwec kwec kwec*'.

2 BARN OWL *Tyto alba* L 35 cm. Note pale appearance and upright stance. Habitat: near buildings, caves and Hamerkop nests; not in true forest. Voice: very high, loud, shivering '*whururururu*' and drawn-up shrieking '*frrrruuuui*' ('*-i*' short).

3 SOKOKE SCOPS-OWL *Otus ireneae* L 15 cm. Very variable like all scops-owls. Coloured rufous, brown or grey. Stance slim with strikingly outstanding ears, or thick and round. Habitat: <250 m. Dry forests and miombo. E (Kenya)

4 COMMON SCOPS-OWL *Otus scops* L 20 cm. (Includes *Otus senegalensis* [African Scops-owl] now recognised as independent species, only distinguishable by voice.) Very variable in colouring and stance. Grey form (b) seen more than buff (a) and brown (not shown) forms. More distinctly striped than other scops-owls. Habitat: <2000 m. More or less wooded habitats, including gardens. Voice: call from *senegalensis* very high '*prriur*' ('*ur*' slightly lower) and low hooting '*trjuuh trjuuh -*' (with 4 sec between each) and from *scops*, high, clear '*hjuuh hjuuh -*' (with 2 sec between each). (NM)

5 PEMBA SCOPS-OWL *Otus pembaensis* L 20 cm. (Not recently heard or seen.) Habitat: plantations with densely foliaged trees. E (Tanzania)

6 BRUCE'S SCOPS-OWL *Otus brucei* L 25 cm. Note regular, narrow and thin striped lines on underparts and general tawny-grey colouring. May hunt by day. Habitat: dry, open, slightly wooded and bushed, natural and cultivated areas.

7 WHITE-FACED SCOPS-OWL *Otus leucotis* L 25 cm. Habitat: <1750 m. Dry more or less bushed and wooded natural and cultivated areas. Voice: high, hooting '*wuh wûuh*' or mid-high, cooing '*rrrroo-Woouu*' ('*-Woo-*' much higher, falling abruptly like a whip lash).

8 PEARL-SPOTTED OWLET *Glaucidium perlatum* L 20 cm. Note long tail and pseudo face at back of head. Habitat: <2250 m. Dry, open woodland and bushed areas with some large trees. Voice: very high, piercing, descending shrieks '*piiiuuu*' (like fireworks) and high '*piuu-piuu-piuu-*' sustained for 20-30 sec, slowly rising and falling in pitch and tempo.

9 RED-CHESTED OWLET *Glaucidium tephronotum* L 20 cm. May hunt by day. Habitat: 750-2250 m. Forests. Voice: high, mellow, gliding, hooting '*too-too-too-*' (2-30 times) or '*tutju tutju -*' or '*huu-huu-huu-*'.

10 AFRICAN BARRED OWLET *Glaucidium capense* L 25 cm. (Not all races shown.) Race *castaneum* (a) (rare) in W Uganda. Note regular head barring and prominent white stripe along mantle. Habitat: <1250 (&>) m. More or less dense forests. Voice: high, slightly rising '*wuh-wuh-wuh-wuh-wuh-wuh-*' and very high, staccato '*pjupjupjupjupjupju*'.

11 LITTLE OWL *Athene noctua* L 25 cm. Note short tail. May hunt by day. Habitat: rocky country and dry areas with scattered trees, shrub and some grass cover. Voice: high, melancholy '*Wjooo Wjooo -*' ('*Wj-*' rapidly lowered in pitch) and alarm '*kip-kip-kip*'.

12 PEL'S FISHING-OWL *Scotopelia peli* L 70 cm. Habitat: <1750 m. Well-wooded streams and mangroves. Voice: high, loud, sinister, rapidly gliding down, howling '*wjôêjaaaaagh*'.

▶

43

13 AFRICAN WOOD-OWL *Strix woodfordii* L 35 cm. Note dark eyes. Habitat: <2750 m. Dense woodland, plantations and suburban gardens. Voice: mid-high hoots like warning barks of quite large dog '*woo-woo-wooberdewoo*'.

14 LONG-EARED OWL *Asio otus* L 45 cm. Note long upright stance especially when disturbed but may perch also with fluffed-out feathers and no visible ear plumes. Habitat: 2000-3500 m. Forest edges and giant heath.

15 AFRICAN MARSH-OWL *Asio capensis* L 35 cm. Note seemingly large eyes and buff barring of flight feathers. Active in twilight at sunset and sunrise. Habitat: <3000 m. Short grass- and moorland, marshes and swamps. Voice: loud explosive shrieks, mid-high duck-like barking '*whuuwhu*' and mid-high snipe-like '*crèèk*'. (AM)

16 SHORT-EARED OWL *Asio flammeus* L 40 cm. Active all day. Habitat: open marshes and wet grasslands. Voice: soft, pushed-out '*booh-booh-booh-booh-*'. NM

17 VERREAUX'S EAGLE-OWL *Bubo lacteus* L 65 cm. Note pink eyelids. Habitat: <2000(&>) m. Well-wooded streams and other areas with some large trees. Voice: extra low, barking '*proôproôproôproo*'.

18 CAPE EAGLE-OWL *Bubo capensis* L 55 cm. Note blotched, only sparsely striped underparts and distinct white edge of scapulars. Crown striped lengthwise. Habitat: 1750-4250 m. Montane moorland with scattered trees and forest patches. Voice: very low, hooting '*hoot hoottooh*'.

19 FRASER'S EAGLE-OWL *Bubo poensis* L 55 cm. Race *p. poensis* (a) in SW Uganda, race *vosseleri* (b) (Nduk Eagle-Owl) in NE Tanzania. Note overall striping and blue eyelids. Habitat: 1500-2250 m (a), 750-1500 m (b). Forests. Voice: *p. poensis* with high, crescendoing, plaintive '*uuuuuuuh*' and very low, pigeon-like rolling '*rrrrru rrrrru*'.

20 COMMON EAGLE-OWL *Bubo bubo* L 60 cm. Note very pale tawny colouring. Habitat: rocky desert and sparsely wooded semi-desert. Voice: very low, pigeon-like '*oohoo*'.

21 SPOTTED EAGLE-OWL *Bubo africanus* L 50 cm. (Not all races shown.) Race *cinerascens* (a) from N Uganda and N Kenya northwards. Habitat: <2250 m. Prefers rocky ravines; also in dry open woodland. Voice: low, short pressed-out '*ooh ooh -*' (with a gap of 6 sec between each '*ooh*').

Plate 44

1 BATES'S NIGHTJAR *Caprimulgus batesi* L 30 cm. Note large, very dark rufous and grey-capped appearance. The ♀ with rufous-brown (not grey) crown and without white in tail and wings. Habitat: <1000 m. Rainforests. Voice: loud, rapid '*whow-whow-whow-*' (5-20 times).

2 SWAMP NIGHTJAR *Caprimulgus natalensis* L 25 cm. Note overall spotted and blotched feathering, short tail with white (♂) or partly buff (♀) tail edges. Habitat: 500-2250 m. Wet grassland, edges of swamps, marshes and lagoons, forest clearings and edges. Voice: high, sustained, staccato '*cuckcuckcuckcuckcuckcuck-*'.

3 SLENDER-TAILED NIGHTJAR *Caprimulgus clarus* L 30 cm. Note white (or buff in ♀) line along trailing wing-edge and (in flight) along forewing, large white throat-patch and white (or buff in ♀) tail edges. The ♂ has lengthened middle tail-feathers. Habitat: <2000 m. Dry, wooded and bushed habitats. Voice: high, sustained, staccato, rapid rattle '*rirrirriri-*' (like a fast sewing machine).

4 GABON NIGHTJAR *Caprimulgus fossii* L 25 cm. Note white tail edges and white line along trailing wing-edge, along forewing and over primaries (all buff in ♀). Large white throat-patch. Habitat: <2000 m. Grassy and sandy areas, often at woodland edges. Voice: mid-high, rapid, staccato rattle '*rururu-riririri-*' ('*ruru-*' 10-30 times and lower and softer than '*riri-*'[20-30 times]).

5 FIERY-NECKED NIGHTJAR *Caprimulgus pectoralis* L 25 cm. Note rather dark appearance, rufous chin, black and white mantle margins and narrow white band over primaries. White tail-areas of ♀ smaller and more buff. Habitat: <1500 m. Open woodland, miombo, plantations and gardens. Voice: high '*tjuuû tuwûwirrrr*' ('*tjuuu*' distinctly drawn up).

6 BLACK-SHOULDERED NIGHTJAR *Caprimulgus nigriscapularis* L 25 cm. Note grey upperparts, buff-rufous underparts and white black-bordered throat-patch. Habitat: <1500 m. Rainforests, dense woodland and moist bushland. Voice: high, liquid '*tjuuû tjuderrr*' ('*tjuuu*' drawn up 'tjude[*rrr*]' short).

7 MONTANE NIGHTJAR *Caprimulgus poliocephalus* L 25 cm. Race *p. poliocephalus* (a) (Abyssinian Nightjar) in NE Tanzania, Kenya and Ethiopia, race *guttifer* (b) (Usambara Nightjar) in NE and SW Tanzania. Note white (buff in ♀) tail edges. Habitat: 1000-3000 m. Open forests, moist woodland, suburban gardens and parks. Voice: very high, fluting '*pêeujûu-tirrr*'.

8 RWENZORI NIGHTJAR *Caprimulgus ruwenzori* L 20 cm. Note grey upperparts and buff underparts. No full white collar and tail only partly white. Habitat: forest edges and glades. Voice: extra high, piercing '*piêe-pirrrr*'.

9 DONALDSON-SMITH'S NIGHTJAR *Caprimulgus donaldsoni* L 20 cm. Note small size and rufous appearance. Habitat: <1250 m. Dry bush- and scrubland near water-holes and dry streams. Voice: very high, hurried '*puwêêt-wirr*' ('*-wêêt*' swept up).

►

44

10 PLAIN NIGHTJAR *Caprimulgus inornatus* L 25 cm. Rather unmarked, light greyish-buff appearance. Shoulder slightly darker. Habitat: <2000 m. Dry, wooded and bushed areas with more or less grass cover. Voice: sustained churr. (AM)

11 STAR-SPOTTED NIGHTJAR *Caprimulgus stellatus* L 25 cm. Note plain upperparts, buff belly and white throat spots. Habitat: semi-desert and low-bushed areas with some grass cover.

12 NUBIAN NIGHTJAR *Caprimulgus nubicus* L 20 cm. Note brown-rufous chequered colouring. Habitat: 500-1000 m. Dry bushland with thickets. Voice: very high, yelping '*whowhow whowhow -*'.

13 FRECKLED NIGHTJAR *Caprimulgus tristigma* L 30 cm. Note large, almost black appearance. Habitat: 500-2000 m. Bare or sparsely overgrown rocky outcrops and ravines. Voice: very high, irregular, staccato yelping '*whowhow whowhow whow whowwhowwhowwhow*'.

14 EGYPTIAN NIGHTJAR *Caprimulgus aegyptius* L 25 cm. No white in opened wing. Habitat: desert and semi-desert. Voice: mid-high, sustained, rapid '*corrcorrcorrcorrcorr-*' like a car engine ticking over. AM

15 DUSKY NIGHTJAR *Caprimulgus fraenatus* L 25 cm. Note black and white scapulars. The ♀ has dusky (no white) tail corners. Habitat: <3250 m. Rocky outcrops in dry areas with scattered scrub and some grass cover. Voice: low, rapid rattle '*rrrrrr-*' like a fast electric sewing machine.

16 EURASIAN NIGHTJAR *Caprimulgus europaeus* L 25 cm. Note grey, rather dark, appearance. No distinct neck-collar. Habitat: <3000 m. Bushed and wooded, natural and cultivated habitats. Voice: mid-high, sustained '*rrrrrr-*' (narrowed to '*rrruu*' at irregular intervals); like a rapid mechanical sewing machine. NM

17 LONG-TAILED NIGHTJAR *Caprimulgus climacurus* L 30 cm (excluding tail streamers). Note long tail, white (buff in ♀) bar over wing coverts and along trailing wing edge. Large white throat-patch. Habitat: semi-desert, bushed and wooded grassland, extensive fields and open woodland. Voice: high or low fast rattle '*r-rrrrrr-*' like a fast electrical sewing machine. (AM)

18 STANDARD-WINGED NIGHTJAR *Macrodipteryx longipennis* L 25 cm. In n-br plumage, looking small without white in wing or tail. Buff scapulars and hind-collar. Habitat: 500-1500 m. Bushed and more or less wooded habitats. Voice: extra high, sharp, sustained twitter '*tititititititititi-*' with slight slackenings. AM

19 PENNANT-WINGED NIGHTJAR *Macrodipteryx vexillaria* L 30 cm. The ♂ in n-br plumage like ♀ without long pennants. Habitat: <3000 m. Miombo and other wooded and bushed natural and cultivated habitats in stony hilly areas. Voice: extra high, sharp, shivering, rather short-phrased twitters '*sisisisisisi-*'. AM

Plate 45

1 BOEHM'S SPINETAIL *Neafrapus boehmi* L 10 cm. Note extremely short black tail and sharp demarcation between black and white on throat. Large white rump-patch. Habitat: <1500 m. Open miombo and other woodland especially near baobabs. Voice: very high, twittering, fast trill '*srisrisisitweeh*'.

2 CASSIN'S SPINETAIL *Neafrapus cassini* L 15 cm. Note narrow white line over tail base. Demarcation on breast less distinct than Boehm's Spinetail. Habitat: <1500 m. Forests. Voice: extra high, soft, twittering cries.

3 SABINE'S SPINETAIL *Rhaphidura sabini* L 12 cm. Note bluish sheen on upperparts. Black tail concealed between white coverts. Habitat: 500-1750 m. Rainforest edges, often over water. Voice: extra high, sharp '*tititututu-tu-tu-tu*'.

4 MOTTLED SPINETAIL *Telacanthura ussheri* L 14 cm. Note white belly-patch (not so in Little Swift) and wing shape. Habitat: <2000 m. Forest edges and dry woodland especially near baobab. Voice: very high, dry '*tchu-tchu tchrrrchrrr*' or mid-high rattling '*rururururururrrrruru*'.

5 SCARCE SWIFT *Schoutedenapus myoptilus* L 15 cm. Note pale rather large throat-patch sharply contrasting with black eye-patch. Smaller than other all-dark swifts and with different voice. Habitat: 2000-3000 m. Breeds on rocky cliffs, mountain sides and ravines, but feeds over forests. Voice: combination of extra high, Blacksmith Lapwing-like (31.4) '*tictictic*' (diagnostic) and high '*weetweetwêet-ruhrururuh*'.

6 AFRICAN PALM SWIFT *Cypsiurus parvus* L 15 cm. Note very slim, long-tailed and pale appearance. Habitat: <1500(&>) m. Any habitat with palm trees. Voice: extra high, sharp, twittering chatter '*tiwiwiwiwiwiwi-*'.

7 MOTTLED SWIFT *Tachymarptis aequatorialis* L 20 cm. Note barring and large size. Voice: extra high, sweeping, short, rasping '*srreep*'.

8 ALPINE SWIFT *Tachymarptis melba* L 20 cm. Habitat: 1750-4500 m. Rocky mountains and cliffs. Voice: extra high, very fast, piercing '*swiswiswiswitititi*' and very high '*wuutwitwitwêêtwitweet*'. (NM)

45

Plate 46

1 AFRICAN BLACK SWIFT *Apus barbatus* L 20 cm. Separation of pale throat-patch from breast gradually scaled. Belly, rump and underwing feathers pale-fringed, inner secondaries (seen from above) paler than rest of upperparts. Habitat: breeds in rocky mountains but feeds in lowland areas.
Voice: extra high, sharp scream '*tsjeeeeah tsjeeeah -*' ('*tsjeeee-*' slightly more trilling than Eurasian Swift).

2 FORBES-WATSON'S SWIFT *Apus berliozi* L 20 cm. Throat-patch rather large and ill-defined. General appearance rather pale. Habitat: <3000 m. Breeds in rocky mountains and coastal caves but feeds over all sorts of country. Voice: screams shorter and slightly lower than Eurasian Swift. AM

3 PALLID SWIFT *Apus pallidus* L 15 cm. General appearance rather pale. Throat-patch rather large, wing tips rather blunt and body rather broad. Eye very distinctly marked. Belly and flanks rather mottled. Habitat: prefers coastal areas. Voice: extra high, 2-noted, short shrieks '*shrêgh shrêgh*'. NM

4 NYANZA SWIFT *Apus niansae* L 15 cm. All-black with small, well-defined, sometimes finely striped, throat-patch. Transparent, rather pale, triangle in wing seen from below. Habitat: <3000 m. Breeds in rocky caves and buildings. Voice: as Eurasian Swift.

5 EURASIAN SWIFT *Apus apus* L 15 cm. Note sooty black colouring and well-defined pale throat-patch. Race *pekinensis* (not shown) however more like Forbes-Watson's Swift. Habitat: 500-2000 m. Any open area. Voice: extra high, sharp screams '*tsjeeetsjeeee tsjeeee -*' (each '*tsjeeee*' slightly falling off). NM

6 WHITE-RUMPED SWIFT *Apus caffer* L 15 cm. White on rump restricted to upperside. Note long forked tail. Habitat: <3000 m. 'Steals' nests from swallows under rocks, bridges and roofs. Voice: high, running-up, short chatter '*pupupupupupupu*'.

7 HORUS SWIFT *Apus horus* L 15 cm. White of rump extends to flanks. Tail-points rather short. Habitat: 1500-3000 m. Breeds in holes of bee-eaters, kingfishers and martins. Often seen over water. Voice: high, plover-like, fluting '*piû-pju piû-pju*'.

8 LITTLE SWIFT *Apus affinis* L 14 cm. Screaming, intertwining 'balls' of birds seen high over towns are likely to be this species. Habitat: <3000 m. Breeds under overhanging roofs, bridges and rocks, normally in cities, towns and villages. Voice: extra high, gliding up and down '*pirrrrrpirrrrrrpirrrrrr-*'.

46

Plate 47

1 **BLUE-NAPED MOUSEBIRD** *Urocolius macrourus* L 35 cm. Note bluish rump and upper tail-coverts. Imm without blue nape. Habitat: <1750 m. Dry, more or less wooded and bushed, natural and cultivated areas.

2 **RED-FACED MOUSEBIRD** *Urocolius indicus* L 35 cm. Note bluish rump and upper tail-coverts, rather pale tail and short crest. Habitat: wooded scrub- and bushland, mangroves, plantations and gardens

3 **SPECKLED MOUSEBIRD** *Colius striatus* L 35 cm. Habitat: open forests, wooded grassland, orchards, plantations and suburban gardens.

4 **WHITE-HEADED MOUSEBIRD** *Colius leucocephalus* L 30 cm. Habitat: <1500 m. Dry bushland with thickets, often near streams.

5 **CHOCOLATE-BACKED KINGFISHER** *Halcyon badia* L 20 cm. Habitat: 500-1500 m. Undergrowth of well-wooded streams.

6 **BROWN-HOODED KINGFISHER** *Halcyon albiventris* L 20 cm. Note all-red bill. Habitat: <2000 m. Open forests and wooded habitats including gardens and parks, especially near ponds and streams.

7 **GREY-HEADED KINGFISHER** *Halcyon leucocephala* L 20 cm. (Not all races shown.) Race *pallidiventris* (a) from S Uganda and SW Kenya southwards. Habitat: <2250 m. Dry, more or less natural and cultivated wooded and bushed areas. Not necessarily near water. (AM)

8 **BLUE-BREASTED KINGFISHER** *Halcyon malimbica* L 25 cm. Habitat: 500-2000 m. Forests and mangroves.

9 **WOODLAND KINGFISHER** *Halcyon senegalensis* L 20 cm. Note bicoloured bill and light grey head and breast. Habitat: <1500(&>) m. More or less wooded and bushed areas, often near streams.

10 **MANGROVE KINGFISHER** *Halcyon senegaloides* L 20 cm. Note all-red bill and pale buff head and breast. Habitat: mangroves, forests, more or less wooded grassland, cultivation, lake margins and river banks.

11 **STRIPED KINGFISHER** *Halcyon chelicuti* L 15 cm. Unobtrusive when perched, but striking pale blue when flying away. Note black eye-stripe and bicoloured bill. Habitat: <2500 m. More or less wooded and bushed habitats; often away from water.

12 **WHITE-COLLARED KINGFISHER** *Halcyon chloris* L 15 cm. Habitat: mangroves.

13 **AFRICAN PYGMY KINGFISHER** *Ceyx picta* L 12 cm. Underparts, including chin and throat, uniformly pale rufous. Cheeks pink. Habitat: <1500 (&>) m. Ground-strata of dry wood-, bush- and scrubland; often away from water.

14 **AFRICAN DWARF KINGFISHER** *Ceyx lecontei* L 10 cm. Note rufous crown. Habitat: 500-1500 m. Dense forest undergrowth and connected well-wooded streams.

15 **SHINING-BLUE KINGFISHER** *Alcedo quadribrachys* L 20 cm. Note dark blue (not orange-rufous) cheeks. Habitat: 500-1250(&>) m. Ponds and streams in forests; also at wooded reedy fringes of lakes and rivers.

16 **HALF-COLLARED KINGFISHER** *Alcedo semitorquata* L 15 cm. Note blue cheeks. Generally lighter than Shining-blue Kingfisher. Habitat: 1000-2000 m. Rivers, streams, lakes and lagoons with overhanging trees.

17 **MALACHITE KINGFISHER** *Corythornis cristata* L 14 cm. Note red bill. Eyebrow and crest blue (not rufous). Habitat: <3000 m. Reed beds, papyrus and shrubbery along lakes, dams, ponds, rivers, streams and creeks.

18 **WHITE-BELLIED KINGFISHER** *Corythornis leucogaster* L 13 cm. Note white underparts, rufous chest-collar and white belly. Habitat: 500-1250 m. Dense swampy forests near streams.

19 **PIED KINGFISHER** *Ceryle rudis* L 25 cm. Plunge-dives for fish from hovering flight. Habitat: <2500 m. Lakes, dams, rivers, creeks, estuaries and coral lagoons.

20 **GIANT KINGFISHER** *Megaceryle maxima* L 40 cm. Habitat: <2750 m. Streams, ponds and lagoons with overhanging trees and shrubs. May be seen at garden pools.

Plate 48

1 **NARINA'S TROGON** *Apaloderma narina* L 30 cm. Habitat: <3000 m. More or less open forests and suburban gardens. Voice: low, loud, crescendoing, hooting '*oooh-oh-oooh-oh-Oooh- Oh- OH-OH*'.

2 **BAR-TAILED TROGON** *Apaloderma vittatum* L 30 cm. Very unobtrusive. Habitat: 1500-3000 m. Forest mid-strata. Voice: high, loud, crescendoing, yelping '*hoo-hoo-hoo-Hoo- Hoo-HOo-HOO-HOO*'.

3 **BLUE-HEADED BEE-EATER** *Merops muelleri* L 20 cm. Habitat: forest edges and interiors.

4 **BLACK BEE-EATER** *Merops gularis* L 20 cm. Habitat: 500-2000 m. Forest edges and interiors.

5 **LITTLE BEE-EATER** *Merops pusillus* L 15 cm. Very similar to Blue-breasted Bee-eater but no white in face. Note rufous in wing. Habitat: <2000 m. Marshes and bushed areas, often near water.

6 **BLUE-BREASTED BEE-EATER** *Merops variegatus* L 20 cm. Note rufous wings, white cheeks and (in good light) purple (not black) gorget. Habitat: tall grassy areas at forest edges or lake sides.

7 **CINNAMON-CHESTED BEE-EATER** *Merops oreobates* L 20 cm. Note green (not rufous) wings and white cheeks. No rufous in tail. Habitat: 1250-3000 m. More or less open forests, cultivation, roadsides, suburban gardens and parks.

8 **SWALLOW-TAILED BEE-EATER** *Merops hirundineus* L 20 cm. Habitat: <1500 m. Wooded and bushed grassland.

9 **CARMINE BEE-EATER** *Merops nubicus* L 40 cm. Race *n. nubicus* (a) in Ethiopia, Somalia, Uganda, Kenya and NE Tanzania, race *nubicoides* (b) (uncommon) in W and S Tanzania and (rare) in S Kenya. Habitat: <1250 m. Wooded and bushed, natural and cultivated areas, including roadsides.

10 **WHITE-FRONTED BEE-EATER** *Merops bullockoides* L 25 cm. Habitat: <2000 m. Wooded and bushed areas, swamp edges and other areas not too far from its breeding colonies in sand cliffs.

11 **RED-THROATED BEE-EATER** *Merops bullocki* L 20 cm. Habitat: <2000 m. Bushed grassland along streams near sand cliffs.

12 **SOMALI BEE-EATER** *Merops revoilii* L 15 cm. Fulvous wing-patches in flight. Habitat: <1000 m. Arid areas with scarce bush and extensive cultivation.

13 **WHITE-THROATED BEE-EATER** *Merops albicollis* L 30 cm. Habitat: <1500 (&>) m. Wooded and bushed areas; also in forests, plantations and gardens. (AM)

14 **LITTLE GREEN BEE-EATER** *Merops orientalis* L 25 cm. Note rufous in wing. Habitat: dry woodland and bushed areas with scarce grass cover; sometimes near watersides and other less dry areas. AM

15 **BOEHM'S BEE-EATER** *Merops boehmi* L 25 cm. Note all-green wing and black tail tip. Habitat: <1500 m. Forest edges near rivers and streams.

16 **BLUE-CHEEKED BEE-EATER** *Merops persicus* L 30 cm. Note coppery underwing in flight. Habitat: <1500 m. Open wooded and bushed grassland, mangroves, and lake and swamp edges. (AM) (NM)

17 **OLIVE BEE-EATER** *Merops superciliosus* L 30 cm. Eyebrow may be blue instead of white as depicted. Habitat: <1500 m. Bushed and wooded grassland, mangroves and lake and swamp edges. (AM)

18 **EURASIAN BEE-EATER** *Merops apiaster* L 30 cm. Habitat: <3000 m. More or less wooded areas including suburban gardens and parks. Often seen and heard passing overhead in loose, seemingly aimless, flying flocks. Voice: high, melodious, liquid, short flutes '*jup*' or '*prjuup*'. NM

48

Plate 49

1 **RUFOUS-CROWNED ROLLER** *Coracias naevia* L 35 cm. Note short tail and shaggy appearance. Habitat: <1250(&>) m. Dry areas with tall trees and bush.

2 **RACQUET-TAILED ROLLER** *Coracias spatulata* L 40 cm. Note intense blue colour of wings and tail. Underparts more green than blue. Habitat: open miombo.

3 **EURASIAN ROLLER** *Coracias garrulus* L 30 cm. Crown, especially of imm, often more green than blue. Habitat: <1500 m. Forest edges and more or less wooded and bushed, natural and cultivated areas. NM

4 **LILAC-BREASTED ROLLER** *Coracias caudata* L 40 cm. Race *c. caudata* (a) from Uganda and C Kenya southwards, race *lorti* (b) from C Kenya north and eastwards. Habitat: <2000(&>) m. Dry, bushed and wooded, natural and cultivated areas including suburban gardens. (AM)

5 **ABYSSINIAN ROLLER** *Coracias abyssinica* L 45 cm. Mantle darker than other rollers. Habitat: <1000 m. Semi-desert and open, more or less wooded and bushed areas, including gardens. (AM)

6 **BLUE-THROATED ROLLER** *Eurystomus gularis* L 25 cm. Habitat: 500-2000 m. More or less extensively cultivated areas with forest-patches. Voice: very high, piping '*pju pju pjupu-pjupu*'.

7 **BROAD-BILLED ROLLER** *Eurystomus glaucurus* L 25 cm. Habitat: <2000 m. Forest glades and edges, wet woodland, grass- and farmland with scattered trees near streams and marshes. Voice: mid-high, magpie-like cries and chatters '*èèèh èèèh èhèhèhèh*'. (AM)

8 **FOREST WOOD-HOOPOE** *Phoeniculus castaneiceps* L 30 cm. Dark-headed (a) and pale-headed (b) forms shown. No white in plumage and straight black bill. Habitat: 100-2500 m. Forest canopies, not on the ground. Voice: extra high, fast, trilling cackling '*tritrutritritritritrutritri-*' and high, slightly hoarse fluting '*wuut-wuut-wuut-wuut-wuut- wuut-wuut*'.

9 **WHITE-HEADED WOOD-HOOPOE** *Phoeniculus bollei* L 35 cm. Imm has dark head, but no white in tail and wing. Habitat: 750-3000 m. Forest interiors and edges, often along streams. Voice: very high, liquid chatters '*chachachachacha-*'.

10 **BLACK-BILLED WOOD-HOOPOE** *Phoeniculus somaliensis* L 40 cm. Bill sometimes red-based. Habitat: 1500-2000 m. Dense bush with some trees.

11 **GREEN WOOD-HOOPOE** *Phoeniculus purpureus* L 40 cm. Note green head and mantle. Habitat: <3000 m. Open wood- and bushland, well-wooded streams and parks. Voice: high to mid-high, magpie-like, excited shouts and fast chatters '*chachachachacha-*'.

12 **VIOLET WOOD-HOOPOE** *Phoeniculus damarensis* L 40 cm. Bill sometimes black at base. Note dark purple-violet mantle and dark coppery head. Habitat: <1500 m. Dry bush- and scrubland, often near water. Voice: mid-high, excited, cackling '*rachararararararahrahcharara*' (with typical '*-ah-*' sound).

13 **ABYSSINIAN SCIMITARBILL** *Phoeniculus minor* L 25 cm. Race *minor* (not shown) from Somalia, Ethiopia and N Kenya has white bar over primaries. Habitat: <1500(&>) m. Bushed and wooded areas.

14 **SCIMITARBILL** *Phoeniculus cyanomelas* L 30 cm. Habitat: <2500 m. Dry wood- and bushland. Often in palm plantations. Voice: very high, upswept, fluting '*pewêêh-pewêêh-pewêê*'.

15 **BLACK WOOD-HOOPOE** *Phoeniculus aterrimus* L 25 cm. Note short tail and rather straight bill. Habitat: <2000 m. Dry wooded and bushed areas. Voice: high, fluting, slightly rising and descending '*weetweetweetweetweetweetweet*'.

16 **HOOPOE** *Upupa epops* L 30 cm. (Not all races depicted.) NM race *e. epops* (a) from C Kenya northwards, race *africana* (b) from C Kenya southwards. African race is darker and has a wing bar less. Habitat: <2000 m. Normally foraging in short grass of more or less bushed and wooded habitats including suburban gardens. Voice: mid-high, regular hooting '*oopoop oopoop -*'. (AM) (NM)

49

Plate 50

1 **BLACK-AND-WHITE-CASQUED HORNBILL** *Ceratogymna subcylindricus* L 75 cm (♂), 70 cm (♀). Note dark bill. White confined to second half of outer tail-feathers. Only outer primaries black. Habitat: 500-2750 m. Forest and surrounding wooded areas, including gardens.

2 **WHITE-THIGHED HORNBILL** *Ceratogymna cylindricus* L 70 cm. Note pale bill, white-black-white pattern of tail and bare red eye-area. Habitat: 750-1500 m. Dense forests.

3 **SILVERY-CHEEKED HORNBILL** *Ceratogymna brevis* L 75 cm (♂), 65 cm (♀). No white in flight feathers. Habitat: <2750 m. Forests, suburban gardens (common in Nairobi) and parks.

4 **PIPING HORNBILL** *Ceratogymna fistulator* L 60 cm (♂), 55 cm (♀). Naked eye-area dark slate-grey (not red). Note black-patch on bill and extensive white in wing. Habitat: <1500 m. Forests and plantations.

5 **TRUMPETER HORNBILL** *Ceratogymna bucinator* L 65 cm, (♂), 60 cm (♀). Note red eye-area and white trailing edge of secondaries. Habitat: <1500 m. Forests and connected well-wooded streams.

6 **BLACK-CASQUED WATTLED HORNBILL** *Ceratogymna atrata* L 80 cm. Habitat: 500-1000 m. Dense forests and surrounding wooded areas.

7 **WHITE-CRESTED HORNBILL** *Tockus albocristatus* L 65 cm. (No recent recorded sightings.) Habitat: 500-750 m. Dense forests and surrounding areas. Voice: very high yelping, gliding up to extra high '*egeoouUWW*' ('*-UWW*' lashing).

8 **BLACK DWARF HORNBILL** *Tockus hartlaubi* L 35 cm. Coloured a rather aberrant green (for hornbills). Habitat: 500-1000 m. Forest canopies. Voice: high, mellow, staccato '*weekweekweekweekweekweek*'.

9 **RED-BILLED DWARF HORNBILL** *Tockus camurus* L 35 cm. Habitat: 500-750 m. Dense swampy forests. Voice: Very high tooting '*toottoottoottoottoottoottoottoot*' (descending 4 notes from beginning to end).

10 **AFRICAN PIED HORNBILL** *Tockus fasciatus* L 50 cm. Note tail pattern. Habitat: 500-1250 m. Forests and surrounding wooded areas. Voice: extra high, rather short '*fjuck-fjuck-fjuck-fjuckfjuck-fjuckfjuckfjuckfjuckfjuck*'.

11 **CROWNED HORNBILL** *Tockus alboterminatus* L 50 cm. Note yellow eye and white outer tail-corners. Habitat: <3000 m. More or less dense forests and woodland. Voice: very high, shrieking, rapid '*wutweetweetweetweet-*' lowering to the end.

12 **PALE-BILLED HORNBILL** *Tockus pallidirostris* L 45 cm. Note all-yellow bill. Habitat: <1250 m. Dry miombo.

13 **AFRICAN GREY HORNBILL** *Tockus nasutus* L 50 cm. Note ♂ and ♀ bill patterns. Habitat: <1750 m. Dry, more or less wooded areas with some bush. Voice: extra high, piping and hooting '*pipipipipipipiupleepeehpiupleepeeh*' (after first '*-piu-*' 2 notes lower).

14 **EASTERN YELLOW-BILLED HORNBILL** *Tockus flavirostris* L 50 cm. Normally feeds on the ground. Habitat: <1500(&>) m. Dry, more or less wooded and bushed habitats.

15 **VON DER DECKEN'S HORNBILL** *Tockus deckeni* L 50 cm (♂) 45 cm (♀). Feeds mainly on the ground. Habitat: <1750 m. Dry, more or less bushed and wooded habitats. Voice: mid-high, chicken-like cackling '*tock tock tock-tock-tocktocktocktocktock*'.

16 **JACKSON'S HORNBILL** *Tockus jacksoni* L 50 cm (♂) 45 cm (♀). (Species level as by Britton.) Feeds mainly on the ground. Only a few secondaries partly white. Bill mainly red with yellow tip. Habitat: 250-1500(&>) m. Dry, wooded and bushed habitats.

17 **RED-BILLED HORNBILL** *Tockus erythrorhynchus* L 45 cm. Feeds mainly on the ground. Bill strongly curved and yellow-based. Habitat: <2000 m. Dry, wooded and bushed habitats and overgrazed grasslands. Voice: mid-high, excited, yelping '*weck-weck-weckweckweckweck weck-*' slightly varying in pitch and volume.

18 **HEMPRICH'S HORNBILL** *Tockus hemprichii* L 60 cm. Feeds on the ground as well in trees. Note tail pattern and dark red bill. Habitat: 750-1500 m. Dry, rocky slopes, particularly with large candelabrum trees.

19 **SOUTHERN GROUND HORNBILL** *Bucorvus cafer* L 105 cm. Habitat: <3000 m. Wooded and bushed habitats.

20 **ABYSSINIAN GROUND HORNBILL** *Bucorvus abyssinicus* L 105 cm. Habitat: 500-1000(&>) m. Arid or dry, open, wooded and bushed areas with more or less grass cover.

50

Plate 51

1 **SPECKLED TINKERBIRD** *Pogoniulus scolopaceus* L 10 cm. Habitat: 500-2000 m. Forests and surrounding wooded areas. Voice: low, slightly irregular, interspersed '*hoot-hoothoot -*' and mid-high, short dry rattles '*titititidae titititidae -*'.

2 **MOUSTACHED GREEN TINKERBIRD** *Pogoniulus leucomystax* L 9 cm. Habitat: 250-3000 m. Forested slopes and suburban gardens. Voice: very high to extra high, loud, sharp, speedy '*widuduwi-wididiwi-widuwi*' sometimes uttered as rattles.

3 **RED-RUMPED TINKERBIRD** *Pogoniulus atroflavus* L 13 cm. Note white face lines and red rump. Habitat: 500-1000(&>) m. Forests. Voice: low, monotonous, hollow '*hoot hoot hoot -*' or high '*trrri trrri trrri*'

4 **EASTERN GREEN TINKERBIRD** *Pogoniulus simplex* L 8 cm. Habitat: <1000 m. Dense forests. Sometimes in woodland. Voice: high, slow-trilled, repeated '*prrruh prrruh -*'.

5 **WESTERN GREEN TINKERBIRD** *Pogoniulus coryphaeus* L 9 cm. No white eye-stripe. Habitat: 2000-2500 m. Forests and wooded habitats. Voice: extra high, loud, sharp, shivering '*bibibiwi-bibibibiwi*' and high, rapid, rattling '*tudurrur-tudurrur-tudurrur*'.

6 **YELLOW-THROATED TINKERBIRD** *Pogoniulus subsulphureus* L 10 cm. Face stripes and chin uniformly green (not white) with breast. Yellow (not white) stripe on forehead over bill. Habitat: 500-2250 m. Forest clearings. Voice: very high, sustained, hurried '*puck-puck-puck-puck-*' (a '*puck*' in every 2-7 is left out); also rapid '*puckpuckpuckpuck-*'.

7 **RED-FRONTED TINKERBIRD** *Pogoniulus pusillus* L 9 cm. Face less finely striped than Yellow-fronted Tinkerbird. Habitat: <2250 m. Dry conifer forests, wood- and bushland and gardens. Voice: extra high, slightly descending, rapid '*bicbicbicbicbicbicbic-*' and mid-high, sustained, monotonous '*buc-buc-buc-buc-buc-*'.

8 **YELLOW-RUMPED TINKERBIRD** *Pogoniulus bilineatus* L 10 cm. Chin and stripes in face white (not yellow or green). Habitat: <3000 m. Forest undergrowth, woodland and suburban gardens. Voice: mid-high, regular, wooden '*pook-pook-pook-pook-*' (a '*pook*' in every 2-7 is left out) and mid-high, hooting, trilled '*prrru-prrru-prrru-*'.

9 **YELLOW-FRONTED TINKERBIRD** *Pogoniulus chrysoconus* L 9 cm. Face rather finely striped. Forehead orange-yellow (not red). Habitat: <1500 m. More or less wooded, natural and cultivated areas. Voice: high, regular, uninterrupted '*puck-puck-puck-puck-*'.

10 **WHITE-EARED BARBET** *Stactolaema leucotis* L 15 cm. Habitat: <2750 m. Forests, often near streams. Voice: very high, shrieking, irregular '*peehpeehpeehpickpickpeekpickper*'.

11 **WHYTE'S BARBET** *Stactolaema whytii* L 15 cm. Habitat: 750-2500 m. Mainly in miombo. Voice: high, hooted, sighing '*hooh hooh hooh-*'.

12 **GREEN BARBET** *Stactolaema olivacea* L 15 cm. (Not all races depicted.) Race *woodwardi* (a) in SE Tanzania. Habitat: <2000 m. Forests and dense woodland. Voice: high, unhurried, slightly accelerated '*tjip tjip tjip-*'.

13 **YELLOW-SPOTTED BARBET** *Buccanodon duchaillui* L 15 cm. Habitat: 1000-2250 m. Forest canopies. Voice: high, owl-like, hollow '*rrrrruu*' and very high, loud, shivering, fast '*bibibiwi-bibibiwi*'.

14 **GREY-THROATED BARBET** *Gymnobucco bonapartei* L 20 cm. Note pale eye and yellow bristle in nostril. Habitat: 750-2750 m. Forest glades. Voice: extra high, sharp chatters and trills.

15 **YELLOW-BILLED BARBET** *Trachyphonus purpuratus* L 25 cm. Note unbarbet-like upright stance. Often perches quietly. Habitat: 500-3000 m. Dense forest undergrowth often at edges and near streams. Voice: mid-high, monotonous '*hoot hoot -*' (2 sec in between each '*hoot*').

16 **YELLOW-BREASTED BARBET** *Trachyphonus margaritatus* L 20 cm. Note yellow head, reddish bill and pale underparts. Habitat: <2000 m. Dry open wood-, bush- and scrubland with some grass cover. Voice: high, loud, jubilant '*tiuɯ tiuɯ tiuɯ -*' in an excited unsynchronised duet.

17 **D'ARNAUD'S BARBET** *Trachyphonus darnaudii* L 15 cm. Note red edge of upper tail-coverts. Habitat: 2000 m. Dry, open wood-, bush- and scrubland with some grass cover. Voice: high, excited, up-and-down, rapid, cackling '*keckkêckerec-keckêckerec-*' in duet.

18 **USAMBIRO BARBET** *Trachyphonus usambiro* L 15 cm. (Species level as by Britton.) All upper tail-coverts yellow (not partly red). Habitat: 1000-1250 m. More or less wooded and bushed areas.

19 **CRESTED BARBET** *Trachyphonus vaillantii* L 20 cm. Note dark grey bill and wide black breast-band. Habitat: <1500 m. Dry open wood-and bushland. Voice: very high, coppery, long trill '*prrrrrrrrrrruh*', extra high, cackling trill '*tritritritrutritritrut*' and high, slightly hoarse, fluting '*wuut-wut-wuut-wuut-wuu-wuut*'.

20 **RED-AND-YELLOW BARBET** *Trachyphonus erythrocephalus* L 25 cm. Note red head, orange-red bill and yellow underparts. Habitat: dry, open, more or less wooded and bushed areas with some scrub and grass cover. Voice: mid-high, excited, descending, cackling '*kêhkerehkọkêhkerehkọ-*' in duet.

51

Plate 52

1 HAIRY-BREASTED BARBET *Tricholaema hirsuta* L 15 cm. Note striped white chin and green black-blotched underparts. Habitat: 500-2000 m. Forests and connected well-wooded streams. Voice: mid-high, regular, fast, rapid or slow, hollow, hooting '*hoothoothoothoothoot*'.

2 RED-FRONTED BARBET *Tricholaema diademata* L 13 cm. Note plain underparts and yellow and white eyebrow. Habitat: 500-2250 cm. Dry open wood- and bushland with dense thickets, sometimes along streams.

3 MIOMBO PIED BARBET *Tricholaema frontata* L 13 cm. Note spotted breast and red crown patch. Habitat: dense miombo.

4 SPOT-FLANKED BARBET *Tricholaema lacrymosa* L 13 cm. Note orange eye (black in ♀), spotted flanks, plain white-edged mantle and plain yellow-edged wing coverts. Habitat: <2000 m. Forest edges and wooded and bushed areas, often near water.

5 BLACK-THROATED BARBET *Tricholaema melanocephala* L 13 cm. (Not all races depicted.) Race *flavibuccalis* (a) in C Tanzania. Habitat: <1500 m. Arid and dry areas with more or less trees, bush, scrub and grass cover often near water.

6 BANDED BARBET *Lybius undatus* L 15 cm. Habitat: 250-3250 m. Wood- and scrubland, often near water. [E] (Ethiopia)

7 VIEILLOT'S BARBET *Lybius vieilloti* L 15 cm. Note red (not black and red) breast. Habitat: dry, mor or less wooded and scrubbed, natural and cultivated areas. Voice: strange, rather low piping, scops owl-lik '*hoot-hoot hoot hoot-hoot-hoot-hoot-*', magpie-like chatters and high goose-like shouts.

8 WHITE-HEADED BARBET *Lybius leucocephalus* L 15 cm. (Not all races depicted.) Race *albicauda* (a) in S Kenya and N Tanzania, race *l. leucocephalus* (b) in W Kenya, Uganda and NW Tanzania. Other races differ by colour (white or brown) of different body parts but all have white head. Habitat: <2000 m. Dry open wood- and bushland including suburban gardens and cultivation; often near streams. Voice: high, loud shrieks '*peec-peec peec-peec*' and high, loud, sharp, tinkling chatters '*pipipipipipeh*'.

9 RED-FACED BARBET *Lybius rubrifacies* L 15 cm. Note brown unmarked wing coverts and chin. Habitat: 1000-1500 m. More or less wooded, natural and cultivated habitats.

10 BLACK-BILLED BARBET *Lybius guifsobalito* L 15 cm. Note striped wing coverts and red chin. Habitat: 500-2000 m. Open, more or less wooded and bushed, natural and cultivated areas.

11 BLACK-COLLARED BARBET *Lybius torquatus* L 15 cm. (Not all races depicted.) Race *zombae* (a) in S Tanzania. Upperparts plain except yellow edging of flight feathers. Habitat: <1750 m. Woodland, grass- and farmland with scattered trees. Voice: combination of low, hurried, miauling '*tjauw-tjauw-*', high, loud, bouncing '*-Bêêdidder-*' and duet '*tjauw-tjauw-tjauw-tjauwBêêdiddertjauwBêêdidder-*'.

12 BROWN-BREASTED BARBET *Lybius melanopterus* L 15 cm. Habitat: <1500 m. Open woodland and farmland with trees and hedges.

13 BLACK-BACKED BARBET *Lybius minor* L 15 cm. Habitat: <1500 m. Forests, bush- and scrubland, farmland with trees and hedges.

14 DOUBLE-TOOTHED BARBET *Lybius bidentatus* L 25 cm. Note red wing bar and black rump. Habitat: 750-2500 m. Undergrowth of forests, woodland and cultivation. Voice: mid-high, tinkerbird-like hooting '*pook-pook-pook-pook pook-pook-*'.

15 BLACK-BREASTED BARBET *Lybius rolleti* L 30 cm. Habitat: 750-1250 m. Dry open woodland, plantations and farmland with scattered trees.

52

Plate 53

1 **WESTERN GREEN-BACKED HONEYBIRD** *Prodotiscus insignis* L 9 cm. White outer tail-feathers not visible when perched. Note greenish mantle, yellowish wings and light brown (not grey) head. Habitat: 500-2250 m. Forests and surrounding areas.

2 **EASTERN GREEN-BACKED HONEYBIRD** *Prodotiscus zambesiae* L 9 cm. White outer tail-feathers not visible when perched. Note yellowish wings, greenish mantle and greenish (not brownish) head. Habitat: 750(&<)-2000 m. Forest edges and woodland, especially miombo.

3 **BROWN-BACKED (or WAHLBERG'S) HONEYBIRD** *Prodotiscus regulus* L 10 cm. Broad dark brown edges of white tail feathers only visible in flight. Note all-brown appearance. Habitat: <2000 m. Miombo, wooded and bushed areas, plantations and cultivation. Voice: high, dry, insect-like trill '*shriiiiiiii*'.

4 **ZENKER'S HONEYGUIDE** *Melignomon zenkeri* L 13 cm. White in tail only visible in flight. Note long slender bill, brown head changing to yellow-brown mantle, wings and tail. Habitat: <1000(&>) m. Forests.

5 **LYRE-TAILED HONEYGUIDE** *Melichneutes robustus* L 20 cm. More often heard than seen in its dense forest habitat. Voice: extra high, piercing '*feeFeefeefeefeeFeefeefee-*'. Also a mechanical 'tail-song': a long, loud sequence of bleating, short toy trumpet-like '*mèhèh-mèhèh-mèhèh-*' slightly speeded-up (dipping at the end) as the bird flies around over the canopy.

6 **GREATER HONEYGUIDE** *Indicator indicator* L 20 cm. Not difficult to identify. Note small head and typical honeyguide-bill. The ♀ with plain underparts. Habitat: <3000 m. Well-wooded areas. Voice: very high, unhurried, piercing '*wêet-three wêet-three wêet-three -*' ('*weet*' sweeping).

7 **SPOTTED HONEYGUIDE** *Indicator maculatus* L 20 cm. White tail feathers only visible in flight. Note plain forehead and crown. Pale spotting and striping on underparts from chin to under tail-coverts. Habitat: 750-1000 m. Forests and surrounding areas.

8 **SCALY-THROATED HONEYGUIDE** *Indicator variegatus* L 20 cm. White tail feathers only visible in flight. Note white spotting on forehead and chin. Pale spotting and striping from chin to flanks. Belly and under tail-coverts pale yellow. Habitat: <3500 m. Forests, bamboo and more or less wooded grassland. Voice: very high, rather short, drawn-up trill '*rrrrrrruh*'.

9 **THICK-BILLED HONEYGUIDE** *Indicator conirostris* L 15 cm. Upperparts striped dark and golden yellow. Crown and nape green (not brown). Faint black striping on lower flanks. Habitat: 500-2500 m. Dense forests and connected well-wooded streams.

10 **LESSER HONEYGUIDE** *Indicator minor* L 14 cm. White in tail only visible in flight. Note more or less striped chin. Mantle and wings only slightly striped golden-green. Habitat: <3000 m. Forest edges, wood-, bush- and scrubland, cultivation and grassland with scattered trees. Voice: extra high, sharp, lashing, level '*weew-weew-weew-weew-*' or very high, slower '*weew weew -*'.

11 **LEAST HONEYGUIDE** *Indicator exilis* L 11 cm. White in tail only visible in flight. Note pure white chin and distinct black stripes on lower flanks. Mantle and wings more yellow than brown. Habitat: 500-2500 m. Forests and surrounding wooded cultivations. Voice: extra high, sharp '*weew-weew-weew-*' (each '*weew*' swooping down slightly).

12 **WILLCOCKS'S HONEYGUIDE** *Indicator willcocksi* L 11 cm. White in tail not visible in perched bird. In face only faintly darker malar stripe. Note pale olive-green (not grey or brown) underparts and narrow dark stripes on lower flanks. Habitat: 1000-2000 m. Forests and connected well-wooded streams. Voice: extra high, fluting '*uweew-uweew-uweew-*' (each '*uweew*' slightly swept up).

13 **DWARF HONEYGUIDE** *Indicator pumilio* L 10 cm. White in tail only visible in flying bird. Crown and nape rather green. Note white moustachial stripe. Flank striping faint. Habitat: 1500-2500 m. Moist forests.

14 **PALLID HONEYGUIDE** *Indicator meliphilus* L 10 cm. Note brown crown and nape, plain-looking golden-yellow wings and almost white underparts. No white in tail visible in perched bird. Habitat: <2000 m. Miombo and other tall woodland.

53

Plate 54

1 NORTHERN WRYNECK *Jynx torquilla* L 15 cm. Often feeds on the ground. Note eye-stripe. Habitat: more or less wooded grassland, farmland and gardens. Voice: high, rapid, bleating '*tjutjutjutju*' (often running up). AM

2 RUFOUS-BREASTED WRYNECK *Jynx ruficollis* L 20 cm. Often feeds on the ground. Note absence of dark eye-stripe. Habitat: 1500 (&<)-3000 m. Open, more or less wooded, natural and cultivated areas. Voice: high, bleating '*tjuuk-tjuuk-tjuuk*'.

3 NUBIAN WOODPECKER *Campethera nubica* L 20 cm. Note heavily striped cheeks, barred upperparts and spotted underparts. The ♀ has long white-spotted malar stripe. Habitat: <2500 m. Miombo and other more or less wooded habitats. Voice: mid-high, loud, excited, accelerated '*weetweetweetweet-*' (lasting 4 sec) often in duet.

4 BENNETT'S WOODPECKER *Campethera bennettii* L 20 cm. Race *b. bennettii* (a) in W Tanzania, race *scriptoricauda* (b) from SW to NE Tanzania. Note plain white cheeks of ♂ and brown cheek of ♀ *b. bennettii*. Combination of barred upperparts and spotted underparts diagnostic. Feeds in trees as well as on the ground. Habitat: <1750 m. Open woodland. Voice: mid-high, excited cackling '*rrrrrutiwêêtiewêêtiewêêtie-*' ('*rrrru-*' running up).

5 GOLDEN-TAILED WOODPECKER *Campethera abingoni* L 20 cm. (Not all races depicted.) Race *mombassica* (a) (full species level by Short) in E Somalia, E Kenya and NE Tanzania. Note striped cheeks and rather short malar stripes. Combination of striped underparts and barred upperparts (spotted in *mombassica*) diagnostic. Habitat: <2000 m. Woodland, often near streams. Voice: mid-high, bleating '*piuèèèèèh*'.

6 GREEN-BACKED WOODPECKER *Campethera cailliautii* L 15 cm. (Not all races depicted.) Race *permista* (a) in SW Uganda. Note red and black forehead of ♂ and yellow frontal patch at bill base of ♀. Habitat: 1750(&<)-2250 m. Forests and other more or less wooded habitats. Voice: (a) very high, swept up and down, slightly bleating '*wiâeh*'.

7 TULLBERG'S WOODPECKER *Campethera tullbergi* L 20 cm. Only woodpecker barred from chin to under tail-coverts. Note yellow-tipped tail. Habitat: 1500-3000 m. Canopy of moist forests.

8 BUFF-SPOTTED WOODPECKER *Campethera nivosa* L 14 cm. Note combination of striped cheeks and brown-scaled pale olive underparts. Habitat: 500-2000 m. Dense forests. Voice: high, slightly plaintive and slightly descending '*pièèèh*'.

9 BROWN-EARED WOODPECKER *Campethera caroli* L 20 cm. Only woodpecker spotted white from chin (and most of face sides) to under tail-coverts. Habitat: 500-2000 m. Forests. Voice: high, drawn-out, rising and gliding-down, fluted '*piuûuuijh*'.

10 AFRICAN PICULET *Sasia africana* L 8 cm. Note small size (as your middle finger or even shorter). Found on stems but also on horizontal twigs and branches near the ground. Habitat: 500-750 m. Dense ground-strata of forest edges.

54

Plate 55

1 SPECKLE-BREASTED WOODPECKER *Dendropicos poecilolaemus* L 13 cm. Note plain golden-green mantle, unmarked belly and golden-yellow rump. Habitat: 500-2250 m. More or less wooded and bushed, natural and cultivated areas. Voice: high, sharp, rasping, speedy '*tethrêe-tethrêe-tethrêe*'.

2 GABON WOODPECKER *Dendropicos gabonensis* L 14 cm. Upperparts, including primaries and rump, all-green. Forehead brown. Habitat: 500-1500 m. Open forests; also in natural and cultivated areas with tree-stands and scattered trees. Voice: very high, level trill '*rrrrrrri*'.

3 STIERLING'S WOODPECKER *Dendropicos stierlingi* L 15 cm. Note plain olive-brown upperparts, distinct face marks and barred scales on underparts. Habitat: miombo.

4 ELLIOT'S WOODPECKER *Dendropicos elliotii* L 15 cm. Only woodpecker with unmarked buff face-sides. Habitat: 1000-2000(&>) m. Forests.

5 CARDINAL WOODPECKER *Dendropicos fuscescens* L 13 cm. (Not all races depicted.) Race *lepidus* (a) in SW Kenya, S Uganda, NW Tanzania and W Ethiopia, race *hemprichii* (b) in NE Uganda, N and E Kenya, Somalia and NE Tanzania. Many races exist but all have more or less mantle barring, barred wings and striped underparts. Habitat: <2750 m. Forests and other wooded and bushed habitats. Voice: extra high, rapid, twittering cry '*tututeetêeteeteetge*' and high, dry rattle '*shree-shree-shree*' (thrush-like alarm cry).

6 ABYSSINIAN WOODPECKER *Dendropicos abyssinicus* L 15 cm. Note face stripes and red rump. Habitat: 1500(&<)-3000 m. More or less wooded areas often with candelabrum trees. [E] (Ethiopia)

7 BEARDED WOODPECKER *Dendropicos namaquus* L 25 cm. Note more or less distinct body barring. Habitat: <3000 m. Open forests, wood- and bushland with some large trees. Voice: high, loud, rapid '*cluclû-cluclu*' (rather irregular but generally descending).

8 GREY WOODPECKER *Dendropicos goertae* L 20 cm. Race *rhodeogaster* (a) in N Tanzania and SW and C Kenya, race *centralis* (b) in Uganda, W Kenya and NW Tanzania. Note belly colour of ♂. Habitat: 500-2000 m. Open forests and other, more or less wooded, natural and cultivated areas including gardens. Voice: very high, slightly descending sharp chatter '*tititritritritritritritrri*'.

9 YELLOW-CRESTED WOODPECKER *Dendropicos xantholophus* L 25 cm. Note plain (not spotted or barred) brown mantle. Habitat: Forests and surrounding areas. Voice: very high, shrill, excited cries and trills like '*tierrrr-tierrr-tututututwi*'.

10 OLIVE WOODPECKER *Dendropicos griseocephalus* L 20 cm. (Not all races depicted.) Race *ruwenzori* (a) in SW Uganda and W Tanzania. Main difference between races is belly colour (red or not). May interbreed with Grey Woodpecker. Habitat: 75-3750 m. Dense forests.

11 BROWN-BACKED WOODPECKER *Picoides obsoletus* L 14 cm. Rump barred white (not red), back brown (not yellowish green). Habitat: <2500 m. Open, more or less wooded and bushed habitats. Voice: mid-high, hurried, sharp, nasal '*tui-tui-trUû-tui*'.

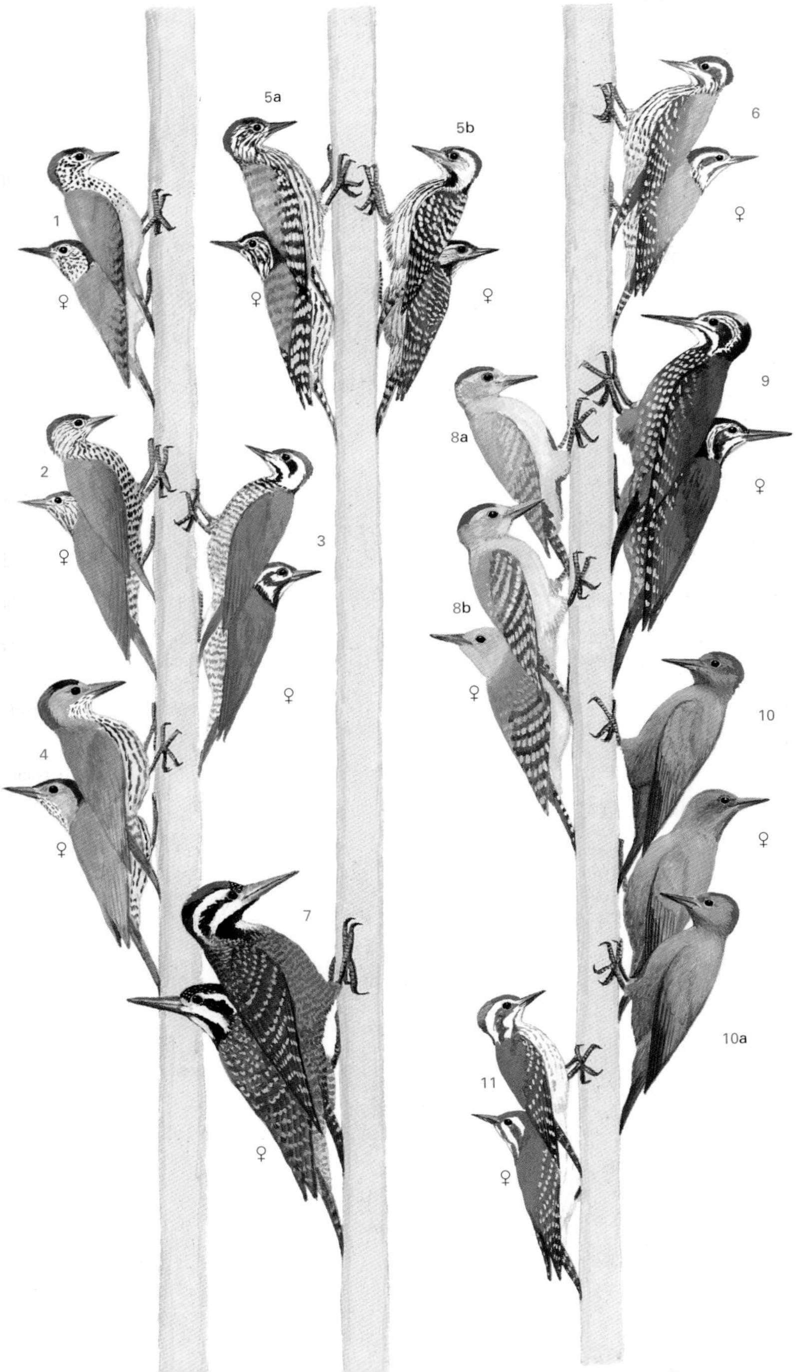
1
♀
5a
♀
5b
♀
6
♀
2
♀
3
♀
4
♀
7
♀
8a
8b
♀
9
♀
10
♀
10a
11
♀

55

Plate 56

1 **GREEN-BREASTED PITTA** *Pitta reichenowi* L 15 cm. Habitat: 1000-1500 m. Forest floors. Voice: high, fluting, pressed-out, short '*fjull fjull fjull*'.

2 **AFRICAN PITTA** *Pitta angolensis* L 20 cm. Habitat: floor under dense shrub patches in wooded areas. Voice: strange, compressed '*puWêe*' ('*pu-*' low and frog-like, '*-Wee*' very fluting). AM

3 **AFRICAN GREEN BROADBILL** *Pseudocalyptomena graueri* L 12 cm. Habitat: 2000-2250 m. Main forest mid-strata and canopies, bamboo.

4 **AFRICAN BROADBILL** *Smithornis capensis* L 13 cm. Flanks white (not pale buffish). Habitat: <1800 m. Mid-strata of forests, bamboo and connected habitats. Voice: low, toy trumpet-like '*prrufêhh*'.

5 **RUFOUS-SIDED BROADBILL** *Smithornis rufolateralis* L 12 cm. Habitat: 500-1500 m. Forest undergrowth, often near streams. Voice: high, rather level, toy trumpet-like '*trrrui*'.

6 **SPIKE-HEELED LARK** *Chersomanes albofasciata* L 12 cm. White tail-corners, long decurved bill, white throat contrasting with light rufous breast. Habitat: 1250-1750 m. Dry areas with more or less short grass cover. Voice: high, unlark-like, more wader-like, rapid, bouncing '*tseeptseeptseeptseep-*'.

7 **DESERT LARK** *Ammomanes deserti* L 14 cm. All races from E Africa rather dark with plain mantle. Wing- and tail feathers dark with rufous margins (excluding central tail-feathers). Habitat: arid, stony and rocky plains or hillsides with sparse grass cover and occasionally some scrub. Voice: very high '*tchrruêe*' ('*tchrru-*' drawn back, '*-ee*' very short and sharp).

8 **BIMACULATED LARK** *Melanocorypha bimaculata* L 17 cm. Note facial pattern, concentrated black breast patches and white corner tips to tail. Habitat: bare or sparsely short-grassed stony habitats. Voice: very high, partly shrill, partly mellow, fluted, hurried twitter with many sudden stops. NM

9 **OBBIA LARK** *Spizocorys obbiensis* L 13 cm. Note face pattern and narrow white tail margins. Habitat: sandy, partly grassed and scrubbed plains and hills near coast. E (Somalia)

10 **MASKED LARK** *Spizocorys personata* L 15 cm. Note face mask, plain upperparts and white throat contrasting with buff breast. Habitat: 750-1500 m. Bare and sparsely grassed areas with some small scrub and bush.

11 **GREATER SHORT-TOED LARK** *Calandrella brachydactyla* L 13 cm. Note small black line under eye, small breast patches and pale eyebrow separating cap from rest of face. Habitat: dry areas, bare fields and overgrazed grassland. Voice: mid-high, liquid, hurried twitter '*trititwitwee*'.

12 **LESSER SHORT-TOED LARK** *Calandrella rufescens* L 13 cm. Note small size and pale appearance. Habitat: stony grass plains. Voice: sustained medley of trills, rattles, whistles and twitters. NM

13 **AFRICAN SHORT-TOED LARK** *Calandrella cinerea* L 14 cm. Habitat: 1250 (&<)-3000 m. Dry, bare and more or less grassed and scrubbed areas. Voice: extra high, unstructured, unhurried twitter including sharp, descending '*tweeeeeh-*'.

14 **SOMALI SHORT-TOED LARK** *Calandrella somalica* L 13 cm. General colouring variable from rufous to pale brown but always distinctly dark striped. No red in wing. Habitat: 1000-1750 m. Short grass plains with sparse bush and scattered trees. NM

15 **SUN LARK** *Galerida modesta* L 14 cm. Note rather stout bill, black moustachial stripe and breast streaking. Some rufous in opened wing. Habitat: open, flat or hilly areas, often with rocky outcrops and occasional large tree stands. Also on pasture land, bare fields and airstrips. Voice: very high, rather sharp, twittering '*sritisrititwee*'.

16 **SHORT-TAILED LARK** *Pseudalaemon fremantlii* L 14 cm. Note bold face pattern and long bill. Habitat: 1000-1750 m. Open areas often with some grass cover, scrub and trees, near rocky outcrops and settlement.

17 **CRESTED LARK** *Galerida cristata* L 17 cm. Note conspicuous crest. Very similar to Thekla Lark but slightly larger and more elongated, slightly longer crested, seemingly down-curved bill and fainter breast striping. Habitat: 250-1000 m. Flat, sandy, partly grassed areas with some occasional bush and trees; also bare fields and roadsides. Voice: extra high, hurried '*tuchêetuchêetywee*'.

18 **THEKLA LARK** *Galerida malabarica* L 16 cm. (See Crested Lark.) Habitat: 250-1500 m. Bare and partly grassed rocky areas and lava; also sand dunes and bare fields. Voice: call like Crested Lark. Song richer and more varied.

19 **FICHER'S SPARROWLARK** *Eremopterix leucopareia* L 12 cm. Habitat: <2000 m. Dry areas with some short grass cover.

20 **CHESTNUT-HEADED SPARROWLARK** *Eremopterix signata* L 12 cm. Habitat: <1500 m. Arid stony areas often with some grass cover.

21 **BLACK-CROWNED SPARROWLARK** *Eremopterix nigriceps* L 12 cm. Note white frontal patch and unstriped back. Habitat: open areas with some grass cover near streams, dry rivers or seashore. Voice: extra high hurried '*puwêêt-wee puwêêt-wee puwêêt-wee*'.

56

22 CHESTNUT-BACKED SPARROWLARK *Eremopterix leucotis* L 13 cm. Note red back of ♂. No white on forehead. Habitat: <2000 m. Open, sandy and stony areas with some grass cover. Voice: '*wuwuch TWuee*' ('*wuwuchi*' rapid, muttered twitter, '*TWuee*' mid-high, short, clear stroke).

Plate 57

1 DEGODI LARK *Mirafra degodiensis* L 14 cm. Note small dull appearance, dark cheek and light eyebrow. Habitat: arid country with some occasional bush or scrub. E (Ethiopia)

2 FAWN-COLOURED LARK *Mirafra africanoides* L 14 cm. General colouring variable from rufous to pale brown. White eye-ring and eyebrow. Breast stripes made of small black triangles. Habitat: 500-2000 m. Open and more or less wooded areas with some grass cover and scrub. Voice: very high, happy, descending, accelerated '*fi fi-fi-fifjuweehweehjuh*'.

3 AFRICAN SINGING BUSHLARK *Mirafra cantillans* L 13 cm. Note short white-edged tail and buff wing patch. Habitat: <2000 m. Open and bushed habitats. Voice: very high, continuous '*tjip-tjip-tjip-*' larded with trills, chatters and short flutes (airborne or perched). (AM)

4 WHITE-TAILED BUSHLARK *Mirafra albicauda* L 13 cm. Note black-marked upperparts, bicoloured bill, white outer tail-feathers and rufous wing. Habitat: 500-2000 m. Open and sparsely bushed habitats. Voice: long sequences of harsh and mellow whistles, without trills.

5 FLAPPET LARK *Mirafra rufocinnamomea* L 13 cm. Very variable in colour (rufous (a) and normal (b) forms shown) but upperparts always rather unicoloured, underparts (plus wing patch) more expressive buff and tail without white. Habitat: <1500(&>) m. Open miombo, bushed and wooded grass plains. Voice: dry, short bursts of wing flaps (like a distant motorbike exhaust) with extra high, up-and-down, hurried twitter '*witweetreewêeh*'.

6 COLLARED LARK *Mirafra collaris* L 13 cm. Note black collar and rufous upperparts. Habitat: 1000-1500 m. Dry areas with some grass cover, bush and trees. Voice: plaintive whistle.

7 RUFOUS-NAPED LARK *Mirafra africana* L 20 cm. (Not all races depicted.) Race *athi* (a) in W and C Kenya and N Tanzania, race *harterti* (b) in SE Kenya and NE Tanzania. Note large size, small rufous crest, red wing patch and absence of white in tail. Habitat: 1000(&<)-3000 m. Open and bushed, partly bare, sometimes overgrazed grassland and pasture land. Voice: extra high, sharp, two-toned, short, fluted '*tee-tjûwęh*' or '*tiû-ûwęęh*'.

8 RED-WINGED LARK *Mirafra hypermetra* L 25 cm. Often perches on bush. Note large size, black breast striping and rufous wing. Habitat: <1500 m. Sparsely bushed, rough grassland. Voice: long, loud, whistled phrases.

9 SOMALI LARK *Mirafra somalica* L 20 cm. Note large size, long bill, rufous appearance and white tail edges. Habitat: arid areas with some grass. E (Somalia)

10 ANGOLA LARK *Mirafra angolensis* L 20 cm. Note large size, long heavy bill, white throat, finely barred wing feathers and white outer tail-feathers. Habitat: rather dry grass plains. Voice: 3- or 4-noted trill.

11 PINK-BREASTED LARK *Mirafra poecilosterna* L 15 cm. Note pale slim appearance, pinkish-buff face-sides and breast streaking. Habitat: <1800 m. Bushed and wooded habitats. Voice: accelerated, descending trill given from perch.

12 GILLETT'S LARK *Mirafra gilletti* L 14 cm. Note beautiful buff-tawny appearance. Wings paler than mantle, and underparts white. Habitat: 1000-1500 m. Hilly, sandy and stony areas with rocky outcrops and some grass and scrub.

13 WILLIAMS'S LARK *Mirafra williamsi* L 13 cm. Note very dark, slightly streaked upperparts, black breast streaking, rusty wing patch and white outer tail-feathers. Habitat: 500-1500 m. Dry, short grass with some occasional bush patches. E (Kenya)

14 FRIEDMANN'S LARK *Mirafra pulpa* L 13 cm. Colourful appearance and white outer tail-feathers. Habitat: 500-1000 m. Sparsely bushed grassland.

15 DUSKY LARK *Pinarocorys nigricans* L 20 cm. Note all-dark, often rather pale-scaled, upperparts. Habitat: open miombo, burnt ground, bare fields. Voice: high, sharp '*Zzeeep-Zzeeep-Zzeeep*'. (AM)

16 RUFOUS-RUMPED LARK *Pinarocorys erythropygia* L 20 cm. Note rufous rump and flanks. Habitat: wooded grassland, burnt ground, bare fields. Voice: high, sharp, fluted, descending '*tûuuu-tûuuu*' and '*têetiuutêetuitee*'.

17 ASH'S LARK *Mirafra ashi* L 14 cm. Note thin bill, darkish upperparts, clear rufous wing patch and white tail edges. Habitat: rocky, rough grass plains near seashore. E (Somalia)

18 SIDAMO LARK *Heteromirafra sidamoensis* L 14 cm. Note creamy-scaled parts of dark mantle and wing and buff-fawn tail-feather edges. Habitat: dry areas with some rough grass cover and low scrub. E (Ethiopia)

▶

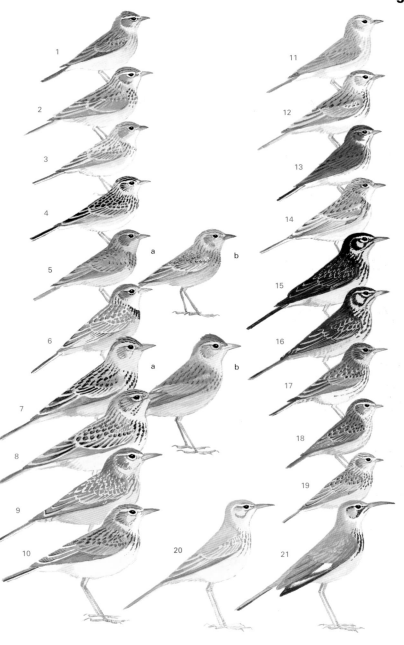

57

19 ARCHER'S LARK *Heteromirafra archeri* L 14 cm. Note short-tailed appearance. No wing patch. Habitat: 1500 m. Open rocky areas with some short grass cover and sparse bush. E (Somalia)

20 LESSER HOOPOE-LARK *Alaemon hamertoni* L 20 cm. Note dark primaries. Breast striping more or less forms a breast-band. Habitat: open plains with rough grass. E (Somalia)

21 HOOPOE-LARK *Alaemon alaudipes* L 20 cm. Striking wing pattern only visible in flight. Habitat: sandy plains with hardly any vegetation. Voice: slowly rising, almost human whistle, with sudden accelerations and slackenings '*piuu-piuu-piuu piuu-piuu-* '.

Plate 58

1 ANGOLA SWALLOW *Hirundo angolensis* L 15 cm. Note large chestnut throat patch, short streamers, buffish under wing-coverts and pale (not white) underparts. Habitat: open and bushed habitats, edges of rivers, lakes, swamps, forest and settlement.

2 ETHIOPIAN SWALLOW *Hirundo aethiopica* L 14 cm. Note interrupted throat-collar and pure white underparts. Habitat: <2750 m. Open areas near woodland and settlement. Also in coastal areas.

3 WHITE-THROATED SWALLOW *Hirundo albigularis* L 15 cm. (Seen only once, in 1957.) Note full throat-collar. Habitat: open grass plains, inundations, dams and rivers. Also in open woodland and near settlements. Voice: extra high '*srueeeh*' and very high, short, rapid twittering '*srisrisrituweeh*' ('*-tuweeh*' one octave lower). AM

4 RED-CHESTED SWALLOW *Hirundo lucida* L 15 cm. Note large chestnut throat patch, dusky under wing-coverts, white underparts and large white tail spots. Habitat: 1750-2750 m. Grassland, marshes, lakes and rivers.

5 BARN SWALLOW *Hirundo rustica* L 20 cm. Note small chestnut throat patch, long tail streamers and pale buff underparts. Habitat: open and half-open areas, forest edges and swamp edges. Voice: mid-high, happy, nasal twitters with inhaled longer trills. NM

6 WIRE-TAILED SWALLOW *Hirundo smithii* L 13 cm. Note almost complete black ring between pure white belly and under tail-coverts. Habitat: <2250(&>) m. Forest edges, woodland, settlement and grassland, often near rivers and lakes. Voice: extra high '*twittwit srièèh*' (like extra high Barn Swallow).

7 PEARL-BREASTED SWALLOW *Hirundo dimidiata* L 15 cm. No white in tail. Habitat: more or less wooded and bushed habitats, often near swamps and settlement. Voice: mid-high, sweeping, nasal, well-spaced '*sreet*', '*sreet-sreet*' and '*sriauw-sriauw*'.

8 WHITE-TAILED SWALLOW *Hirundo megaensis* L 15 cm. Habitat: arid plains with scarce grass, bush or trees. E (Ethiopia). (Note that map 58.8 on p.246 is wrong: White-tailed Swallow occurs only in a small area in S Ethiopia.)

9 MOSQUE SWALLOW *Hirundo senegalensis* L 25 cm. Note rufous-buff cheeks and whitish chin and under wing-coverts. Habitat: <2600 m. Forest edges and more or less wooded areas. Voice: mid- and very high, nasal, miauling '*twits*' and '*treeeehs*'.

10 RUFOUS-BREASTED SWALLOW *Hirundo semirufa* L 20 cm. Note black cheek. Chin and under wing-coverts only slightly paler than rest of underparts. Habitat: 500-1750 m. Open and bushed habitats with some scattered trees, often near water. Voice: mid-high, sharp, explosive '*tit-tiTriUOOH*'.

11 RED-RUMPED SWALLOW *Hirundo daurica* L 20 cm. Note black under tail-coverts. Habitat: 1000(&<)-3000 m. Rocky hillsides. Also near Lake Victoria and the seacoast. (NM)

12 LESSER STRIPED SWALLOW *Hirundo abyssinica* L 15 cm. Habitat: <2250 m. Open forests, woodland, dry bushed grass- and farmland; also in areas near cliffs and buildings needed for nesting. Voice: high, often reed warbler-like, '*whit wheet wit wit -*'.

13 GREATER STRIPED SWALLOW *Hirundo cucullata* L 20 cm. (Last seen in 1929.) Note pale chestnut cheek and upper tail-coverts. Generally with more buffy underparts and finer striping than Lesser Striped Swallow. Habitat: open grassland. Voice: mid-high '*trrit treet trrit -*'. AM

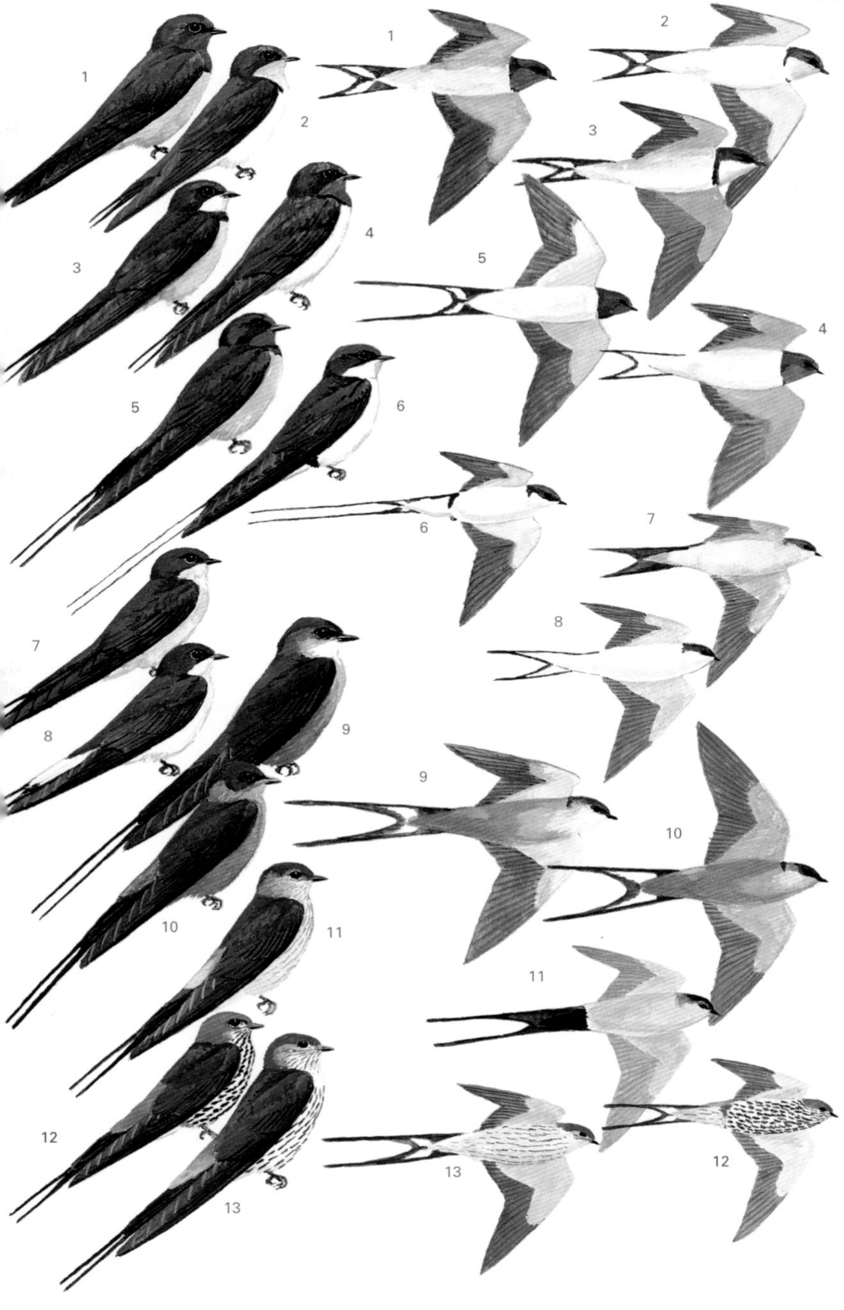
1
2
3
4
5
6
7
8
9
10
11
12
13

58

Plate 59

1 **BANDED MARTIN** *Riparia cincta* L 15 cm. Note white under wing-coverts, white eyebrow, distinct breast-band and square tail. Habitat: 1500(&<)-3000 m. Open and bushed grassland, marshes, dams and ponds. Voice: mid-high, reed warbler-like, hurried twittering.

2 **BROWN-THROATED SAND-MARTIN** *Riparia paludicola* L 13 cm. Dark (a) and pale-bellied (b) forms shown. Note plain-coloured head, tail without spots and uniformly dark under wing. Habitat: 1000-3000 m. Areas near rivers, lakes and dams. Voice: mid-high, rasping shrieks and liquid twitters.

3 **COMMON SAND-MARTIN** *Riparia riparia* L 13 cm. Note dark under wing-coverts and distinct breast-band. Habitat: <1250 m. Open grassland, swamps, rivers and lakes. Voice: mid-high, rasping, hurried twitters. NM

4 **MASCARENE MARTIN** *Phedina borbonica* L 13 cm. Be warned that the striped underparts are difficult to see from some distance. Habitat: open woodland. AM

5 **ROCK MARTIN** *Hirundo fuligula* L 15 cm. Bicoloured appearance not very distinct in the field. White tail spots only visible in opened tail and against a dark background. Habitat: 1500(&<)-3000 m. Open, bushed and wooded areas near cliffs and buildings. Voice: high, dry, sharp rattles '*tchrreeh*' and '*tuchirrr*'.

6 **CRAG MARTIN** *Hirundo rupestris* L 15 cm. Under wing-coverts are darkest area underneath. White tail spots only visible in opened tail. Habitat: <3500 m. Areas near cliffs and buildings. NM

7 **WHITE-THROATED BLUE SWALLOW** *Hirundo nigrita* L 15 cm. Habitat: well-wooded rivers and lake edges; also in mangroves.

8 **(ETHIOPIAN) CLIFF SWALLOW** *Hirundo* species L 15 cm. Recently discovered, not yet named, cliff swallow from Ethiopian rift valley, resembling Red Sea Cliff Swallow but with rufous (not grey) rump and South African Cliff Swallow, but with ill-defined dark (not with clearly streaked) throat and chest. E? (Ethiopia)

9 **GREY-RUMPED SWALLOW** *Pseudhirundo griseopyga* L 14 cm. Note grey head and rump and absence of white in tail. Habitat: 750-2250 m. Sheltered areas with some grass cover, often near water. Voice: mid-high, shrieking '*shree-frih wih shree*'.

10 **WESTERN HOUSE-MARTIN** *Delichon urbica* L 14 cm. Note white rump, white feet and white underparts (including under wing-coverts). No white in tail. Habitat: 1500(&<)-3000 m. Open and half-open areas, often near cliffs and buildings. Voice: very high, liquid '*pri-wip pri-wrip*'. NM

11 **BLUE SWALLOW** *Hirundo atrocaerulea* L 20 cm. Tail form (with long narrow streamers) differs from saw-wing tails. Habitat: 1750-3000 m. Open, bushed and wooded grassland occasionally near swamp edges or forest edges. Voice: high, reed warbler-like, rapid '*weetweetweetweet-*' mixed with short flutes and chirps. AM

12 **BLACK SAW-WING** *Psalidoprocne pristoptera* L 20 cm. Colour of under wing-coverts varies from white (Ethiopian races) to black (most Kenyan, Tanzanian and Ugandan races). Race *orientalis* (S Tanzanian, treated as full species by Short) has white under wing-coverts. Habitat: 1500-3250 m. Forest glades, more or less wooded grassland and moorland; often near settlement.

13 **WHITE-HEADED SAW-WING** *Psalidoprocne albiceps* L 20 cm. The ♀ crown is only partly white. Habitat: 500-1500 m. Forest glades, miombo and sparsely wooded areas.

59

Plate 60

1 **RICHARD'S PIPIT** *Anthus novaeseelandiae* L 15 cm. Note distinct face pattern and pale buff outer tail-feathers. Distinct streaks restricted to upper breast. Habitat: <3500 m. Any open habitat. Voice: very high, liquid, level '*tjeetjeetjee*' and level, fast, twittering '*tweetweetweetweetwee*'.

2 **TAWNY PIPIT** *Anthus campestris* L 15 cm. Note almost unstreaked upperparts, plain breast and wide pale margins to upper wing-feathers. Habitat: <2000 m. Dry, short grassland often with some bush and trees. Voice: high, sharp, short '*tchuwi*'. NM

3 **RED-THROATED PIPIT** *Anthus cervinus* L 14 cm. Note pale buff head and breast colouring of n-br bird and extensive streaking of underparts. Habitat: lake shores and seashore, moorland and wet grass. Voice: extra high, slightly descending, shrill '*teeu teeu*'. NM

4 **TREE PIPIT** *Anthus trivialis* L 15 cm. Streaking extends to lower flanks. Habitat: 1700(&<)-3000 m. Open forests and other wooded habitats, suburban gardens and parks. NM

5 **BUFFY PIPIT** *Anthus vaalensis* L 15 cm. Note plain upperparts and faint upper-breast streaking. Outer tail-feathers like rest of tail. Habitat: dry short grassland. Voice: very high, rapid '*triowhee*' as part of an unstructured and well-spaced sequence. (AM)

6 **PLAIN-BACKED PIPIT** *Anthus leucophrys* L 15 cm. Note warm brown appearance and faint striping of upperparts. Habitat: 500-2250 m. Dry, open, bushed and wooded habitats with some grass cover. Voice: unstructured, monotonous, well-spaced '*tjeeh tjup three tweeh tjeeh -*'.

7 **LONG-BILLED PIPIT** *Anthus similis* L 20 cm. Note large size, faint mantle striping, distinct chest striping and white outer tail-feathers. Habitat: 1000(&<)-2000(&>) m. Miombo, dry rocky slopes, stony grassland with some bush. Voice: high, monotonous, well-spaced '*tjup thrêe tjup tjup thrêe -*'.

8 **STRIPED PIPIT** *Anthus lineiventris* L 15 cm. Note faint greenish wing and tail edging, long streaks on underparts and almost plain mantle. Habitat: 1000-2000 m. Rocky wooded hillsides often near water. Voice: very high, rich, loud '*twittwittwêehtwit-twit-tuèh*'.

9 **BUSH PIPIT** *Anthus caffer* L 11 cm. Note small size, white outer tail-feathers and dense black overall striping and streaking. Habitat: 1000(&<)-2000(&>) m. Wooded and bushed grassland with bare sandy patches. Voice: high, rather nasal '*mèèh-tjih mèèh-tjih -*' ('*mèèh*' rising).

10 **SHORT-TAILED PIPIT** *Anthus brachyurus* L 11 cm. Note small size and short, white-edged tail and rather heavy striping and streaking. Habitat: 1000-1500 m (in Uganda) or 1750-2000 m (in Tanzania). Short grassland. Voice: high, very short, rapid, rather grating '*tuweeh weeh-weeh wheeh threeohweeh*'.

11 **SOKOKE PIPIT** *Anthus sokokensis* L 14 cm. Note beautiful contrasting colouring with clear white wing stripes. Habitat: open forests and woodland.

12 **MALINDI PIPIT** *Anthus melindae* L 15 cm. Most distinct feature is dark breast streaking contrasting with white throat. No white or buff in tail. Habitat: grasslands near Tana River and seashore.

13 **GOLDEN PIPIT** *Tmetothylacus tenellus* L 15 cm. Habitat: <1000(&>) m. Dry bushed and shrubbed grassland. Voice: rather grating, warbling, hurried, short '*trittritthrêedidderruh*'.

14 **YELLOW-THROATED LONGCLAW** *Macronyx croceus* L 20 cm. Note bright yellow of eyebrow and throat. Yellow on both sides of black chest-collar identical. Habitat: <2250 m. Open and bushed habitats, often near marshes, inundations, rivers, lakes and moorland. Voice: mid-high, drawn-up '*mèèèh*' and chattering '*chattûhchattûh-*'.

15 **FUELLEBORN'S LONGCLAW** *Macronyx fuelleborni* L 20 cm. Unstreaked underparts less yellow than throat. Habitat: 1750-2750 m. Short grass- and moorland. Voice: mid-high, loud, rather unvaried whistle '*wi-êh wrrît*'.

16 **ROSY-THROATED LONGCLAW** *Macronyx ameliae* L 20 cm. Habitat: 500-2250 m. Rough grass near lakes, dams, inundations and marshes. Voice: high, hardly varied '*wêe-tjihwêe-tjih-*'.

17 **PANGANI LONGCLAW** *Macronyx aurantiigula* L 20 cm. Throat-patch more orange-yellow than eyebrow and breast. Black collar rather narrow and streaks on breast rather extensive. Habitat: <1000(&>) m. Dry bushed and slightly wooded areas with some grass.

18 **SHARPE'S LONGCLAW** *Macronyx sharpei* L 15 cm. Looks like a small slim yellow pipit. Neck-collar striped (not full like other adult longclaws). Habitat: 2000-3500 m. Rough grassland. E (Kenya)

19 **ABYSSINIAN LONGCLAW** *Macronyx flavicollis* L 20 cm. Note orange-yellow throat, yellow forehead and wing thumb. Habitat: 1000-4250 m. Grass- and moorland. E (Ethiopia)

60

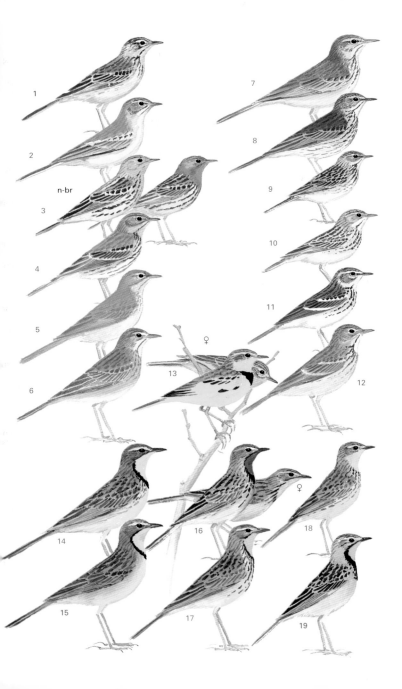

1

2

n-br

3

4

5

6

7

8

9

10

11

♀

13

12

14

15

♀

16

17

18

19

Plate 61

1 **CAPE WAGTAIL** *Motacilla capensis* L 15 cm. Note brownish buff appearance, black chest-collar and white throat. Habitat: 750-3000 m. Wet open woodland, grass- and pasture land, swamp and lake edges. Voice: very high '*sweep tèdèdjèh*'.

2 **CITRINE WAGTAIL** *Motacilla citreola* L 20 cm. Note white (not yellowish) under tail-coverts. Habitat: wet, rough grass especially in coastal areas. NM

3 **YELLOW WAGTAIL** *Motacilla flava* L 20 cm. Visiting races include *flava* (a), *thunbergii* (b), *lutea* (c), *beema* (d), *feldegg* (e), *leucocephala* (g) and *superciliosus* (f). Note yellow (not white) under tail-coverts in all plumages and races. Often near large grazing animals. Habitat: <3000 m. Short grass in open bushland also at river banks, lake shores, marsh and swamp edges. Voice: very high, unstructured, shrill shrieks '*sree-sreeh*' and '*tuwiet wheet*'. NM

4 **AFRICAN PIED WAGTAIL** *Motacilla aguimp* L 20 cm. Habitat: <3000 m. Wood- and shrubland, fields and grassland, suburban gardens and parks and everywhere near water. Voice: high, sharp, sweeping '*tweeêt*' and sharp, liquid, rapid '*quickquick-trêêt*' ('*trêêt*' very high).

5 **PIED WAGTAIL** *Motacilla alba* L 20 cm. Race *a. alba* (a), race *yarrellii* (b) (not in E Africa). Note white (or pale) forehead. Habitat: river banks, lake shores, marsh edges, farmland, settlement, large lawns and parks. Voice: extra high compressed '*tutwuut*' and '*tuwêeh*'. NM

6 **GREY WAGTAIL** *Motacilla cinerea* L 20 cm. Note absence of white wing-bars. Habitat: 1500-3000 m. Wooded, rocky mountain streams. Voice: extra high, sharp '*tweet-tweet wheet*' ('*wheet*' just within ear reach). NM

7 **MOUNTAIN WAGTAIL** *Motacilla clara* L 15 cm. Note narrow black necklace and pure white underparts. Habitat: 500-3000 m. Well-wooded rocky streams. Voice: very high, gliding '*sreeeeeeh*' and '*trêedrurrûp*'.

8 **BLACK CUCKOOSHRIKE** *Campephaga flava* L 20 cm. Black (a) and yellow-shouldered (b) forms shown. Note uniformly black-blue (not blue and purple) colouring and rather small yellow gape. Habitat: <3000 m. Open forests, plantations and other wooded and bushed habitats. Voice: extra high, silvery, rather short insect-like trills. (AM)

9 **RED-SHOULDERED CUCKOOSHRIKE** *Campephaga phoenicea* L 20 cm. Red shoulder-patch might be yellow-orange. The ♀ has less yellow in wing and finer striped mantle than the Black Cuckooshrike. Habitat: rather dense parts of more or less extensive forests and woodland patches.

10 **PETIT'S CUCKOOSHRIKE** *Campephaga petiti* L 20 cm. Note purplish gloss on underparts and rather large yellow gape. Habitat: 1250-2000 m. Tall trees at forest edges and surrounding areas.

11 **PURPLE-THROATED CUCKOOSHRIKE** *Campephaga quiscalina* L 20 cm. Note beautiful purple and green (not bluish) gloss. Habitat: 1500(&<)-2500 m. Montane forests.

12 **WHITE-BREASTED CUCKOOSHRIKE** *Coracina pectoralis* L 25 cm. Habitat: <1400(&>) m. Large trees in open miombo and other woodland. Voice: very high '*shrêê-shrêê witwit*' ('*witwit*' much lower).

13 **GREY CUCKOOSHRIKE** *Coracina caesia* L 25 cm. Note grey (not white or pale buff) underparts and dark grey (not white) forehead. Shorter-billed than White-breasted Cuckooshrike. Habitat: 750(&<)-3000 m. Tall forest trees and well-wooded streams. Voice: extra high '*shreeuu*' and slow twittering just within ear reach.

14 **GRAUER'S CUCKOOSHRIKE** *Coracina graueri* L 20 cm. Habitat: 1000-2000 m. Forests.

15 **BLUE CUCKOOSHRIKE** *Coracina azurea* L 20 cm. Habitat: 1000-1250 m. Forests.

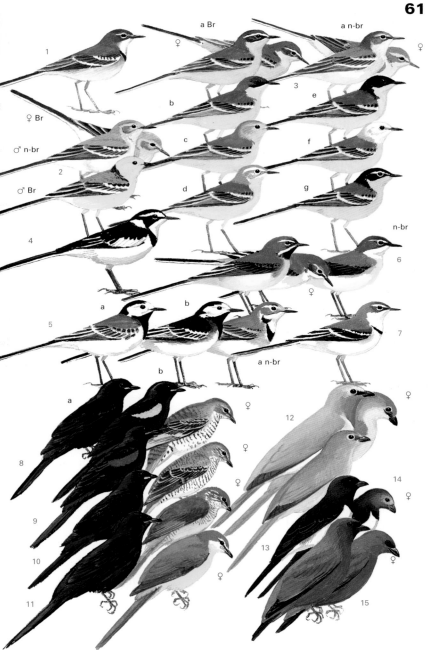

61

Plate 62

1 LITTLE GREENBUL *Andropadus virens* L 15 cm. Note short bill, reddish brown wings, rump and tail, faint pale eye-ring and slightly darker breast. Habitat: <1500(&>) m. Midstrata and undergrowth at forest edges. Voice: mid-high, reed warbler-like, fast *'prrrkprrrrktjerp-fuwit'*.

2 GREY GREENBUL *Andropadus gracilis* L 15 cm. Note reddish brown upperparts, yellowish rump and flanks. Mantle slightly darker (and browner) than breast. Habitat: 500-1500(&>) m. Midstrata of forests. Voice: very high to extra high, up and down *'wietûptoûp'*.

3 ANSORGE'S GREENBUL *Andropadus ansorgei* L 15 cm. Note white eye-ring, dark grey head and greenish edges of flight feathers. Tail more reddish brown than rest of body. Habitat: 1500-1750 m. Forest midstrata. Voice: very high, rapid *'wêêtwjutweet'*.

4 PLAIN GREENBUL *Andropadus curvirostris* L 20 cm. Note pale chin separated from greenish underparts by light grey breast-band. Tail reddish brown. Habitat: midstrata and undergrowth of forests and connected forest strips and patches. Voice: mid-high *'pêêtje-cruuu'* and *'wêê-tu-wee-tu'*.

5 SLENDER-BILLED GREENBUL *Andropadus gracilirostris* L 15 cm. Note thin pointed bill and plain upperparts contrasting with pale brownish grey underparts. Habitat: 500-2500 m. Canopy of forest edges and interiors. Also surrounding well-wooded areas. Voice: very high, descending, rather short *'tjûuu'* and mid-high, miauling *'nieauû'*.

6 MOUNTAIN GREENBUL *Andropadus tephrolaemus* L 20 cm. Race *kikuyensis* (a) in Uganda and SW Kenya, race *nigriceps* (b) in S Kenya and N Tanzania. Note white eye-ring, striped cheek and grey throat. Habitat: 1250-3500 m. Forests and bamboo. Voice: high, 3-noted *'it's-not-so-chilly'*.

7 STRIPE-CHEEKED GREENBUL *Andropadus milanjensis* L 20 cm. Note all-green upperparts and grey-striped cheeks. Eye may be yellow. Habitat: 750-2000 m. Forest edges and surrounding areas. Voice: mid-high, 2-noted *'tjash tjerk-tjerk-tjerk-trrrrr'*.

8 SHELLEY'S GREENBUL *Andropadus masukuensis* L 15 cm. Note pale (not white) eye-ring and grey head with dark grey-brown (not grey-blue) crown. Habitat: 1500(&<)-2500 m. Forests and surrounding well-wooded areas. Voice: rather quiet *'wit-wit-wit'*.

9 YELLOW-WHISKERED GREENBUL *Andropadus latirostris* L 20 cm. Yellow whiskers very distinct. Habitat: 500-3000 m. Forests, bamboo, suburban gardens. Voice: mid-high, unstructured, up-and-down, unhurried *'tjash tjesh tjish-tjush tjash -'*.

10 SOMBRE GREENBUL *Andropadus importunus* L 20 cm. Note yellow-brown appearance and pale eye. Imm may have a yellow eye-ring. Habitat: <2000 m. (Coastal) scrub, more or less wooded and bushed, natural and cultivated habitats. Voice: high, fast, warbling *'fwirofwifwifwi-tru-tri'*.

11 COMMON BULBUL *Pycnonotus barbatus* L 20 cm. (Not all races shown.) Race *dodsoni* (a) in NE Kenya, C, S and E Ethiopia and Somalia. Habitat: <3000 m. Forest edges, gardens, more or less wooded and bushed areas. Voice: high, up and down happy whistle *'I'm côming hôme'*.

12 SWAMP GREENBUL *Thescelocichla leucopleura* L 20 cm. Habitat: 500-750 m. More or less wooded swamps with palms. Voice: low, slightly rising, rapid miauling chatters *'whittauwittauwitwit'*.

13 YELLOW-THROATED GREENBUL *Chlorocichla flavicollis* L 20 cm. Note pale yellow throat contrasting with dark grey cheeks. Habitat: 750-1500(&>) m. Open woodland, well-wooded streams, moist bushland, thickets and gardens. Voice: high, miauling, scolding, rather short calls *'pirruri riuw riuw -*

14 SIMPLE GREENBUL *Chlorocichla simplex* L 20 cm. Note white chin, white eye-ring in dark brown head and (less) brown upperparts. Habitat: 500-750 m. Undergrowth of forest edges, dense bush and hedges. Voice: high, short, fast, miauling chatter *'miauauchêtchêt'*.

15 YELLOW-BELLIED GREENBUL *Chlorocichla flaviventris* L 20 cm. Note chocolate-brown head with white eye-ring, pale brownish breast and moss-green wing edges. Habitat: 500-1750(&>) m. Undergrowth of forest edges and coastal shrub. Voice: mid-high miauling *'tji-tjûû tjuu-tjuu-tjuu'*.

16 JOYFUL GREENBUL *Chlorocichla laetissima* L 20 cm. Note golden-green appearance with narrow yellow eye-ring. Habitat: 1250-2500 m. Canopy of forest edges and nearby well-wooded areas. Voice: mid-high, fast, bubbling *'wapwapwapwapwapwap-there he is'* ('*there he is*' running up).

17 EASTERN BEARDED BULBUL *Criniger chloronotus* L 20 cm. Note whitish often fluffed-out 'beard' contrasting with dark head, grey-brown breast and reddish tail. Habitat: <2000 m. Forests. Voice: mid-high, trilled whistle *'tutututjiuu'*.

18 RED-TAILED BULBUL *Criniger calurus* L 20 cm. Note pure white often fluffed-out 'beard' (sharply contrasting with chocolate-brown head) and reddish green tail. Habitat: 500-1500 m. Forest undergrowth and nearby wooded areas. Voice: high, repeated *'tuwêêt'* and *'tu-tu-tjîou'*.

19 COMMON BRISTLEBILL *Bleda syndactyla* L 20 cm. Note long pointed bill, black moustachial area and red tail. Habitat: 500-2250 m. Forest undergrowth and moist thickets. Voice: mid-high, miauling chatter *'kiuuu-kiuuu-kiuuu'* and many other thrush- and magpie-like whistles changing in speed, pitch and volume, often with crescendos.

▶

62

20 GREEN-TAILED BRISTLEBILL *Bleda eximia* L 20 cm. Note yellow lores and yellow tail corners. Habitat: 500-1250 m. Forest edges and interiors. Voice: very high, twittered, fluted '*titjituu-tuu*' continued with rolls, trills and clear whistles.

Plate 63

1 FISCHER'S GREENBUL *Phyllastrephus fischeri* L 15 cm. Note pale eye, whitish eye-ring and pale yellow belly. Habitat: <1750 m. Forest undergrowth. Voice: mid-high, reed warbler-like '*tjrrrt tjrrrt-trit-trit-trit*'.

2 OLIVE MOUNTAIN GREENBUL *Phyllastrephus placidus* L 15 cm. (Species level as by Britton.) Note rather dark appearance with striped cheek, whitish eye-ring and buff wing-feather edges. Habitat: 1500(&<)-2750 m. Forest undergrowth.

3 LEAFLOVE *Pyrrhurus scandens* L 20 cm. Note large size, grey head, pale breast (but darker than rest of underparts), buff edging of flight feathers. Habitat: 500-1250 m. Forests, often near streams and swampy places. Also in surrounding areas. Voice: mid-high, melodious, jackdaw-like chatters '*piûpiû-piew-pû-pû-pû-pû*'.

4 TERRESTRIAL BROWNBUL *Phyllastrephus terrestris* L 20 cm. Note pale chin rather contrasting with rest of colouring, rather dark breast and flanks, and small pale eye-ring. Habitat: <500 m. Groundstrata of moist forests and thickets. Voice: low grating and chattering screeches.

5 NORTHERN BROWNBUL *Phyllastrephus strepitans* L 15 cm. Note rather rufous appearance with pale eye-ring. Habitat: <1000(&>) m. Undergrowth of forest patches, woodland and bush.

6 GREY-OLIVE GREENBUL *Phyllastrephus cerviniventris* L 20 cm. Note buffish underparts and greyish head and mantle. No eye-ring. Habitat: 250-2000 m. Undergrowth of dense moist forests and bamboo, often near streams.

7 OLIVE GREENBUL *Phyllastrephus cabanisi* L 15 cm. Note rather dark breast, tawny-brown wings and tail and greenish brown mantle. Habitat: 1000-2250 m. Forests.

8 SASSI'S GREENBUL *Phyllastrephus lorenzi* L 15 cm. Note dark cap. Habitat: <1500(&>) m. Forests.

9 YELLOW-STREAKED GREENBUL *Phyllastrephus flavostriatus* L 20 cm. Note grey head and greenish upperparts with more buff wing-feather edges. Habitat: <2500 m. Forests. Voice: fast, reed warbler-like tremolo '*tjrrrt*' continued with high, slow, fluted '*keh keh keh tjip tjup-tjup*'.

10 TORO GREENBUL *Phyllastrephus hypochloris* L 15 cm. Note greyish flanks and pale yellow underparts. Habitat: 500-2000 m. Forest undergrowth, often near streams.

11 XAVIER'S GREENBUL *Phyllastrephus xavieri* L 15 cm. Note slightly paler eyebrow and yellow underparts with darker breast. Habitat: 500-1500 m. Forest undergrowth and nearby wooded habitats. Voice: very high, staccato, fluted '*tju-têe-tu*' and '*têe-tju-têe*'.

12 ICTERINE GREENBUL *Phyllastrephus icterinus* L 15 cm. Underparts uniformly pale yellow. Eye colour variable. Habitat: 500-1250 m. Forest undergrowth and surrounding wooded areas. Voice: high, rapid, miauling '*weck-weck weck-weck -*' mixed with low, drawn-out miaulings.

13 WHITE-THROATED GREENBUL *Phyllastrephus albigularis* L 15 cm. Note pure white throat, sharply demarcated from mainly grey head. Habitat: 750-2000 m. Dense forest undergrowth. Voice: high, melodious, bubbling '*witwitwêetwittjuutjuutjuu*' (first part very rapid).

14 TINY GREENBUL *Phyllastrephus debilis* L 13 cm. Note small size, long thin bill, grey cheeks, all-green upperparts and yellowish flight-feather edges. Habitat: <1500 m. Forest undergrowth, miombo and coastal shrub. Voice: low, running-up, nasal '*mau-miau-miau-miau-trreeh*'.

15 HONEYGUIDE-GREENBUL *Baeopogon indicator* L 20 cm. Habitat: 500-2000 m. Forest canopies. Voice: high, fluted, falling-off '*pipiupi-pjiiuuuw*' and '*piiijuuuuuw*' (gliding down and up).

16 SPOTTED GREENBUL *Ixonotus guttatus* L 15 cm. Social. Habitat: 750-1250 m. Forest canopies. Voice: very high, wren-like '*tjitjerk -*'.

17 WHITE-THROATED NICATOR *Nicator gularis* L 15 cm. Habitat: dense forest undergrowth and scrub. Voice: mid-high, melodious, fast '*quick-corrr-quickerquêet*' ('*queet*' lashed up very high).

18 COMMON NICATOR *Nicator chloris* L 20 cm. Habitat: <1300(&>) m. Forest undergrowth, wood- and bushland. Voice: high, level '*weet-weet-weet-weet-weet kisch kisch*' ('*kisch kisch*' loud and explosive).

19 YELLOW-THROATED NICATOR *Nicator vireo* L 14 cm. Habitat: 500-1000 m. Forest undergrowth.

20 GREY HYPOCOLIUS *Hypocolius ampelinus* L 25 cm. Seen once in Ethiopia, in 1850. Habitat: 'green' places with palms in deserts. OM

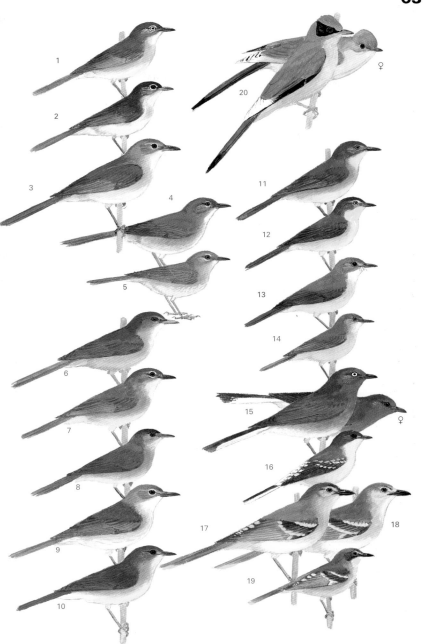

63

Plate 64

1 **ISABELLINE WHEATEAR** *Oenanthe isabellina* L 15 cm. Cheek unmarked (except eye-line), wing coverts uniformly pale, terminal ⅓ of tail black and eyebrow white in front of eye. Habitat: <2500 m. (Very) dry habitats occasionally with scarce bush and trees. NM

2 **NORTHERN WHEATEAR** *Oenanthe oenanthe* L 15 cm. Terminal half of tail black. Habitat: <3000 m. Rocky areas often with some grass cover, bush and trees. NM

3 **BLACK-EARED WHEATEAR** *Oenanthe hispanica* L 15 cm. Imm white-throated form (a), adult white-throated form (b) and black-throated form (c). In n-br plumage not distinguishable from Pied Wheatear. Note narrow black terminal band and mainly black outer tail-feathers. Habitat: <1000(&>) m. Bare fields and rocky areas with some short grass cover and trees. NM

4 **DESERT WHEATEAR** *Oenanthe deserti* L 15 cm. Black of wing (in br plumage) connected with black throat. Note almost all-black tail (but white rump). Habitat: dry, flat, stony and sandy areas with sparse vegetation. NM

5 **PIED WHEATEAR** *Oenanthe pleschanka* L 15 cm. Imm ♂ like imm ♂ of Black-eared Wheatear. Note narrow black terminal band and mainly black outer tail-feathers. Habitat: 250-1500(&>) m. Open areas with some grass, bush and trees, bare fields, rocky hill sides and moorland. Voice: very high, scratchy, short, fast, whistles 'tsjatsja-tsjaa'. NM

6 **HOODED WHEATEAR** *Oenanthe monacha* L 20 cm. Note all-white tail (apart from middle tail-feathers) of ♂. Habitat: bare desert slopes. NM

7 **RED-BREASTED WHEATEAR** *Oenanthe bottae* L 14 cm (a), 20 cm (b). Race *heuglini* (a) in NW Ethiopia, W Kenya and Uganda, race *frenata* (b) in C,W and E Ethiopia. Note plain upperparts and short white eyebrow. Habitat: <4250 m. Rocky areas with some short grass. Voice: for race *heuglini*, high, unstructured, scratchy reed warbler-like whistles 'tjickturrr-tjick-tjicktjick-tjirktjirk'. AM

8 **CAPPED WHEATEAR** *Oenanthe pileata* L 15 cm. The only wheatear with black chest-collar. Habitat: semi-desert and other open stony areas with some grass. Also montane moorland and coastal shrub. Voice: babbling medley of clicking, fluted, grating and hissing notes.

9 **MOURNING WHEATEAR** *Oenanthe lugens* L 15 cm. Race *schalowi* (a) (Schalow's Wheatear) in S Kenya and N Tanzania, race *lugubris* (b) in Ethiopia, race *vauriei* (c) in Somalia. Note red or buff tail, buff rump and black (not white) chest. No distinct white eyebrow. Habitat: 1000-3000 m. Rocky slopes and slightly bushed areas with some rough grass cover.

10 **RED-TAILED WHEATEAR** *Oenanthe xanthoprymna* L 14 cm. Note white (not black) breast, dark grey (not black) mantle and white eyebrow. Habitat: arid rocky areas, occasionally with some grass or scrub. NM

11 **WHITE-CROWNED BLACK WHEATEAR** *Oenanthe leucopyga* L 15 cm. Habitat: rocky desert, also near settlement. Voice: high, loud, happy, short, fast whistles 'ratsjsja-sjarara'. NM

12 **SOMALI WHEATEAR** *Oenanthe phillipsi* L 14 cm. Habitat: stony areas occasionally with some grass or bush.

13 **WHITE-FRONTED BLACK CHAT** *Pentholea albifrons* L 13 cm. (Scientific name as by Britton.) Note small size and bluish sheen. Habitat: 750-2500 m. Bare stony places in bushed and wooded areas. Voice: very high, swept-up 'ohwêetjee-ohwêetjee-wêetjee' interwoven with imitations, mainly of other birds.

14 **SPOTTED MORNING-THRUSH** *Cichladusa guttata* L 15 cm. Habitat: dense thickets along dry streams. Voice: high, continuous, 4-5 toned, up-and-down song with short whistles.

15 **COLLARED MORNING-THRUSH** *Cichladusa arquata* L 20 cm. Habitat: <1500 m. River thickets with palms near settlement. Voice: high, unhurried sequence of fluted notes and short phrases 'wêetwuutwut weetwêetwit'.

16 **WHITE-HEADED BLACK CHAT** *Myrmecocichla arnotti* L 20 cm. Habitat: 750-1750 m. Bare ground in miombo and other woodland. Voice: very high, canary-like hurried twittering with some rasping notes.

17 **MOCKING CLIFF CHAT** *Myrmecocichla cinnamomeiventris* L 20 cm. (Has black rump in Ethiopia.) Habitat: 500-2250 m. Well-wooded areas, often near lake shores with rocky outcrops, slopes or buildings. Voice: very varied; extra high whistles, sunbird-like twitters and nightingale-like strophes.

18 **WHITE-WINGED CLIFF CHAT** *Myrmecocichla semirufa* L 20 cm. Habitat: stony ground, cliffs and rocky outcrops, often near forests. [E] (Ethiopia)

19 **RUEPPELL'S BLACK CHAT** *Myrmecocichla melaena* L 20 cm. (Only black chat in Ethiopia.) Habitat: >1750 m. Cliffs and ravines. [E] (Ethiopia)

20 **NORTHERN ANTEATER-CHAT** *Myrmecocichla aethiops* L 20 cm. (Not in Ethiopia.) Habitat: 1500-3000 m. Termite mounds in dry short grassland. Voice: high, loud, rather slow whistle 'pêe-pee-pju tjufju'.

▶

64

21 SOOTY ANTEATER-CHAT Myrmecocichla nigra L 20 cm. White restricted to coverts. Flight feathers all black. Habitat: 1000-1750 m. Termite mounds in (almost) open short grassland. Voice: high, loud, even-spaced, rather slow whistle '*pju-pû-pee-pi-piju*'.

Plate 65

1 **BLUETHROAT** Luscinia svecica L 14 cm. Race *svecica* (a), race *cyanecula* (b). Note rufous at tail base. Habitat: reeds, papyrus and shrubbery near water and swamps. NM

2 **THRUSH-NIGHTINGALE** Luscinia luscinia L 15 cm. Generally less warm brown than Nightingale. Tail more rufous-brown than rump and mantle. Breast and flanks slightly mottled. Habitat: <1500 m. Wood-and bushland with leafy undergrowth. Voice: continuous, unhurried, rich flow of single or repeate harsh fluted trilling rattles and liquid notes. NM

3 **NIGHTINGALE** Luscinia megarhynchos L 15 cm. Note warm brown colouring, almost red tail and large eye. Habitat: dry undergrowth of woodland and scrub. Voice: very rich flow of very variable short phrases with rolls, rattles and the famous crescendo '*tjuu-Tjuu-TJuu- TJUu-TJUU-*'. NM

4 **COMMON STONECHAT** Saxicola torquata L 13 cm. (Not all races depicted.) Races *axillaris* (a) in NW Tanzania and *promiscua* in NE Tanzania (*axillaris* has even smaller chestnut bib than *promiscua*). NM race *albofasciata* (b) in Ethiopia, NM race *variegata* (c) and NM race *hemprichii* (*variegata* has larger white tail base than *hemprichii*). The ♀ of all races has no distinct eyebrow while mantle is faintly streaked. Habitat: areas with some scattered bush and shrubs, moorland and swamp edges. Voice: short, nervous rattle '*trrrut-trrut*'. (NM)

5 **WHINCHAT** Saxicola rubetra L 13 cm. The ♀ has distinct eyebrow, distinctly streaked mantle and white outer tail-basis. Habitat: 250-3000 m. Open, not too dry woodland and other more or less wooded, natural or cultivated habitats. Voice: nervous '*jûu tec-tec*'. NM

6 **LITTLE ROCK-THRUSH** Monticola rufocinerea L 15 cm. Habitat: 1250-2500 m. Rocky ravines and outcrops in more or less wooded and bushed areas.

7 **COMMON ROCK-THRUSH** Monticola saxatilis L 20 cm. The ♂ has white back-patch; ♀ with dark and white spots and stripes all over. Habitat: <2000(&>) m. Open areas with high look-out posts like buildings or telephone wires. NM

8 **BLUE ROCK-THRUSH** Monticola solitaria L 20 cm. Note dark upperparts of ♂ without rufous in tail. Habitat: <4000 m. Areas with rocky outcrops. NM

9 **MIOMBO ROCK-THRUSH** Monticola angolensis L 15 cm. Habitat: 500-2000 m. Hilly open miombo. Voice: mid-high, short whistles '*mieuuhweetohweet*' ('*mieuuh-*' gliding down).

10 **FAMILIAR CHAT** Cercomela familiaris L 15 cm. Note rufous rump and tail with inverted black 'T'. Habitat: 250-1750 m. Wooded and bushed areas with rocky outcrops and small streams. Voice: extra high, slightly rising '*wheet wheet wheet -*'.

11 **BROWN-TAILED CHAT** Cercomela scotocerca L 13 cm. Note brown tail and upright stance. Habitat: 250-1250 m. Dry bushed areas with rocky outcrops.

12 **BLACKSTART** Cercomela melanura L 14 cm. Note black tail and grey-brown back. Habitat: dry rocky slopes, often with some scrub and bush. Voice: very high, simple rapid warble '*frrrfrrri-didnôtsee*'.

13 **SOMBRE ROCK-CHAT** Cercomela dubia L 14 cm. Note rather dark appearance. Tail uniformly brown with rest of upperparts. Habitat: not known, but supposed to be rocky areas with some bush.

14 **ALPINE CHAT** Cercomela sordida L 15 cm. Note white tail with inverted black 'T'. Habitat: 2250-4500 m. Alpine, rocky grass- and moorland.

15 **EURASIAN REDSTART** Phoenicurus phoenicurus L 14 cm. Race *p. phoenicurus* (a), race *samamisicus* (b). Note white forehead and pale underbelly. Habitat: 750-2000 m. Dry scrub- and woodland along streams. NM

16 **BLACK REDSTART** Phoenicurus ochruros L 15 cm. Note (dark) grey forehead. Lower belly and under tail-coverts almost uniformly chestnut with breast. Habitat: >1500 m. Rocky slopes with more or less trees. NM

17 **IRANIA** Irania gutturalis L 15 cm. The ♀ has buff flanks and black tail. Habitat: 500-1500 m. Thickets o open bush- and scrubland often near scattered settlements.

18 **BROWN-BACKED SCRUB-ROBIN** Cercotrichas hartlaubi L 15 cm. Note dark chest-striping and contrasting rufous rump and tail. Habitat: 750-2250 m. Tall grass near forests and cultivation. Voice: very high fluted whistles '*fjêetuwêedu*' ('*fjee-*' extra high).

19 **NORTHERN BEARDED SCRUB-ROBIN** Cercotrichas leucosticta L 15 cm. Note wing pattern, plain unstreaked breast and dark cheek. Habitat: <1500 m. Undergrowth of forest interiors often near termite mounds. Voice: very high, sharp, rapid, 3-noted strophe '*fjutuweetweetutjeeweetweet*'.

▶

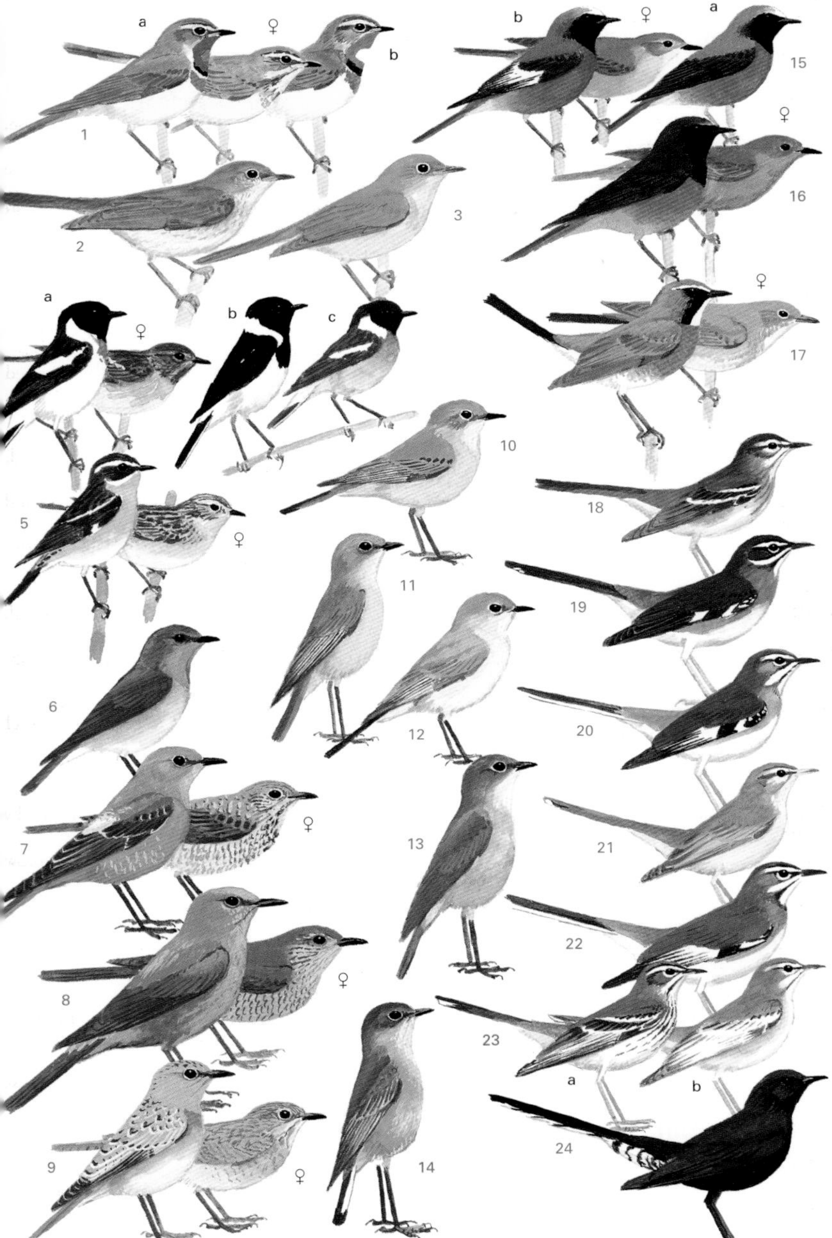
1
a
♀
b
2
3
15
b
♀
a
16
♀
17
♀
a
b
c
♀
4
10
5
♀
18
19
11
6
12
20
21
7
♀
13
8
♀
22
23
a
b
9
♀
14
24

65

20 EASTERN BEARDED SCRUB-ROBIN *Cercotrichas quadrivirgata* L 15 cm. Very similar to Miombo Bearded Scrub-Robin but not in same area. Habitat: <1000(&>) m. Undergrowth of dry forests, bushland, scrub and gardens.

21 RUFOUS SCRUB-ROBIN *Cercotrichas galactotes* L 15 cm. Note reddish tail. Habitat: <1000 m. Any dry, wooded area including plantations and gardens. Voice: high, sharp, hurried thrush-like warbles '*trrrrweetweet*' and '*trrrrtjutjuweetweet*'. (NM)

22 MIOMBO BEARDED SCRUB-ROBIN *Cercotrichas barbata* L 15 cm. Cheek colour as breast and rump. Habitat: 1000-1500 m. Miombo and well-wooded streams.

23 WHITE-BROWED SCRUB-ROBIN *Cercotrichas leucophrys* L 15 cm. Many races exist of which is shown a type of red-rumped races (a) and a type of white-winged races (b). Note double white wing-bar. Habitat: <1500(&>) m. Dense weed patches in more or less wooded and bushed areas. Voice: very high, loud, fast whistles repeated 2-3 times, '*weeduweet*'.

24 BLACK SCRUB-ROBIN *Cercotrichas podobe* L 20 cm. Habitat: areas with palms, trees and thickets in dry semi-desert. Voice: high, rather short or prolonged thrush-like warbling.

Plate 66

1 RED-THROATED ALETHE *Alethe poliophrys* L 15 cm. Habitat: 1500-3000 m. Undergrowth of forest and bamboo.

2 FIRE-CRESTED ALETHE *Alethe diademata* L 20 cm. Note white in tail. Habitat: 500-1500 m. Forest undergrowth. Voice: mid-high, simple whistle '*fuu-uu*' ('*uu*' slightly lower) and high '*fju weh*'.

3 BROWN-CHESTED ALETHE *Alethe poliocephala* L 15 cm. Note upright stance, grey head and buff upperparts. Habitat: 500-3000 m. Forest floors and undergrowth, and nearby wooded areas. Voice: high, fluted, descending whistle '*fjû-fjû-fjû-fju-fju-fjufju*'.

4 WHITE-CHESTED ALETHE *Alethe fuelleborni* L 20 cm. Note clear white underparts with sparsely but distinctly barred flanks. Habitat: 750(&<)-2750 m. Undergrowth of forest edges. Voice: high, monotonous, sweeping, fluted '*uWeeet uWeeet -*'.

5 DAPPLED MOUNTAIN-ROBIN *Arcanator orostruthus* L 14 cm. Note long bill, buff and greenish head. Habitat: 750-1250(&>) m. Undergrowth of moist forests.

6 SPOT-THROAT *Modulatrix stictigula* L 14 cm. Note long bill, reddish rump and generally warm brown colouring. Habitat: 750-2000 m. Forest groundstrata; also in gardens.

7 USAMBARA AKALAT *Sheppardia montana* L 13 cm. Note general olive-brown colouring and warm brown rump. May show rufous spot in front of eye. Habitat: 1500-2500 m. Forest undergrowth. E (Tanzania)

8 IRINGA AKALAT *Sheppardia lowei* L 13 cm. Note more or less uniformly coloured underparts, throat more rufous and belly rather whitish. Habitat: 1250-2500 m. Dry forests. E (Tanzania)

9 SHARPE'S AKALAT *Sheppardia sharpei* L 13 cm. Colour uniform except pale orange throat and small white eyebrow. Habitat: 750-2750 m. Dense forest undergrowth and bamboo.

10 COMMON AKALAT *Sheppardia cyornithopsis* L 13 cm. Similar to Equatorial Akalat but distinguished by larger size, altitude and song. Note short stumpy bill, greyish cheeks, orange flanks and rump. Habitat: 500-1250 m. Undergrowth of more or less swampy forests. Voice: very high, varied, calm warbling strophes (2-3 sec) with melodious rattles and rolls.

11 EAST-COAST AKALAT *Sheppardia gunningi* L 13 cm. Note uniformly coloured upperparts (including rump). Eyebrow mainly grey. Habitat: <500 m. Dense moist forest undergrowth.

12 EQUATORIAL AKALAT *Sheppardia aequatorialis* L 13 cm. Similar to Common Akalat but separated by size, altitude and voice. Habitat: 1500-2250 m. Forest undergrowth. Voice: mid-high, simple, rolling flute '*prurr prurrr -*'.

13 BOCAGE'S AKALAT *Sheppardia bocagei* L 14 cm. Lores (if present) pale grey, tail and wings brown, rump warm brown. Habitat: 1250-2500 m. Forest floors.

14 FOREST-ROBIN *Stiphrornis erythrothorax* L 12 cm. Note black face and white spot before eye. Habitat: 500-2000 m. Undergrowth of swampy forests. Voice: extra high, sharp hurried whistle '*feetjeetowee*', '*feetjeeweeteewo*' and '*sri-Sweep-srêeppersrêep-sreepsreep-Sweep*'.

15 WHITE-STARRED ROBIN *Pogonocichla stellata* L 15 cm. Note yellow margins of outer tail-feathers (which are however absent in the race occurring on Mt Elgon). White spots near eyes and on throat normally concealed. Habitat: 1500(&<)-3500 m. Midstrata and undergrowth at forest edges, bamboo and giant heath. Voice: very high, clear, single or repeated, rather short phrases often sounding like carefree human whistling.

16 SWYNNERTON'S ROBIN *Swynnertonia swynnertoni* L 14 cm. Note white breast-patch and all-dark tail. Habitat: 1000-1750 m. Forest undergrowth. Voice: very high '*pwêe-fwee-fwee*'.

66

17 FRASER'S ANT THRUSH *Neocossyphus fraseri* L 20 cm. Note orange outer tail-feathers and partly orange primaries. Habitat: 500-1500 m. Forest canopies and midstrata. Voice: mid-high, slightly descending, drawn-out whistle '*uweeet uweeet-uweeet-weet*' and mid-high, swept-up '*uwreeêt uwreeêt-*'.

18 WHITE-TAILED ANT THRUSH *Neocossyphus poensis* L 20 cm. Note black tail with white corners and partly rufous-brown flight feathers. Habitat: 500-1500 m. Midstrata and undergrowth of forests. Voice: extra high, swept-up '*fueeet*' and mid-high '*weeet-weeet-weet*'. Also an unhurried, fluted whistle.

19 RED-TAILED ANT THRUSH *Neocossyphus rufus* L 20 cm. Note rufous appearance, brown head and mantle. Habitat: 500-1500 m. Forests, moist bush- and scrubland. Voice: extra high, trilling '*fifififififiisruu fjui weee*' ('-*sruu*' rapidly descending, '*weee*' as a high, loud, level whistle).

20 GREY-WINGED ROBIN-CHAT *Cossypha polioptera* L 15 cm. Note narrow black eye-stripe, dark grey (not black) crown, short stumpy bill and uniformly reddish brown tail. Habitat: 1000-2000 m. Forest undergrowth and connected well-wooded streams. Voice: very high, sharp whistling of varied pitch, interspersed with clicks and short tempo changes, often resembling unstructured human whistling.

21 ARCHER'S ROBIN-CHAT *Cossypha archeri* L 15 cm. Note warm rufous-brown colouring, dark face and white eyebrow. Habitat: 1500-4000 m. Undergrowth of forests, bamboo and giant heath. Voice: very high '*firra-tweet-twêet-tweet*'.

22 OLIVE-FLANKED ROBIN-CHAT *Cossypha anomala* L 15 cm. (Not all races depicted.) Race *macclounii* shown. Note orange rump, buff-brown upperparts and rusty olive tail. Other races may have inverted black 'T' on tail and very dark breast. Habitat: 1500-2750 m. Groundstrata of forests, often near glades and streams.

23 WHITE-BELLIED ROBIN-CHAT *Cossyphicula roberti* L 15 cm. Note bicoloured tail, black lores, short white eyebrow, pale throat, orange breast and cheeks. Habitat: <1750 m. Forests.

Plate 67

1 AFRICAN THRUSH *Turdus pelios* L 25 cm. Note white underparts, grey (not olive) breast and olive upperparts. Habitat: 500-2000 m. Forests, woodland, gardens. Voice: loud, unhurried, typical thrush-like variations on '*tertjee tee-tju tee tjuwiet*'.

2 OLIVE THRUSH *Turdus olivaceus* L 25 cm. Race *helleri* (b) from SE Kenya. In most other races (a) little or no white on belly. Throat streaking not usually obvious. Habitat: 1500(&<)-3500 m. Forests, woodland, bamboo, giant heath, suburban gardens and parks. Voice: high, full, short, up-and-down whistled phrases, each ending in a varied trill, like almost level '*wheetohweetohthrrree*'.

3 SOMALI BLACKBIRD *Turdus ludoviciae* L 25 cm. Note throat streaking. Habitat: montane forests. E (Somalia)

4 GROUNDSCRAPER THRUSH *Psophocichla litsitsirupa* L 20 cm. Note bold face pattern and unspotted wing coverts. Habitat: 750-2000(&>) m. Giant heath, bamboo, forests, woodland and open bush. Voice: mid-high, slightly rasping whistles '*tictictweedhohwheeh*'.

5 SONG THRUSH *Turdus philomelos* L 20 cm. Note unstructured face pattern and small wing spots. Habitat: areas with some trees and bush. NM

6 SPOTTED GROUND-THRUSH *Zoothera guttata* L 20 cm. Note bold face pattern and large wing spots. Habitat: groundstrata of humid forests and woodland. Voice: high, loud, plaintive, fluted whistle '*tweeohtweehtitthrrric*'. AM

7 BLACK-EARED GROUND-THRUSH *Zoothera cameronensis* L 20 cm. Note rather pale brown colouring of upperparts, small malar stripe, pale chin and throat, and orange belly. Habitat: 500-1500 m. Groundstrata of lowland forests.

8 PRIGOGENE'S GROUND-THRUSH *Zoothera kibalensis* L 20 cm. Note general intensive colouring, distinct malar stripe, pale chin and orange throat and chest. Habitat: montane forests. E (Uganda)

9 ORANGE GROUND-THRUSH *Zoothera gurneyi* L 20 cm. Note all-brown upperparts (only forehead is slightly orange-brown). Habitat: 750-2000(&>) m. Groundstrata of forests. Voice: high, loud, piping whistles '*tututjuweehêehêetju*', very high fluted '*fiu fiufiu fiu-few-tjee*' and other whistles sounding almost like human song fragments.

10 ABYSSINIAN GROUND-THRUSH *Zoothera piaggiae* L 20 cm. Note rufous forehead and crown. Habitat: 1750-2500(&>) m. Groundstrata of bamboo and forests. Voice: very high, rather sharp, fluted, slightly hurried '*pipipjipju*'.

11 OBERLAENDER'S GROUND-THRUSH *Zoothera oberlaenderi* L 20 cm. Note rufous face. Habitat: 500-1000 m. Groundstrata of forests. Voice: high, unstructured, up-and-down '*peeeuuwip-tothree* and '*riuriu-reep-reepreep*'.

12 KIVU GROUND-THRUSH *Zoothera tanganjicae* L 20 cm. (Species level as by Britton.) Note rufous forehead, crown and nape. Habitat: 1500-3000 m. Groundstrata of forests.

▶

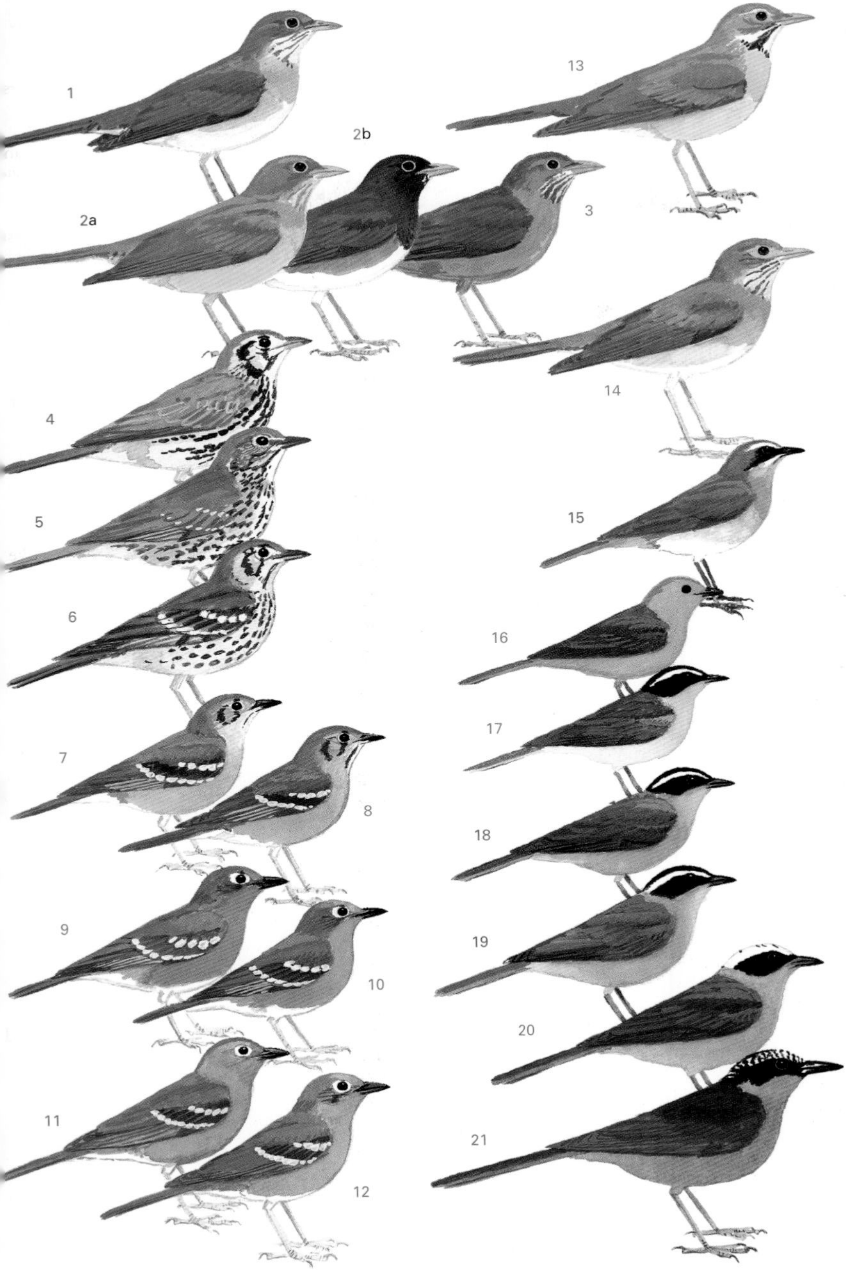
1
2a
2b
3
4
5
6
7
8
9
10
11
12
13
14
15
16
17
18
19
20
21

Plate 67 (continued)

13 **KURRICHANE THRUSH** *Turdus libonyanus* L 25 cm. Note black malar stripe and grey (not olive) breast. Habitat: <2000 m. Miombo, bushland, plantations and gardens. Voice: very high, loud, short fluted whistles '*wheetohwheet*' and '*wheetohweetthrêe*'.

14 **BARE-EYED THRUSH** *Turdus tephronotus* L 20 cm. Note bare orange eye area, pale orange underparts, olive breast and distinct throat striping. Habitat: <1750 m. Arid bush and cultivations.

15 **COMMON ROBIN-CHAT** *Cossypha caffra* L 15 cm. Note face pattern, short malar stripe, white belly and pale olive flanks. Habitat: 1000-3500 m. Gardens, cultivations, open forests and giant heath. Voice: high, short, fluted whistles '*tuh-twitwii-rurutwêerêerêe*' immediately followed by other strophes.

16 **RED-CAPPED ROBIN-CHAT** *Cossypha natalensis* L 15 cm. Habitat: <2250 m. Forest undergrowth, wood- and bushland and gardens. Voice: call is '*uwêeeh-rrur*'; song is a continuous flow of often repeated rich, fluted notes and short phrases incorporating adapted imitations.

17 **BLUE-SHOULDERED ROBIN-CHAT** *Cossypha cyanocampter* L 20 cm. Note shining light orange underparts and blue shoulder. Habitat: 500-2000 m. Wet forest undergrowth especially along streams. Voice: mid-high to high, liquid, rich, unhurried whistles repeated 1-3 times (like a person happily whistling).

18 **RUEPPELL'S ROBIN-CHAT** *Cossypha semirufa* L 20 cm. Differences with Heuglin's Robin-Chat include darker middle tail-feathers, slightly greyer mantle and incomplete orange neck-collar. Habitat: 1250-2500 m. Forest patches and gardens with dense shrub. Voice: high, melodious '*puwêêt puwêêt puwêêtpuwêêtpuwêêt*' and many other variations and imitations, mainly of other birds.

19 **HEUGLIN'S ROBIN-CHAT** *Cossypha heuglini* L 20 cm. Differences with Rueppell's Robin-Chat include slightly paler central tail feathers, browner mantle and almost complete orange neck-collar. Habitat: 2250 m. Open forests, bushland and gardens with dense shrub. Voice: high, melodious, crescendoing '*pêepipupurtupêepiperpurtu-*' endlessly varied and interwoven with imitations, mainly of other birds.

20 **SNOWY-CROWNED ROBIN-CHAT** *Cossypha niveicapilla* L 20 cm. Note narrow black area between white forehead and bill and all-orange (not partly black) chin. Habitat: 750-2000 m. Forest edges, undergrowth of moist woodland and gardens. Voice: beautiful, rich, liquid, sustained whistling with perfect imitations, mainly of other birds.

21 **WHITE-CROWNED ROBIN-CHAT** *Cossypha albicapilla* L 25 cm. Black-scaled white cap reaches bill. Note black and orange (not all-orange) chin. Habitat: swampy woodland thickets. Voice: rich, rather sharp and slightly hurried fluted phrases, normally without imitations.

Plate 68 (continued)

BAMBOO WARBLER *Bradypterus alfredi* L 14 cm. Note olive-brown upperparts and grey underparts. Habitat: 1000-2500 m. Dense forest undergrowth and bamboo.

FAN-TAILED WARBLER *Schoenicola platyura* L 15 cm. Habitat: 750-2000 m. Tall grass and shrubbery, often near water. Voice: extra high, unstructured, piercing '*sweeh sweeh sweeh -*'.

ICTERINE WARBLER *Hippolais icterina* L 13 cm. Note peaked crown, yellow overall wash and pale wing-panel. Habitat: <3000 m. Open wood- and bushland and gardens. Voice: high to very high sustained, varied strophes, full of sharp powerful rattles and chuckles, every phrase repeated 2-4 times. NM

UPCHER'S WARBLER *Hippolais languida* L 14 cm. Note peaked crown, dark tail and wings. Habitat: dry wood- and bushland. NM

OLIVE-TREE WARBLER *Hippolais olivetorum* L 15 cm. Note peaked crown, long bill, pale wing-panel and light underparts. Habitat: <2500 m. Dry, more or less wooded and bushed areas. Voice: mid-high, reed warbler-like, unhurried chattering. NM

OLIVACEOUS WARBLER *Hippolais pallida* L 13 cm. Note peaked crown, pale appearance and faint wing-panel. Wings and tail slightly darker than rest of upperparts. Habitat: <2000 m. Arid and dry wood- and bushland, gardens and cultivation. Voice: very high rasping warble, sounding like a slightly speeded-up reed warbler. NM

Plate 68

1 **GRASSHOPPER WARBLER** *Locustella naevia* L 13 cm. Note striped, very long under tail-coverts and streaked mantle. Habitat: <2000 m. Swamp edges. Voice: extra high, shrill, cicada-like sustained trill, like a very fast electric sewing machine. NM

2 **RIVER WARBLER** *Locustella fluviatilis* L 14 cm. Note 'barred' very long under tail-coverts and distinctly streaked chest. Habitat: shrubland undergrowth, reed beds and herbage in cultivation. Voice: extra high level trill, like a mechanical sewing machine. NM

3 **SAVI'S WARBLER** *Locustella luscinoides* L 14 cm. Note very long under tail-coverts and only faintly striped chest. Habitat: reedy habitats, often near streams and marches. Voice: extra high buzz. NM

4 **SEDGE WARBLER** *Acrocephalus schoenobaenus* L 13 cm. Note faint mantle streaking and white eyebrow contrasting sharply with dark cap. Habitat: reed beds, papyrus and other vegetation near or over water. Voice: mid-high, very varied medley of fluted, hoarse, rattling, sharp and sweet notes and phrases repeated 2-20 times. NM

5 **BLYTH'S REED WARBLER** *Acrocephalus dumetorum* L 12 cm. Note short eyebrow (lighter than eye-ring), faint rusty rump and flat high forehead. Habitat: mangroves. Voice: very varied medley of well-spaced phrases. NM

6 **AFRICAN REED WARBLER** *Acrocephalus baeticatus* L 13 cm. Note general rusty colouring and brown wings and tail. Habitat: <2000 m. Tall grass, reed beds and other lush herbage, not necessarily near water. Voice: high, loud, chattered, sustained, rapid syllables '*chritchrittjitji weetcarreweetweettri--*' each syllable repeated twice.

7 **EURASIAN REED WARBLER** *Acrocephalus scirpaceus* L 13 cm. Note warm brown upperparts, dark cap and white throat. Eye-ring dominates eyebrow. Habitat: reed beds over lakes and rivers. Voice: mid-high, unhurried, sustained, rasping '*kritteritkrit-tirrr-tretietie- carrecarre-trêettrêet-*' randomly changing in pitch. NM

8 **MARSH WARBLER** *Acrocephalus palustris* L 13 cm. Eye-ring dominates eyebrow. Note dark pale-fringed flight feathers. May look hippolais warbler-like (see 68.21-24) especially with raised crest. Habitat: thickets, reed beds, tall herbage not necessarily near water. Voice: very high, powerful, rapid warble, each short phrase repeated 3-7 times with perfect imitations and short canary-like rolls like '*wêetwêetochrêechrêeweetictictie-*'. NM

9 **GREAT REED WARBLER** *Acrocephalus arundinaceus* L 20 cm. Note large size, pale eyebrow and rather heavy bill. Habitat: reed beds, thickets and dense shrubbery near or away from water. Voice: mid-high, very loud, hoarse unhurried '*carre-carre-kêetkêet-weet-*'. NM

10 **CLAMOROUS REED WARBLER** *Acrocephalus stentoreus* L 20 cm. Note large size, long bill and distinct eyebrow. Habitat: mangroves and papyrus. NM

11 **BASRA REED WARBLER** *Acrocephalus griseldis* L 15 cm. (Species level as by Britton.) Note long bill, pale eyebrow, medium-large size. Habitat: dense bush, tall grass, moist thickets, reeds near or away from water, often at forest edges. NM

12 **LESSER SWAMP WARBLER** *Acrocephalus gracilirostris* L 15 cm. Note warm brown colouring, distinct eyebrow and medium-large size. Habitat: <2500 m. Low shrubs near water and swamp edges. Voice: mid-high sustained medleys of '*weet weet weet -*' and loud, rapid, melodious rattles, flutes and oriole-like warbles.

13 **GREATER SWAMP WARBLER** *Acrocephalus rufescens* L 20 cm. Note dark earth-brown colouring and medium-large size. Habitat: 500-2000 m. Papyrus. Voice: low to very high, unhurried '*tjiptjip-WHâaRo-PJUPJUPJU- -*' with marked contrasts in volume and pitch.

14 **GRAUER'S RUSH WARBLER** *Bradypterus graueri* L 13 cm. Note dark bill, general dark colouring, white throat and face markings. Habitat: 2000-2250 m. Forest swamps.

15 **LITTLE RUSH WARBLER** *Bradypterus baboecala* L 12 cm. Breeds in colonies. Note dark bill, rusty brown crown and mantle, and freckle-striped breast. Habitat: <2500 m. Dense vegetation in swamps and over water. Voice: very high, loud, accelerated, slightly descending '*trwit trwit trwit-trwit-trwit-trwittrwittrwittrwit*'. (AM)

16 **WHITE-WINGED WARBLER** *Bradypterus carpalis* L 13 cm. Habitat: 1000-2000 m. Papyrus and reed beds. Voice: descending chirping whistle concluded with some explosive wing beats.

17 **CINNAMON BRACKEN WARBLER** *Bradypterus cinnamomeus* L 14 cm. Note chestnut-brown colouring, pale eye-stripe and dark bill. Habitat: 2000(&<)-4000 m. Moist thickets, giant heath, forests and bamboo. Voice: extra high, melodious rapid rattles '*fjuût-rrrrrr*' and '*tjuût-weetweetweetweet*'.

18 **EVERGREEN-FOREST WARBLER** *Bradypterus mariae* L 13 cm. Note dark rusty brown colouring, pale chin and olive underparts. Habitat: 1500(&<)-3250 m. Forest undergrowth. Voice: high, hurried rattling '*tjkutjkutjkutjkutjkutjku*' and crescendoing '*tidjú-titjú-titjú-titjú*' like a camaroptera (72.23).

◀

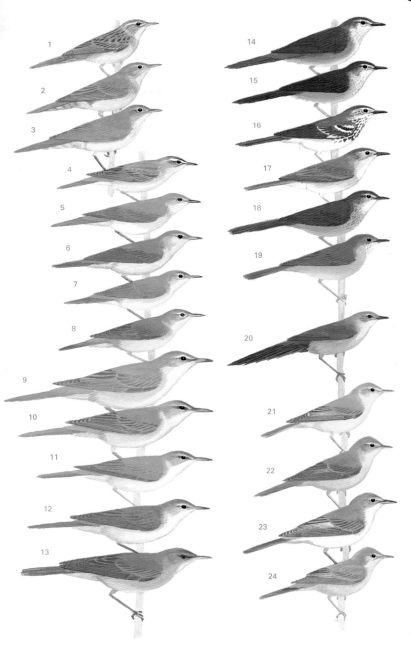

68

Plate 69

1 **MOUSTACHED WARBLER** *Melocichla mentalis* L 20 cm. Habitat: <2000 m. Moist areas with tall grass and other rank herbage in more or less wooded and bush areas. Voice: very high, basically staccato unhurried whistle with sudden accelerated short '*tjup tjup priweetweetweet tjup weedèh*'.

2 **AFRICAN YELLOW-THROATED WARBLER** *Phylloscopus ruficapilla* L 9 cm. Note rufous-brown crown, eye-stripe and nape. Habitat: 750-2500 m. Bamboo and forest interiors and edges. Voice: very high, bouncing, fast '*wêettuttuttwêettuttutwwêettuttuttut*' and short strophes including extra high '*sweetsweettûttût*'.

3 **LAURA'S WARBLER** *Phylloscopus laurae* L 10 cm. Note clear green-yellow colouring. Habitat: >1000 m. Dense forest canopies.

4 **RUSTY-FACED WARBLER** *Phylloscopus laetus* L 9 cm. Note greenish upperparts and buff face and breast. Habitat: 1500-3000 m. Forests and bamboo.

5 **UGANDA WARBLER** *Phylloscopus budongensis* L 10 cm. Note darkish green colouring and slightly yellow-streaked breast. Habitat: 1000-2000 m. Mainly midstrata of dense forests.

6 **BROWN WARBLER** *Phylloscopus umbrovirens* L 10 cm. Note greenish wings and outer tail-feathers. Habitat: 1500-4500 m. Forest undergrowth, bamboo and giant heath.

7 **WOOD WARBLER** *Phylloscopus sibilatrix* L 12 cm. Note yellow-green edges to dark flight- and tail-feathers. Habitat: <3000 m. Forests and woodland. Voice: extra high, rather short, fast, accelerated trill. NM

8 **CHIFFCHAFF** *Phylloscopus collybita* L 11 cm. Note pale buff (not buff stripes on a yellow base) face and breast. Feet rather dark to black. Habitat: 1250-3750 m. Forests and bamboo. Voice: low, soft '*tru-tru-tru*' followed by rhythmic, unstructured '*tri tru tri tri tru -*' (or '*chiff chaff chaff -*'). NM

9 **WILLOW WARBLER** *Phylloscopus trochilus* L 12 cm. Note buff stripes on a green base (not all-buff) face and breast. Feet flesh-brown coloured. Habitat: <2250(&>) m. Voice: rich, full whistle, starting very high and jubilant, gradually descending 5 notes and ending melancholy '*fifififururururu tweet tweet*'. NM

10 **BONELLI'S WARBLER** *Phylloscopus bonelli* L 11 cm. Note general buff colouring and yellow edges of tail feathers. Habitat: arid sparsely wooded areas and coastal bush. Voice: very high '*pjeeh pjeeh pjeeh trititititititee*' and very high short trill '*tseetsitsitsitsi*'. NM

11 **AFRICAN YELLOW WARBLER** *Chloropeta natalensis* L 14 cm. Note complete golden-yellow underparts and wide bill base. Habitat: 750-2500 m. Shrubbery, tall grass and rank herbage in open woodland and suburban gardens. Voice: very high, melodious, staccato trills and rolls connected by dry '*tectec tec*'.

12 **MOUNTAIN YELLOW WARBLER** *Chloropeta similis* L 14 cm. Note yellow throat, chest and belly and pale grey-brown flanks. Habitat: 1750-3500 m. Forest undergrowth and bamboo. Voice: high (sometimes low), sweet, varied '*ti-tu-wu-wu-jujuju-wee-wee-djidjidji-dju-dju-trrril-ti-ti-*'.

13 **PAPYRUS YELLOW WARBLER** *Chloropeta gracilirostris* L 14 cm. Note saffron belly and flanks and pale orange wing-patch. Habitat: papyrus.

14 **RED SEA WARBLER** *Sylvia leucomelaena* L 14 cm. Note sharp division between black head and ash-grey mantle. Habitat: <2000 m. Dry wooded areas.

15 **SUBALPINE WARBLER** *Sylvia cantillans* L 13 cm. The ♂ n-br plumage is like ♀ plumage but with light red eye-ring. Habitat: open wood-, bush- and scrubland. Voice: unstructured medleys of dry, loud '*chuck*' phrases repeated up to 8 times and very high, rapid, melodious warbling. NM

16 **RUEPPELL'S WARBLER** *Sylvia rueppelli* L 14 cm. The ♀ may have white chin without any black. Habitat: bush- and scrubland. NM

17 **MENETRIES'S WARBLER** *Sylvia mystacea* L 14 cm. Black of ♂ head merges into grey of mantle. Habitat: wooded bush- and scrubland, cultivation and gardens. NM

18 **ORPHEAN WARBLER** *Sylvia hortensis* L 15 cm. Note yellowish eye-colour. Habitat: open wood-, bush- and scrubland. Voice: high, unstructured, loud, melodious medleys of flutes, rattles and chuckles. NM

19 **BARRED WARBLER** *Sylvia nisoria* L 15 cm. Barring of n-br plumage not very visible in the field. Habitat: low scrub and undergrowth of wood- and bushland. NM

20 **LESSER WHITETHROAT** *Sylvia curruca* L 14 cm. Note small size, dark (not black) cheek and black (not yellow) eye. Habitat: open bush- and shrubland. Voice: very high, level, melodious rattle and very high, fast rattling warble. NM

21 **COMMON WHITETHROAT** *Sylvia communis* L 14 cm. Note wide buff-rufous margins of wing feathers. Habitat: <1750(&>) m. Scrub and undergrowth of wood- and bushland. Voice: high, rather long strophes, starting unhurriedly but developing to sharp warbles with deep scratchy rattles. NM

▶

1
2
3
4
5
6
7
8
9
10
11
12
13
14
15
♀
16
♀
17
n-br
18
n-br
19
n-br
20
n-br
21
♀
22
23
24
♀

69

22 DESERT WARBLER *Sylvia nana* L 12 cm. Note pale eye and small size. Habitat: dry coastal scrub. Voice: extra high, short, hurried warble '*trreeetrêetrititjee*'. NM

23 GARDEN WARBLER *Sylvia borin* L 14 cm. Note pale grey area behind cheek. Habitat: 750-2000 m. Tall herbage and dense shrubbery in forests, wood- and bushland, cultivation and gardens. Voice: high, long, rapid whistles, slightly speeded up, starting melodiously, more sharp and harsh at the end. NM

24 BLACKCAP *Sylvia atricapilla* L 14 cm. Note black ($\male$) or rufous ($\female$) cap. Habitat: 750-1750($\&$>) m. Forests, bamboo, bush, suburban gardens. Voice: high, rich, chattered, unhurried warbling, starting with some hurried squeaky notes. NM

Plate 70

1 PECTORAL-PATCH CISTICOLA *Cisticola brunnescens* L 9 cm. The $\male$ has tawny, faintly striped crown, and very thin bill. Breast-patches often not visible. Habitat: 1250-2500 m. Dry and moist grass-and moorland. Voice: extra high, rapid '*tzipclaptzipclaptzipclap- -*' (four '*tzip*' per sec, '*clap*' [made by wings] like a pencil tap on a table).

2 WING-SNAPPING CISTICOLA *Cisticola ayresii* L 9 cm. Face rather marked, pale neck-collar, bill thin (not very thin). Breast-patches often visible. Habitat: 1000-4000 m. Dry and moist short grass. Voice: very high, sweet '*trêetreetreetêetêe*' and rapid wing claps '*clapclapclapclapclap-*' (song and wing claps alternate in an irregular way).

3 BLACK-BACKED CISTICOLA *Cisticola eximia* L 9 cm. Note plain brown colouring of crown and nape and stubby tail of $\male$ br plumage. May have pectoral patches. Habitat: 750-1500 m. Dry short grass. Voice: very high '*tret-snap-tret-snap-*' (snap made by wings).

4 ZITTING CISTICOLA *Cisticola juncidis* L 10 cm. Tail not stumpy and streaking of mantle darker than crown. Habitat: <2000($\&$>) m. Dry rough grass. Voice: extra high '*tseet tseet tseet-*' coinciding with dips in very high cruising flight. No wing claps.

5 DESERT CISTICOLA *Cisticola aridula* L 10 cm. Note fine striping of neck and sides of upper breast. Striping of crown as heavy as mantle. General colouring including rump rather uniform. Habitat: <2000 m. Dry short grass. Voice: very high, sharp '*piWi-piWi-piWi-*' and extra high '*tingtingting-ting-tingting-*'. No wing claps.

6 SOCOTRA CISTICOLA *Cisticola haesitata* L 10 cm. Note buff rump and lower flanks. Streaking crown darker than mantle. Habitat: bushed grassland. E (Socotra)

7 CROAKING CISTICOLA *Cisticola natalensis* L 15 cm ($\male$), 13 cm ($\female$). Habitat: <2250 m. Bushed and wooded tall grassland. Voice: mid-high '*wêêêêêwêep*' and '*fwjuuuuwhêep*'.

8 STOUT CISTICOLA *Cisticola robusta* L 16 cm ($\male$), 14 cm ($\female$). Note bright rufous crown, rather short dark tail with pale edging and buff wing-panel. Habitat: 1000-2500 m. Bushed and wooded habitats with moist places. Voice: high, dry, rapid, rattling '*ti-ti-three*'.

9 ABERDARE CISTICOLA *Cisticola aberdare* L 16 cm($\male$), 14 cm ($\female$). Tail all black and mantle broadly streaked black. Habitat: 2250-3750 m. Grasslands. Voice: very high, accentuated '*prreeh prreeh prreeh*' or high, nasal '*preh-preh-preh*'. E (Kenya)

10 WAILING CISTICOLA *Cisticola lais* L 15 cm. Note rather uniform colouring. Mantle and rump greyer. Sides of face uniformly buff with crown. Habitat: 1500-2750 m. Grassland with bush and large rocks or cliffs. Voice: very high, canary-like piping and trilling '*peeppeepprrrrrrt*'.

11 ASHY CISTICOLA *Cisticola cinereola* L 14 cm. Note pale uniform colouring. Habitat: 250-1500 m. Dry bush. Voice: very high, descending, sharp, fluted '*weeweeweh*'.

12 TANA RIVER CISTICOLA *Cisticola restricta* L 13 cm. Note grey mantle, rump and tail. Crown and wing-panel tawny brown. Habitat: dry bush. E (Kenya)

13 RATTLING CISTICOLA *Cisticola chiniana* L 13 cm. (Not all races depicted.) Race *ukamba* (a) in S Kenya, race *heterophrys* (b) in NE Tanzania and SE Kenya. Race *ukamba* has finely striped crown. Wing-panel and tail rusty brown. Race *heterophrys* has faint mantle-streaking and distinct orange head. Habitat: <2000 m. More or less dry bush with tall grass. Voice: very high, sharp, fast '*chachachacharrr*' and extra high '*fiewfiewfiarrr*'.

14 CHURRING CISTICOLA *Cisticola njombe* L 13 cm. Note general warm rufous-brown colouring. Mantle faintly streaked. Bill rather heavy. Habitat: 2000-3000 m. Rough herbage near large rocks. Voice: very high, rattling '*tjerrûptjerrûptjerrûp-*'.

15 RED-PATE CISTICOLA *Cisticola ruficeps* L 14 cm. In br plumage with warm brown upperparts and buff-rufous crown. In n-br plumage with grey and streaked mantle. Habitat: bushed and wooded areas. Voice: extra high '*feeee-ferresh*' ('*feee*' slurred up).

16 TINY CISTICOLA *Cisticola nana* L 11 cm. Note rather short tail, bright buff head and faint mantle striping. Habitat: <1500 m. More or less wooded and bushed, natural and cultivated areas. Voice: extra high, up-and-down '*tjurrêp-tjurrêp-tjurrêp- -*'.

▶

Plate 70 (continued)

17 **SIFFLING CISTICOLA** *Cisticola brachyptera* L 10 cm. Very dull coloured. Habitat: <2250 m. More or less wooded and bushed habitats. Voice: extra high '*fifiwich-fifiwich-fifiwich*' and many other whistles.

18 **FOXY CISTICOLA** *Cisticola troglodytes* L 10 cm. Habitat: wooded grassland.

19 **NEDDICKY CISTICOLA** *Cisticola fulvicapilla* L 11 cm. Race *muelleri* (a) in SE Tanzania, race *angusticauda* (b) in W Tanzania and SW Kenya. Note narrow often cocked tail. Habitat: <1500 m. Open miombo, wood- and bushland. Voice: very high, slow, crescendoing '*wuu-wuu-Wuu-Wuu-WUu--*'

20 **ROCK-LOVING CISTICOLA** *Cisticola aberrans* L 13 cm. Habitat: bare rocky areas, often with some grass or scrub. Voice: extra high, tit-like tinkling '*teetteet*' followed by mid-high, nasal '*tèèhtèèhtèèh*'.

21 **WHISTLING CISTICOLA** *Cisticola lateralis* L 14 cm. Note long firm bill and uniformly coloured upperparts except slightly more buff wing-panel. Habitat: 750-1000 m. Herbage in wood- and bushland, especially along streams. Voice: high, jubilant (or mid-high, nasal) '*pju-pjupuPJuwuweeh*'.

22 **TRILLING CISTICOLA** *Cisticola woosnami* L 13 cm. Note short firm bill, short tail, slightly rusty forehead and buff wing-panel. Habitat: 750-2000 m. Tall grass in forests and more or less wooded and bushed areas, often on rocky hillsides. Voice: extra high, crescendoing, fast trill '*weeweeweeWeeWeeWEeWEeWEEWEE*'.

RED-WINGED GREY WARBLER *Drymocichla incana* L 13 cm. Habitat: 500-1250 m. Damp herbaceous places in woodland. Voice: very high, sweeping whistles '*tweet-tweet-tweet*' and very high, finch-like, fast twitters.

BLACK-FACED RUFOUS WARBLER *Bathmocercus rufus* L 13 cm. Habitat: 500-3000 m. Forest undergrowth. Voice: extra high, sharp '*tjeeeéé-tjeeeéé-tjeeeéé-*'.

MRS MOREAU'S WARBLER *Bathmocercus winifredae* L 15 cm. Habitat: 1500-2250 m. Dense forest undergrowth. Voice: mid-high '*fjuuuuu fjuuuui*' and '*tuui-tuui-tuui-tio-tui-fêe*'. E (Tanzania)

Plate 71

1 **RED-FACED CISTICOLA** *Cisticola erythrops* L 13 cm. Note rusty sides of face and uniformly coloured upperparts (including crown, wings and tail). Habitat: <2500 m. Tall grass, herbage and shrubbery near water. Often in same area as Singing Cisticola but prefers the lower, moister parts of the environment. Voice: mid-high, rather tinkling, rapid '*wéetjewéetjewéetjewéetje*' and very high, lashing '*weepweepweepweep*'.

2 **SINGING CISTICOLA** *Cisticola cantans* L 14 cm. Note rufous crown and reddish tail. Habitat: thick herbaceous undergrowth of woodland, cultivation and gardens. Voice: high, loud, sweeping '*twitTrêet-twitTrêet-twitTrêet*'.

3 **HUNTER'S CISTICOLA** *Cisticola hunteri* L 14 cm. Note dark appearance, faint mantle streaking, rusty brown forehead and crown. Habitat: 1750(&<)-3000(&>) m. Tall grass, herbage and shrubbery in open forests, bamboo and giant heath. Voice: duet of high, undulating, fast trills with a rhythmic counter-song '*weed weed weed -*'.

4 **CHUBB'S CISTICOLA** *Cisticola chubbi* L 14 cm. Note plain mantle and dark area between eye and bill. Habitat: <1500 m. Dense undergrowth at well-wooded streams. Voice: high, undulating, chirping, fast '*tsêetsêeweeohtsêeweeohtsêetsêe- -*' (actually an inseparable duet).

5 **BLACK-LORED CISTICOLA** *Cisticola nigriloris* L 15 cm. Habitat: dense undergrowth of forest edge. Voice: duet of extra high, undulating, shrill piping (like a badly oiled wheel) with faint lower counter-song '*trit trit trit*'. Also other variations.

6 **BORAN CISTICOLA** *Cisticola bodessa* L 13 cm. Note uniformly coloured upperparts and more buff forehead and crown. Habitat: <2250 m. Rocky slopes with some grass and bush. Voice: very high, jubilant fast '*cisticola*'.

7 **WINDING CISTICOLA** *Cisticola galactotes* L 13 cm. Br plumage is pale version of n-br plumage. Habitat: <2500 m. Rough grass and tall herbage near lakes and marshes. Voice: extra high, slightly uplifted, shrill trill '*tssrrrrrrru*' and high '*tuwêe-tuwêe-*'.

8 **CARRUTHER'S CISTICOLA** *Cisticola carruthersi* L 13 cm. Note bright buff head and grey upperparts. Habitat: <2250 m. Interior of papyrus swamps. Voice: rapid trill.

9 **CHIRPING CISTICOLA** *Cisticola pipiens* L 15 cm. Less brightly coloured then Levaillant's Cisticola. Habitat: moist herbage along streams. Voice: very high, loud, decisive '*tHis-tHis thrrrrêeee*' ('*tHis*' finch-like).

10 **LEVAILLANT'S CISTICOLA** *Cisticola tinniens* L 13 cm. Very colourful. Habitat: 2000-3250 m. Swamps, marshes and inundations. Voice: very high, lashing '*jujutHrill*' ('*juju-*' very short, '*tHrill*' sweeping up).

11 **SOCOTRA WARBLER** *Incana incana* L 13 cm. Note long thin bill, warm brown upperparts and near-white margins of primaries. Habitat: <1500 m. Open and bushed grassland. E (Socotra)

12 **GRACEFUL WARBLER** *Prinia gracilis* L 14 cm. Habitat: wooded and bushed, natural and cultivated areas.

13 **TAWNY-FLANKED PRINIA** *Prinia subflava* L 13 cm. Note long white eyebrow. Habitat: <2500 m. Grassy areas in forests and bushland. Also at swamp edges. Voice: extra high, lashing staccato '*WiettuWiettuWiettu-*' and rapid '*tjêeptjêeptju-tjuwickwirwir*'.

14 **WHITE-CHINNED PRINIA** *Prinia leucopogon* L 14 cm. Habitat: 1000-2500 m. Tall herbage and shrubbery in forest glades and cultivation. Voice: extra high, sharp, fast warbling '*fifi-weep-weep-fi*' and '*frifrifrifrifri-*'.

15 **PALE PRINIA** *Prinia somalica* L 12 cm. Note short eyebrow. Habitat: 250-1500 m. Dry, open areas with some grass and bush.

16 **BANDED PRINIA** *Prinia bairdii* L 12 cm. Habitat: 500-750 m and 1500-3000 m. Tall grassy places and shrubbery in forests and woodland. Voice: high, sharp, fast, tinkling '*weetweetweetweet-*' (lasting 30 sec).

17 **CRICKET WARBLER** *Spiloptila clamans* L 13 cm. Habitat: bare desert, often with some scrub. Voice: extra high, irregular mechanical rattle '*weetweetweetweetweetweet-*' and extra high, level, piercing '*weet-weet-weet-weet- -*'.

18 **RED-FRONTED WARBLER** *Spiloptila rufifrons* L 12 cm. Habitat: 250-1500 m. Dry shrubland with some grass.

19 **BUFF-BELLIED WARBLER** *Phyllolais pulchella* L 9 cm. No eye-stripe. Habitat: 500-2000 m. Open acacia woodland. Voice: extra high, dry, short trills '*srrrrr*'.

20 **RED-WINGED PRINIA** *Prinia erythroptera* L 14 cm. Habitat: <1500 m. Tall grassy places in open woodland. Voice: high, bubbling '*fiufiufiufiufiufiu*' and '*djipdjipdjipdjipdjipdjip*'.

◀

71

Plate 72

1. **YELLOW-BREASTED APALIS** *Apalis flavida* L 12 cm. (Not all races depicted). Race *caniceps* (a) in SW and SE Uganda and in SW Kenya. The ♀ has greenish and ♂ grey nape. Habitat: <2250 m. Wood-, bush- and shrubland. Voice: mid-high, dry, rapid, staccato '*tiu-tiu-tiu-tiu-tiu*'.

2. **MASKED APALIS** *Apalis binotata* L 10 cm. Habitat: 1500-3000 m. Forests. Voice: very high, sharp, rapid '*fiu-fiu-fiu-*', high '*fru-fru-fru-fru*' and high, fast '*crrrrk crrrrk kêelerkêelerkêeler*'.

3. **BLACK-THROATED APALIS** *Apalis jacksoni* L 12 cm. Habitat: 1000-2500 m. Forest edges. Voice: very high, sharp, fluted '*tuut tuut tuut*' or in duet '*tuuttuut-tuuttuut-tuuttuut*'. Duets often just out of synchrony.

4. **WHITE-WINGED APALIS** *Apalis chariessa* L 12 cm. (Last seen in 1961.) Habitat: <1250 m. Forests and well-wooded streams.

5. **BLACK-CAPPED APALIS** *Apalis nigriceps* L 10 cm. Habitat: 1000-1500 m. Forest canopies. Voice: extra high, dry trill '*srrrrr srrrrr srrrrr -*' (each one 1½ sec).

6. **BLACK-COLLARED APALIS** *Apalis pulchra* L 13 cm. Habitat: 1500-2500 m. Forest undergrowth. Voice: mid-high, nasal, rapid '*piuw-piuw-piuw-piuw-piuw*'. Sometimes shortened to almost a rattle.

7. **COLLARED APALIS** *Apalis ruwenzorii* L 10 cm. Note all-grey tail and pale rufous (not white) throat. Habitat: 1500-3250 m. Undergrowth of forests and bamboo. Voice: very high, squeaking '*weeweeweeweeweewee*'.

8. **LONG-BILLED FOREST-WARBLER** *Orthotomus moreaui* L 15 cm. No white in tail, note very long bill. Habitat: 750-1000 m. Leafy undergrowth of dense forests.

9. **BAR-THROATED APALIS** *Apalis thoracica* L 12 cm. Habitat: 1250-2750 m. Undergrowth and midstrata of well-wooded slopes and valleys.

10. **GREY APALIS** *Apalis cinerea* L 13 cm. Note white outer tail-feathers. Habitat: 1500-3000 m. Dense forests. Voice: mid-high, rapid '*raprapraprapraprap*' and extra high, insect-like '*trrrrrrt-tit*' sometimes slackened to a rapid '*tit-tit-tit-tit- -*'.

11. **BROWN-HEADED APALIS** *Apalis alticola* L 13 cm. Note white tail-feather tips and rather grey margins of outer tail-feathers. Habitat: 1000-2250 m. Forests.

12. **KARAMOJA APALIS** *Apalis karamojae* L 12 cm. Habitat: thickets and low shrub.

13. **BUFF-THROATED APALIS** *Apalis rufogularis* L 12 cm. Note warm brown mantle and rump, and pale grey (not brown) eye. Habitat: 1500-2500 m. Forest canopies. Voice: high, sweeping, sharp, double-toned, rapid '*wrreetwrreetwrreet- -*'.

14. **KUNGWE APALIS** *Apalis argentea* L 13 cm. Habitat: 1000-2250 m. Forests and bamboo. E (Tanzania).

15. **BLACK-HEADED APALIS** *Apalis melanocephala* L 14 cm. Habitat: <2000 m. Forests and woodland. Voice: very high lashing '*swee-swee-swee-swee-*'.

16. **CHESTNUT-THROATED APALIS** *Apalis porphyrolaema* L 13 cm. Habitat: 1500-3500 m. Forest interiors and edges. Voice: extra high, insect-like double-buzz '*turrrree-turrree*'.

17. **CHAPIN'S APALIS** *Apalis chapini* L 13 cm. Race *c. chapini* (a) in C Tanzania, race *strausae* (b) in SW Tanzania. Habitat: <3500 m. Forest interiors and edges.

18. **RED-CAPPED FOREST-WARBLER** *Orthotomus metopias* L 10 cm. Habitat: 1000-2500 m. Forest undergrowth.

19. **GREY-CAPPED WARBLER** *Hypergerus lepidus* L 15 cm. More often heard than seen. Habitat: 750-2500 m. Undergrowth, tall herbage near water and suburban gardens. Voice: extra high, fast, rattling trill '*tirrrrrr*', high song phrases like '*tutu-tu tû*' and other trills.

20. **GREY BUSH-WARBLER** *Calamonastes simplex* L 13 cm. Habitat: <1500 m. Thick undergrowth of wood- and bushland.

21. **MIOMBO BUSH-WARBLER** *Calamonastes undosus* L 13 cm. Habitat: 750-1750 m. Undergrowth of bush- and woodland (miombo).

22. **BARRED BUSH-WARBLER** *Calamonastes stierlingi* L 13 cm. (Species level as by Britton.) Habitat: <1250 m. Grassy places in miombo and dry bushland. Voice: very high, piercing '*trwiet-trwiet-trwiet-*' (like a badly oiled wheel).

23. **COMMON CAMAROPTERA** *Camaroptera brachyura* L 10 cm. (Not all races depicted.) Race *griseigula* (a) as type for grey-mantled races, race *pileata* (b) as type for green-mantled group. Habitat: <2250 m. Dense undergrowth of forest edges. Voice: mid-high, dry, staccato '*treet-treet-treet-treet-treet*' and mid-high, miauling '*mèh-mèh-mèh*'.

24. **YELLOW-BROWED CAMAROPTERA** *Camaroptera superciliaris* L 10 cm. Habitat: 500-1750 m. Forest undergrowth. Voice: mid-high, miauling '*kiâu-kiau kiâu-kiâu*' and '*yuwêet-yuwêet*'.

72

25 OLIVE-GREEN CAMAROPTERA *Camaroptera chloronota* L 9 cm. Habitat: 500-2000 m. Dense forest undergrowth. Voice: extra high, sustained, gradually descending, sharp, rapid whistle '*sisisisisi-*'.

Plate 73

1 RED-CAPPED SYLVIETTA *Sylvietta ruficapilla* L 10 cm. Note rather long bill and orange cheek. Habitat: miombo. Voice: very high, hurried, fluted warble '*titituwreetuwreethrêe*' ('*-three*' extra high).

2 WHITE-BROWED SYLVIETTA *Sylvietta leucophrys* L 8 cm. Note greenish wing and yellow should Habitat: 1500-2750 m. Undergrowth of forests and bamboo.

3 GREEN SYLVIETTA *Sylvietta virens* L 7 cm. Habitat: 500-1500 m. Midstrata and undergrowth of forests and gardens. Voice: extra high, descending, sharp, fast twitter '*sisêesreesisi*', often followed by slov and lower syllables.

4 RED-FACED SYLVIETTA *Sylvietta whytii* L 10 cm. No eye-stripe. Habitat: <2000(&>) m. Forest edges, dry wood- and bushland. Voice: very high, crescendoing, cicada-like trill (lasting 3 sec).

5 NORTHERN SYLVIETTA *Sylvietta brachyura* L 8 cm. Note white throat. Habitat: <2000(&>) m. Dry wood- and bushland. Voice: extra high, descending, short, hurried, twittering warble '*tutjêettertsjêetuwee*'.

6 LONG-BILLED SYLVIETTA *Sylvietta rufescens* L 10 cm. Habitat: hilly, wooded and bushed habitat with some grass. Voice: very high, shrill '*tuwie-thrêewie-thrêewie-thrée*'.

7 SOMALI SHORT-BILLED SYLVIETTA *Sylvietta philippae* L 9 cm. Note dark eye-stripe and reddish legs. Habitat: dry bushland. E (Somalia)

8 SOMALI LONG-BILLED SYLVIETTA *Sylvietta isabellina* L 10 cm. Note long bill. Habitat: <1000 Dry wood- and bushland.

9 YELLOW-VENTED EREMOMELA *Eremomela flavicrissalis* L 8 cm. Pale yellow area restricted to under tail-coverts. Habitat: <1250 m. Dry wood- and bushland.

10 GREEN-CAPPED EREMOMELA *Eremomela scotops* L 10 cm. Habitat: <2000 m. Miombo, wood- and bushland, gardens. Voice: high '*trrit-trrit-trrit-trrit- -*' and low, shrieking '*tchreettchreettchreet-*'.

11 BROWN-CROWNED EREMOMELA *Eremomela badiceps* L 10 cm. Note rufous crown, forehead a eyebrow. Habitat: 500-1500 m. Canopy of forest edges. Voice: extra high, hurried, siffling '*sisisisisi-*' incorporating very high, reed warbler-like syllables.

12 YELLOW-BELLIED EREMOMELA *Eremomela icteropygialis* L 9 cm. Note extensive yellow area. Habitat: <2000 m. Desert and more or less wooded and bushed habitats occasionally near water. Voice: very high, sharp '*tutuWêeh-tutuWêeh tutuWêeh*' and extra high, sharp, descending, hurried warbl '*sêeesisrititituu-wee*' ('*-tu*' lowest).

13 GREEN-BACKED EREMOMELA *Eremomela canescens* L 10 cm. Habitat: hilly, wooded and bushe habitats often near streams.

14 TURNER'S EREMOMELA *Eremomela turneri* L 10 cm. Note dark brown crown. Habitat: 1500-175 m. Canopies of forest edges. Voice: extra high, complex, unmusical siffling.

15 BROWN PARISOMA *Parisoma lugens* L 12 cm. Habitat: 1250-2500 m. Canopies of more or less ope woodland and gardens.

16 BANDED PARISOMA *Parisoma boehmi* L 12 cm. Habitat: <1750 m. Tree tops of more or less woode and bushed habitats.

17 GREEN HYLIA *Hylia prasina* L 12 cm. Habitat: 500-2000 m. Undergrowth and midstrata of forests and bush.

18 GREY LONGBILL *Macrosphenus concolor* L 13 cm. Habitat: 1000-1500 m. Dense forest undergrowt Voice: very high, hurried twitter descending or with repeated phrases like '*-weetturutuwiet-*'.

19 KRETSCHMER'S LONGBILL *Macrosphenus kretschmeri* L 15 cm. Looks like a small greenbul. Habitat: <2000 m. Forest undergrowth. Voice: high, compressed '*ti tiderrêedip*'.

20 YELLOW LONGBILL *Macrosphenus flavicans* L 13 cm. Habitat: 500-1500 m. Dense forest undergrowth. Voice: descending, slow, fluted '*fjuu fjuu fjuu fjuu fjuu fjuu-fjuu*' starting very high.

21 SHORT-TAILED WARBLER *Hemitesia neumanni* L 13 cm. Habitat: 1500-2500 m. Forest undergrowth.

22 GRAUER'S WARBLER *Graueria vittata* L 15 cm. Habitat: 1500-2500 m. Dense forest undergrowth.

73

Plate 74

1 **AFRICAN SOOTY FLYCATCHER** *Muscicapa infuscata* (formerly *Artomyias fuliginosa*) L 10 cm. Note small thin bill. Habitat: 750-1750 m. Forest glades.

2 **SPOTTED FLYCATCHER** *Muscicapa striata* L 13 cm. Note faintly striped crown. Habitat: <2250(&)> m. More or less wooded and bushed habitats including gardens. NM

3 **GAMBAGA FLYCATCHER** *Muscicapa gambagae* L 10 cm. Note unstriped crown. Habitat: dry, more or less wooded and bushed habitats.

4 **AFRICAN DUSKY FLYCATCHER** *Muscicapa adusta* L 10 cm. May show distinctly streaked throat and pale edges of flight feathers. Habitat: 750-3250 m. Woodland and gardens, often near water.

5 **CHAPIN'S FLYCATCHER** *Muscicapa lendu* L 10 cm. Note stumpy bill and plain upperparts. Habitat: 1500-2250 m. Forests.

6 **SWAMP FLYCATCHER** *Muscicapa aquatica* L 13 cm. Note pure white throat. Habitat: 500-1500 m. Papyrus and reed beds.

7 **CASSIN'S GREY FLYCATCHER** *Muscicapa cassini* L 13 cm. Note very dark colouring. Underparts slightly paler. Habitat: <2000 m. Well-wooded streams.

8 **YELLOW-FOOTED FLYCATCHER** *Muscicapa sethsmithii* L 9 cm. Note yellow feet, white underpar and pale breast. Habitat: forests.

9 **DUSKY BLUE FLYCATCHER** *Muscicapa comitata* L 12 cm. Note white chin. Habitat: 500-1750 m. Midstrata of forest edges.

10 **ASHY FLYCATCHER** *Muscicapa caerulescens* L 13 cm. Note silver-grey upperparts, short pale eyebrow and pale grey breast. Habitat: <2000 m. Forest edges, woodland, well-wooded streams.

11 **GREY-THROATED FLYCATCHER** *Muscicapa griseogularis* L 10 cm. Note black tail and pale edges of grey-brown wing feathers. Habitat: 500-2000 m. Forest streams.

12 **LEAD-COLOURED FLYCATCHER** *Myioparus plumbeus* L 12 cm. Habitat: <2000 m. Forest glades, moist wood- and bushland, wooded grassland.

13 **BOEHM'S FLYCATCHER** *Muscicapa boehmi* L 12 cm. Note triangular breast striping. Habitat: miombo.

14 **COLLARED FLYCATCHER** *Ficedula albicollis* L 13 cm. Race *a. albicollis* (a), race *semitorquata* (b) (Semi-collared Flycatcher). Note partial second wing-bar in all plumages of race *semitorquata*. Note extension of white over primaries of both races. Habitat: miombo and other woodland. NM

15 **PIED FLYCATCHER** *Ficedula hypoleuca* L 13 cm. Primaries almost entirely black. May have (pale) partial second wing-bar. (This species has a form in which black of ♂ br plumage is replaced by dark brown.) Habitat: more or less wooded habitats including gardens. NM

16 **SOUTHERN BLACK FLYCATCHER** *Melaenornis pammelaina* L 20 cm. Note blue gloss. Habitat: <2000 m. More or less wooded and bushed natural and cultivated habitats. Voice: high, loud, melodious, fluted '*feeh-tjuutjuu*' ('*feeh*' extra high).

17 **NORTHERN BLACK FLYCATCHER** *Melaenornis edolioides* L 20 cm. Note sooty black colouring. Habitat: 250-2000 m. Woodland, bushland and gardens.

18 **YELLOW-EYED BLACK FLYCATCHER** *Melaenornis ardesiacus* L 20 cm. Habitat: 1500-2250 m. Dense undergrowth at forest edges.

19 **WHITE-EYED SLATY FLYCATCHER** *Melaenornis fischeri* L 15 cm. Habitat: 1250-3000 m. Woodland, cultivation and gardens.

20 **ABYSSINIAN SLATY FLYCATCHER** *Melaenornis chocolatina* L 15 cm. Note stout bill. Habitat: 1000-3250 m. Forest edges. [E] (Ethiopia)

74

Plate 75

1   PALLID FLYCATCHER *Bradornis pallidus*   L 15 cm. Forehead grey (not white) with unstriped crown. Habitat: wooded and bushed areas including gardens. Voice: high, sharp, weaver-like chattering.

2   GREY FLYCATCHER *Bradornis microrhynchus*   L 13 cm. Note white forehead between bill and striped crown. Habitat: dry wooded and bushed areas.

3   YELLOW-BREASTED HYLIOTA *Hyliota flavigaster*   L 14 cm. Note blue gloss of ♂; ♀ has brown (not black) cheek uniform with crown. Habitat: <2000 m. Bamboo, forests and other more or less wooded areas.

4   SOUTHERN HYLIOTA *Hyliota australis*   L 14 cm. Note black cheeks. Habitat: forest canopies and plantations.

5   FOREST BATIS *Batis mixta*   L 12 cm. Note orange eye, wide black chest-band of ♂ and buff-brown upperparts of ♀. Habitat: <2000 m. Forests.

6   RWENZORI BATIS *Batis diops*   L 12 cm. No (or little) white in neck. Note grey-black upperparts of ♂ and chestnut throat-patch of ♀. Habitat: 1500-2750 m. Forests and bamboo.

7   CHIN-SPOT BATIS *Batis molitor*   L 12 cm. Note white neck-patch. The ♀ has full dark chestnut collar and throat-patch. Habitat: 500-3000 m. Midstrata and undergrowth of more or less wooded and bushed areas, including gardens. Voice: very high, descending, sharp, slow, piping '*it's so sad*'.

8   EAST-COAST BATIS *Batis soror*   L 10 cm. Very similar to Chin-spot Batis. Main difference is pale rufous collar and throat-patch of ♀. Habitat: <1250 m. Miombo and other woodland. Voice: sustained staccato tooting '*tioh tioh tioh*' ('*ti-*' an octave higher than '*-oh*').

9   GREY-HEADED BATIS *Batis orientalis*   L 10 cm. Note black-striped breast sides of ♂ and white throat of ♀. Habitat: 1000-1250 m. More or less wooded areas.

10 PYGMY BATIS *Batis perkeo*   L 8 cm. Note small size, dark brown flight feathers and short white eyebrow. Habitat: <1200 m. Dry, wooded and bushed areas.

11 BLACK-HEADED BATIS *Batis minor*   L 10 cm. Note fully developed eye-stripes connected in neck. Chest-band rather narrow. Habitat: <1750 m. More or less wooded and bushed habitats including gardens.

12 ITURI BATIS *Batis ituriensis*   L 9 cm. Note absence of grey colouring. The ♀ has black chest-collar. Habitat: forest canopies.

13 FOREST FLYCATCHER *Fraseria ocreata*   L 14 cm. (Sci name as by Britton.) Habitat: canopies of forest edges and tree tops of wooded areas.

14 SILVERBIRD *Bradornis semipartitus*   L 20 cm. Habitat: 250-1500 m. Dry bushed grassland.

15 CRESTED SHRIKE-FLYCATCHER *Bias musicus*   L 13 cm. Habitat: tall trees of forests, wooded areas and gardens. Voice: high and mid-high '*tjutjip-tjutjip-tjiptweettweet*'.

16 COMMON SHRIKE-FLYCATCHER *Bias flammulatus*   L 15 cm. Habitat: 500-2250 m. More or less open forests with dense undergrowth. Voice: extra high, very sharp '*sritsruwitsweetwseet*'.

17 BANDED WATTLE-EYE *Platysteira cyanea*   L 13 cm. Habitat: 500-2250 m. Forest edges and other wooded and bushed areas, including gardens.

18 BLACK-THROATED WATTLE-EYE *Platysteira peltata*   L 13 cm. Habitat: <3000 m. More or less wooded and bushed areas, including gardens. Voice: high, sweeping, tit-like '*tsja-tsja-whêetohwhêetohwhêetohwhêet*'.

19 CHESTNUT WATTLE-EYE *Platysteira castanea*   L 10 cm. Habitat: 500-2000 m. Forest undergrowth. Voice: very high, descending '*winwin-win-wgn-wan*' ('*wen*' lowest).

20 JAMESON'S WATTLE-EYE *Platysteira jamesoni*   L 8 cm. Habitat: dense forest undergrowth.

21 YELLOW-BELLIED WATTLE-EYE *Platysteira concreta*   L 9 cm. Habitat: 1750-2500 m. Forests. Voice: mid-high, fluted '*whitwhit tjuu-tjuu whip*' (descending to a lashing '*whip*').

75

Plate 76

1 **RED-BELLIED PARADISE MONARCH** *Terpsiphone rufiventer* L 20 cm. Habitat: 500-2000 m. Forest interiors.

2 **AFRICAN PARADISE MONARCH** *Terpsiphone viridis* L 20 cm (excluding tail streamers). Rufous and white form of race *ferreti* (a) in Uganda, Kenya and N and W Tanzania (often together with other races), (b) type of other races. Individuals of these races may have some white wing feathers too, so that the extent of white in wings (and tail) rather varies. Habitat: forests, wood- and bushland and gardens. (AM)

3 **BLUE MONARCH** *Elminia longicauda* L 14 cm. Note absence of white in tail. Habitat: midstrata and canopies of open forests, moist wooded and bushed areas including gardens and farmland.

4 **WHITE-TAILED BLUE MONARCH** *Elminia albicauda* L 14 cm. Note silver-grey colouring with much white in tail. Habitat: 1500(♂<)-2500 m. Bamboo, forests and woodland.

5 **YELLOW MONARCH** *Erythrocercus holochlorus* L 9 cm. Habitat: <500 m. Forests and moist bushland

6 **LIVINGSTONE'S MONARCH** *Erythrocercus livingstonei* L 10 cm. Habitat: <750 m. Moist wood- and bushland. Voice: combination of a short, low twitter and very high, short, fluted, warble *'tititriwheetohwheetohwheet'* (last *'wheet'* highest).

7 **CHESTNUT-CAPPED MONARCH** *Erythrocercus mccallii* L 10 cm. Habitat: forests.

8 **BLUE-HEADED CRESTED-MONARCH** *Terpsiphone nitens* L 12 cm. Habitat: 500-1000 m. Dense forest undergrowth.

9 **BLUE-MANTLED CRESTED-MONARCH** *Terpsiphone cyanomelas* L 12 cm. Habitat: <2000 m. Dense undergrowth and midstrata of forests. Voice: very varied medley of instrumental sounds like high, nasal *'wheetwhit wheetwhit'*; low, rapid, liquid *'weetweetweetweet'* and fluted trill *'wuruwuwuwuwu'*.

10 **WHITE-TAILED CRESTED-MONARCH** *Elminia albonotata* L 10 cm. Habitat: 750-2750 m. Undergrowth and midstrata of forests. Voice: extra high, wagtail-like *'tweet treet treetohweet'* with high, fluted *'wheet tsio-wheet'*.

11 **WHITE-BELLIED CRESTED-MONARCH** *Elminia albiventris* L 9 cm. Note white belly centre. Habitat: 1500-2250 m. Forest undergrowth.

12 **DUSKY CRESTED-MONARCH** *Elminia nigromitrata* L 9 cm. Underparts hardly paler than upperparts. Habitat: 510-2250 m. Forest undergrowth and moist bushland.

76

Plate 77

1 **SCALY-BREASTED ILLADOPSIS** *Illadopsis albipectus* L 14 cm. Note scaly breast and face sides. Habitat: 500-2250 m. Forest undergrowth. Voice: very high, slightly rising, sharp '*piuu-piuu-peeh*' and extra high, sharp, whistled '*fjuu-fjee-fjêee*'.

2 **PALE-BREASTED ILLADOPSIS** *Illadopsis rufipennis* L 14 cm. Rather social. Note stout (not warbler-like) bill and grey face sides. Crown uniformly coloured with mantle. Habitat: <1750 m. Dense forest undergrowth. Voice: very high, pure, short whistle '*feeeeeee*' with very slight tremolo and crescendo.

3 **MOUNTAIN ILLADOPSIS** *Illadopsis pyrrhopterum* L 14 cm. Habitat: 1500-3000 m. Dense forest undergrowth. Voice: very high, descending '*tipip teeep-tuuup-toooh*' or fluted '*ônetwothree four*' ('*four*' muc lower).

4 **BROWN ILLADOPSIS** *Illadopsis fulvescens* L 15 cm. Note dark crown, grey cheeks, rusty brown wing and tail. Habitat: 500-2000 m. Forest floors and undergrowth. Voice: high '*fweeeee*' and '*djip(-djip)*', low '*fooooo*' and '*trreptrep-trep-terreptrep*'.

5 **GREY-CHESTED ILLADOPSIS** *Kakamega poliothorax* L 15 cm. A truly beautiful bird! Habitat: 1500-2500 m. Forest undergrowth. Voice: high, descending thrush- or oriole-like '*pju-pju-pjuwi*' ('*j*' falsetto).

6 **AFRICAN HILL-BABBLER** *Illadopsis abyssinica* L 13 cm. Social. Note striped breast. Habitat: 1500-3000 m. Undergrowth of damp forests and bamboo. Voice: high, up-and-down, rather unhurried, thrush-like, fluted '*wîpiwîpwupwîwjopwîwup*'.

7 **ABYSSINIAN CATBIRD** *Parophasma galinieri* L 15 cm. Habitat: 2500-3500 m. Dense forests. [E] (Ethiopia)

8 **CAPUCHIN BABBLER** *Phyllanthus atripennis* L 20 cm. Habitat: 500-1000(&>) m. Dense forest undergrowth.

9 **FULVOUS CHATTERER** *Turdoides fulvus* L 20 cm. Note faint striping. Habitat: arid areas with some scrub.

10 **RUFOUS CHATTERER** *Turdoides rubiginosus* L 20 cm. Note brown upperparts and contrasting tawn underparts. Habitat: <1500 m. Open places in dense bush- and shrubland.

11 **SCALY CHATTERER** *Turdoides aylmeri* L 20 cm. Some faint scaling of throat and breast, varying according to race. Habitat: <1500 m. Dry wood- and bushland.

12 **DUSKY BABBLER** *Turdoides tenebrosus* L 20 cm. Habitat: 500-1250 m. Dense forest undergrowth near streams.

13 **BLACK-LORED BABBLER** *Turdoides melanops* L 25 cm. Note white eye. Habitat: 1000-2000(&>) m Bushed and wooded areas.

14 **PIED BABBLER** *Turdoides hypoleucus* L 25 cm. Habitat: 500-2000(&>) m. Wooded and bushed natural and cultivated areas including gardens and parks.

15 **ARROW-MARKED BABBLER** *Turdoides jardinei* L 15 cm. Note eye colour. Habitat: <2250 m. More or less wooded areas, including parks and gardens.

16 **BROWN BABBLER** *Turdoides plebejus* L 25 cm. No black before and around eye. Habitat: 500-1500 n More or less wooded and bushed areas.

17 **WHITE-RUMPED BABBLER** *Turdoides leucopygius* L 20 cm. Note white rump (unique for babblers) Generally very variable in extension of white (and black) especially on head which may be all white. Two variations, (a) and (b), shown. Habitat: 1500-2250 m. Damp wooded and bushed grassland.

18 **HINDE'S BABBLER** *Turdoides hindei* L 20 cm. Note tawny rump and flanks (unique for babblers). Otherwise variable. Tawny feathers and white areas can appear asymmetrical anywhere on head and bod (depending on width of pale feather edges). Habitat: 1250-1500 m. Bush- and shrubland especially in small valleys. E (Kenya)

19 **WHITE-HEADED BABBLER** *Turdoides leucocephalus* L 20 cm. Note naked blue-grey eye area and brown rump, tail and mantle. Habitat: <1000 m. Bushland.

20 **SCALY BABBLER** *Turdoides squamulatus* L 20 cm. Note dark (red) eye and brown (not white or tawny) rump. Habitat: dense bush.

77

Plate 78

1 **NORTHERN GREY TIT** *Parus thruppi* L 12 cm. Note narrow mid-breast stripe. Habitat: <1750 m. Dry, more or less wooded and bushed habitats especially along wooded streams.

2 **MIOMBO GREY TIT** *Parus griseiventris* L 12 cm. Note wide mid-breast stripe and almost completely white wings. Habitat: miombo and other woodland.

3 **STRIPE-BREASTED TIT** *Parus fasciiventer* L 12 cm. Habitat: 1750-3500 m. Forests and giant heath.

4 **RUFOUS-BELLIED TIT** *Parus rufiventris* L 14 cm. Habitat: miombo and other woodland.

5 **RED-THROATED TIT** *Parus fringillinus* L 12 cm. Habitat: 1000-1750 m. More or less wooded and bushed grassland.

6 **NORTHERN BLACK TIT** *Parus leucomelas* L 14 cm. Habitat: <2000 m. Dense or open, more or less wooded and bushed, natural and cultivated areas.

7 **WHITE-BELLIED BLACK TIT** *Parus albiventris* L 14 cm. Habitat: <3500 m. Forest edges and more or less wooded and bushed grassland, including gardens.

8 **WHITE-BACKED BLACK TIT** *Parus leuconotus* L 13 cm. Habitat: >2000 m. Wooded valleys. [E] (Ethiopia)

9 **DUSKY TIT** *Parus funereus* L 13 cm. Habitat: 750-1750 m. Forest canopies.

10 **AFRICAN PENDULINE TIT** *Anthoscopus caroli* L 7 cm. Very small: length including tail is no more than your index finger. Habitat: open forests and other more or less wooded areas. Voice: extra high, hurried *'tsitsiseehtsitsiseeh'* ('-seeh' just within ear-reach).

11 **MOUSE-COLOURED PENDULINE TIT** *Anthoscopus musculus* L 7 cm. Note pale eyebrow and slightly greyish upperparts. Habitat: 250-1750 m. Dry, rocky, more or less wooded areas.

12 **SENNAR PENDULINE TIT** *Anthoscopus punctifrons* L 7 cm. Note striping on forehead and greenish (not greyish) mantle. Habitat: open bushland. Voice: extra high, thin, piercing *'fie fie fie fie -'* alternating with a low, dry trill.

13 **SPOTTED CREEPER** *Salpornis spilonotus* L 15 cm. Habitat: 500-2500 m. Miombo and forest edges.

14 **TIT HYLIA** *Pholidornis rushiae* L 8 cm. Habitat: forest canopies.

15 **ABYSSINIAN WHITE-EYE** *Zosterops abyssinica* L 12 cm. (Not all races depicted.) Race *flavilateralis* (a) in E Kenya and N Tanzania, race *jubaensis* (b) in SE Ethiopia and S Somalia. Note yellow underparts (including flanks) and rather narrow eye-ring. Habitat: <2000 m. Forest edges, wood- and bushland and gardens.

16 **YELLOW WHITE-EYE** *Zosterops senegalensis* L 10 cm. (Not all races depicted.) Race *anderssoni* (a) in SE Tanzania, race *jacksoni* (b) in E Kenya, race *senegalensis* (c) in Uganda, race *stuhlmanni* (d) in NW Tanzania, race *vaughani* (e) on Pemba, race *stierlingi* (f) in SW Tanzania. Note greenish flanks (in most races) and yellow belly. Habitat: <3500 m. Forest edges and interiors, giant heath, woodland and suburban gardens.

17 **MONTANE WHITE-EYE** *Zosterops poliogaster* L 12 cm. (Not all races depicted.) Race *kikuyensis* (a) in C Kenya, race *winifredae* (b) in NE Tanzania, race *eurycricota* (c) in S Kenya and N(E) Tanzania, race *silvana* (d) in SE Kenya, race *mbuluensis* (e) in N Tanzania, race *kulalensis* (f) in NW Kenya. Note grey breast in some and wide white eye-ring in most races. Habitat: 1500-3000 m. Forest edges and gardens.

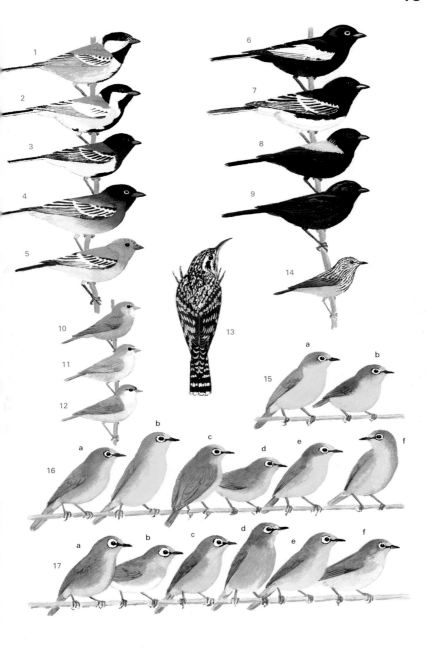

78

Plate 79

1 **VARIABLE SUNBIRD** *Nectarinia venusta* L 10 cm. (Not all races depicted.) Race *albiventris* (a) in NE Kenya, S and SE Ethiopia and Somalia. (Other white-bellied nectarinia sunbirds do not occur in the same area.) Habitat: <3000 m. Forest edges, wood- and bushland, suburban gardens and cultivations. Voice: extra high fluted rattles and hurried twitters.

2 **WHITE-BELLIED SUNBIRD** *Nectarinia talatala* L 11 cm. Occurs only in most southern part of Tanzania. Habitat: <1000 m. Dry, open wood- and bushland.

3 **ANGOLA WHITE-BELLIED SUNBIRD** *Nectarinia oustaleti* L 10 cm. Occurs along western border of Tanzania. Note maroon in breast-band. Habitat: miombo.

4 **SOUTHERN ORANGE-TUFTED SUNBIRD** *Nectarinia bouvieri* L 10 cm. Note purple (not green) forehead and brown (not reflecting) chin. Habitat: 500-2000 m. Forest edges and natural and cultivated areas with small bushes and scattered tall trees.

5 **SHINING SUNBIRD** *Nectarinia habessinica* L 13 cm. Note purple crown and blue wings. Habitat: 250-1000 m. Dry, rocky and sandy bushland.

6 **LITTLE PURPLE-BANDED SUNBIRD** *Nectarinia bifasciata* L 11 cm. Note bluish green colouring and purple breast-band. Habitat: <1500 m. Wood-, bush- and dense shrubland, mangroves and gardens.

7 **VIOLET-BREASTED SUNBIRD** *Nectarinia pembae* L 11 cm. Note beautiful purple-blue-green colouring. Habitat: <1000 m. Wood- and bushland, including gardens.

8 **SPLENDID SUNBIRD** *Nectarinia coccinigaster* L 14 cm. Note purple head and breast. Some pure red feathers in chest-band. Habitat: forest edges and other wooded areas including gardens.

9 **SUPERB SUNBIRD** *Nectarinia superba* L 14 cm. Note long, almost straight bill and maroon belly. Habitat: 500-1750 m. Forest canopies.

10 **COLLARED SUNBIRD** *Anthreptes collaris* L 10 cm. Note grass-green (not purple or blue) colouring. Habitat: <3000 m. Forest edges, wood- and bushland, suburban gardens and parks. Voice: extra high, up-and-down, rather fast '*sêeyousêeyou*' or high, swept up, rapid '*wheêtwheêtwheêtwheêt-*' and extra high '*sweeh sweeh sweeh*'.

11 **NORTHERN PYGMY SUNBIRD** *Anthreptes metallicus* L 8 cm (excluding tail streamers). Note purple (not green) chest-band. Habitat: arid areas with scattered trees and bush.

12 **SOUTHERN PYGMY SUNBIRD** *Anthreptes platurus* L 8 cm (excluding tail streamers). Note green (not purple-banded) chest. Habitat: dry, bushed and wooded areas.

13 **GREEN SUNBIRD** *Anthreptes rectirostris* L 9 cm. Note green (not whitish) throat. Habitat: forest canopies.

14 **BANDED GREEN SUNBIRD** *Anthreptes rubritorques* L 9 cm. Note whitish (not green) throat. Habitat: 750-1750 m. Canopy of forest edges. E (Tanzania)

15 **WESTERN VIOLET-BACKED SUNBIRD** *Anthreptes longuemarei* L 13 cm. Most purple white-bellied anthreptes sunbird. Note blue reflections in rump. Habitat: 500-1500 m. Forest edges and other more or less wooded areas.

16 **EASTERN VIOLET-BACKED SUNBIRD** *Anthreptes orientalis* L 12 cm. Mid-purplish white-bellied anthreptes sunbird. Note green reflections in rump. Habitat: <1500 m. Dry, more or less wooded and bushed areas.

17 **ULUGURU VIOLET-BACKED SUNBIRD** *Anthreptes neglectus* L 13 cm. Most bluish of the white-bellied anthreptes sunbirds. No green or blue in rump. Habitat: 1250-2000 m. Forest interiors and edges, moist wooded and bushed areas.

18 **ANCHIETA'S SUNBIRD** *Anthreptes anchietae* L 10 cm. Habitat: miombo.

19 **SCARLET-TUFTED SUNBIRD** *Anthreptes fraseri* L 11. Note grey head. Habitat: 500-1750 m. Midstrata of forests.

20 **PLAIN-BACKED SUNBIRD** *Anthreptes reichenowi* L 10 cm. Note mainly black (slightly blue-reflecting) throat and forehead. Habitat: <500 m. Forest canopies. Voice: extra high, rapidly descending, Willow Warbler-like '*fiifiifjitit ututut ui*'.

21 **AMANI SUNBIRD** *Anthreptes pallidigaster* L 8 cm. Note bottle-green upperparts. Habitat: <1000 m. Forest canopies. Voice: extra high, amusical, fast twitter.

Note: Some sunbird species (79.1, 2, 3, 6, 11 and 12) also have n-br plumages in which, however, the reflecting wing coverts and rump feathers, the black wing feathers and the elongated middle tail-feathers (79.11 and 12) are retained.

79

Plate 80

1 **OLIVE-BELLIED SUNBIRD** *Nectarinia chloropygia* L 10 cm. Note grass-green colouring and blue (not purple or pale brown) rump. Habitat: 500-1750 m. Forest, moist bushland, cultivation and gardens

2 **TINY SUNBIRD** *Nectarinia minulla* L 8 cm. Note narrow red chest-band and dark brown breast. Habitat: 500-1750 m. Forests.

3 **MONTANE DOUBLE-COLLARED SUNBIRD** *Nectarinia ludovicensis* L 9 cm. (Species level as by Britton.) Note blue-green (not yellow-green) colouring, wide red breast-band and purple upper tail-coverts. Habitat: 2500-3500 m. Forest, bamboo and giant heath.

4 **SOUTHERN DOUBLE-COLLARED SUNBIRD** *Nectarinia chalybea* L 10 cm. (Britton names this species *Nectarinia manoensis*, Miombo Double-collared Sunbird.) Note grass-green (not blue-green) colouring and pale brown rump. Habitat: 1000-1500 m. Miombo and other woodland.

5 **NORTHERN DOUBLE-COLLARED SUNBIRD** *Nectarinia preussi* L 10 cm. Hard to distinguish from Montane Double-collared Sunbird but rump more yellow-green and red chest-band narrower. Habitat: 1250-2750 m. Forest, bamboo and gardens.

6 **REGAL SUNBIRD** *Nectarinia regia* L 11 cm. Habitat: 1500-3000 m. Forest and bamboo.

7 **EASTERN DOUBLE-COLLARED SUNBIRD** *Nectarinia mediocris* L 10 cm. Note grass-green colouring of upperparts and pale orange-buff belly and flanks. Habitat: 750-1500(&>) m. Forest edges, bamboo and gardens.

8 **LOVERIDGE'S SUNBIRD** *Nectarinia loveridgei* L 12 cm. Note yellow (not red) under tail-coverts and orange (not red) breast. Habitat: 1500 (&<)-2000 m. Undergrowth and midstrata of forest edges. E (Tanzania)

9 **MOREAU'S SUNBIRD** *Nectarinia moreaui* L 12 cm. Note moss-green edges of wing feathers. Habitat: 1250-3000 m. Forests. E (Tanzania)

10 **STUHLMANN'S DOUBLE-COLLARED SUNBIRD** *Nectarinia stuhlmanni* L 12 cm. (Species level as by Britton.) Note blue-green (not yellow-green) colouring and pale brown rump. Habitat: 2500-3500 m. Bamboo and giant heath.

11 **RED-CHESTED SUNBIRD** *Nectarinia erythrocerca* L 12 cm (excluding tail streamers). Only black-bellied sunbird with purple rump and upper tail-coverts. Habitat: 500-2000 m. Shrubbery and undergrowth near water, swamps and gardens.

12 **SMALLER BLACK-BELLIED SUNBIRD** *Nectarinia nectarinioides* L 9 cm (excluding tail streamers). Like black-bellied form of Beautiful Sunbird but with shorter tail streamers and orange (not red) breast. Habitat: <1500 m. Dry wood- and bushland.

13 **BEAUTIFUL SUNBIRD** *Nectarinia pulchella* L 12 cm (excluding tail streamers). Green- and black-bellied forms shown. Habitat: 250-2000 m. Dry and moist, more or less wooded and bushed areas, including gardens and cultivations.

14 **LITTLE OLIVE SUNBIRD** *Nectarinia seimundi* L 9 cm. Note short pale bill. Eye stripe and moustachial stripe joined behind eye. Habitat: 500-1500 m. Open forests. Voice: squeaky '*tuip-tuip-tuip*

15 **OLIVE SUNBIRD** *Nectarinia olivacea* L 14 cm. Note dusky green mantle and moss-green edges of wing feathers. Habitat: <2500(&>) m. Forests. Voice: high, loud, almost staccato, fluted '*tu tu tfiFITUTUTWUH*' ('*tu*' very soft, '*tfiFI-*' extra high).

16 **MOUSE-COLOURED SUNBIRD** *Nectarinia veroxii* L 12 cm. May show small red tufts. Habitat: undergrowth of coastal wood- and bushland, gardens and mangroves. Voice: very high, squeaking, fast '*pipipipipipipiri*'.

17 **RUFOUS-WINGED SUNBIRD** *Nectarinia rufipennis* L 12 cm. (Species discovered in 1981.) Habitat: 1000 m. Forest undergrowth. E (Tanzania)

18 **COPPER SUNBIRD** *Nectarinia cuprea* L 11 cm. Habitat: 500-1750 m. Forest edges, more or less wooded and bushed natural and cultivated areas, including gardens.

19 **MARICO SUNBIRD** *Nectarinia mariquensis* L 14 cm. Note large size, maroon chest-band and all-green head and upperparts. Habitat: 1000(&<)-1500(&>) m. Open wood- and bushland.

20 **SHELLEY'S SUNBIRD** *Nectarinia shelleyi* L 12 cm. Note all-green (not partly purplish) head and orange-red chest with partial narrow yellow edges. Habitat: 500-1250 m. Miombo, wood- and bushland and gardens; often along streams.

Note: Some sunbird species (80.10 and 13) also have n-br plumages in which, however, the reflecting wing coverts and rump feathers, the black wing feathers and the elongated middle tail-feathers (80.13) are retained.

Plate 81

1 **PURPLE-BREASTED SUNBIRD** *Nectarinia purpureiventris* L 13 cm (excluding tail streamers). Habitat: 1500-2500 m. Open forests.

2 **TACAZZE SUNBIRD** *Nectarinia tacazze* L 14 cm (excluding tail streamers). Habitat: 1750-4250 m. Open forests, bamboo, heathland, gardens and cultivation.

3 **MALACHITE SUNBIRD** *Nectarinia famosa* L 14 cm (excluding tail streamers). More shining than reflecting green. Tufts not normally visible. Habitat: 1500(&<)-3000(&>) m. Forests, bamboo, moorland, grassland with flowers.

4 **SCARLET-TUFTED MALACHITE SUNBIRD** *Nectarinia johnstoni* L 15 cm (excluding tail streamers). Reflecting (not shining) green with black under tail-coverts. Tufts normally concealed. Habitat: 3000(occasionally <)-4500 m. Alpine moorland.

5 **BRONZE SUNBIRD** *Nectarinia kilimensis* L 14 cm (excluding tail streamers). Habitat: 1000-2500 m. Forest edges, wooded and bushed areas, including gardens and cultivation.

6 **GOLDEN-WINGED SUNBIRD** *Nectarinia reichenowi* L 15 cm (excluding tail streamers). Habitat: 1750(&<)-2500(&>) m. Forests, bamboo, bushed areas, gardens, cultivation, grassland with flowers.

7 **GREEN-HEADED SUNBIRD** *Nectarinia verticalis* L 14 cm. Note olive-green (not saffron) mantle. Habitat: 1000-2500 m. Forest, bamboo, bushland, gardens, cultivation.

8 **BLUE-HEADED SUNBIRD** *Nectarinia alinae* L 14 cm. Note saffron mantle. Habitat: 1250-2750 m. Forest canopies.

9 **BLUE-THROATED SUNBIRD** *Nectarinia cyanolaema* L 14 cm. Habitat: 500-1750 m. Forest canopies.

10 **SCARLET-CHESTED SUNBIRD** *Nectarinia senegalensis* L 15 cm. Green chin and brown rump difficult to see in the field. Yellow-green colouring of forehead reaches crown (not nape). Habitat: 2250(&>) m. Forest edges and more or less wooded and bushed areas, including gardens and parks.

11 **HUNTER'S SUNBIRD** *Nectarinia hunteri* L 14 cm. Note black chin and purple rump. Blue-green colouring of forehead reaches nape. Bill more curved than Scarlet-chested Sunbird. Habitat: <1250 m. More or less wooded and bushed areas.

12 **AMETHYST SUNBIRD** *Nectarinia amethystina* L 14 cm. Appears all-black in field. Chin (if seen) reflects purple (not green). Habitat: <2250 m. Forest edges, woodland, mangroves, gardens and parks.

13 **GREEN-THROATED SUNBIRD** *Nectarinia rubescens* L 13 cm. Appears all black in the field but chin (if seen) reflects mainly green. Habitat: 500-2000 m. Forest edges, gardens and parks.

14 **SOCOTRA SUNBIRD** *Nectarinia balfouri* L 15 cm. Habitat: no information available. E (Socotra)

Note: Some sunbird species (81.1, 2, 3 and 4) also have n-br plumages in which, however, the reflecting wing coverts and rump feathers, the black wing feathers and the elongated middle tail-feathers (if present in br dress) are retained.

81

Plate 82

1 **GREEN-HEADED ORIOLE** *Oriolus chlorocephalus* L 20 cm. Habitat: <1000(&>) m. Forests and woodland. Voice: mid-high, liquid, gliding-up, fast '*tui*'.

2 **MONTANE ORIOLE** *Oriolus percivali* L 25 cm. No green in tail. Habitat: 1500-2750 m. Forests.

3 **AFRICAN BLACK-HEADED ORIOLE** *Oriolus larvatus* L 25 cm. Note tail pattern. Two middle feathers are all-green, the rest is mainly black but yellow area increases from the inner to the outer tail-feathers. Note pale blue (not white) edges of wing feathers. Habitat: <2500 m. Forest edges, woodlan and mangroves. Voice: mid-high, liquid, short, hurried whistle '*weetohwêeoh*'.

4 **WESTERN BLACK-HEADED ORIOLE** *Oriolus brachyrhynchus* L 20 cm. Note tail pattern. Two middle feathers are greenish-yellow; the rest from inside outwards with increasing amounts of greenish-yellow at feather ends, seperated from the greenish-yellow parts by increasing amounts of black Habitat: 500-2000 m. Forest edges.

5 **BLACK-HEADED FOREST ORIOLE** *Oriolus monacha* L 25 cm. Tail pattern exactly like Western Black-headed Oriole but species separated geographically. Some individuals however do not have any black in their tail. Habitat: >1000 m. Forests and wooded grassland. [E] (Ethiopia)

6 **BLACK-WINGED ORIOLE** *Oriolus nigripennis* L 25 cm. Hardly any white in wing. Habitat: <1500 r Forests.

7 **AFRICAN GOLDEN ORIOLE** *Oriolus auratus* L 25 cm. Note complicated wing pattern. Habitat: <2000 m. Forest edges, woodland and open areas with large trees. Voice: high, melodious, flutec '*wêetwêetoh-wêehohweer*'. AM

8 **EURASIAN GOLDEN ORIOLE** *Oriolus oriolus* L 25 cm. Wing almost all black. Habitat: <2000 m. Forest edges, woodland and open forests with large trees. Voice: mid-high, liquid, very melodious, rapid '*wêetwêetohrihôhrool*' and descending miauling cry. NM

9 **ROSY-PATCHED BUSH-SHRIKE** *Rhodophoneus cruentus* L 25 cm. Often on the ground. Habitat: <1500(&>) m. Dry, more or less bushed areas.

10 **BRUBRU** *Nilaus afer* L 13 cm. Race *nigrotemporalis* (a) from C and E Tanzania southwards. Habitat: <2000(&>) m. Wooded and bushed areas. Voice: very high, inquiring, short trill '*prrrrriii?*'.

11 **BLACK-BACKED PUFFBACK** *Dryoscopus cubla* L 15 cm. (Not all races depicted.) Race *affinis* (a) i Somalia, E Kenya and NE Tanzania. Note white (not grey) rump, white (not buff) underparts and black (not brown) wings of ♂ and dark brown wings of ♀. Habitat: <2250 m. Forest edges, woodland, suburban gardens. Voice: high, loud, sweeping whistles like rapid '*weeh-tie-weeh-tie-weeh-tie-*' ('*tie*' dry and low).

12 **NORTHERN PUFFBACK** *Dryoscopus gambensis* L 20 cm. The ♂ has grey rump and brown wing, ♀ is brown with buff edges of wing feathers and buff underparts. Habitat: 750-2250 m. Forest edges, woodlanc and suburban gardens.

13 **PRINGLE'S PUFFBACK** *Dryoscopus pringlii* L 13 cm. Note white belly and brown wings; ♂ has black crown. Habitat: <1000 m. Dry wood-and bushland.

14 **RED-EYED PUFFBACK** *Dryoscopus senegalensis* L 15 cm. Note plain black wings of ♂ and dark brow wings of ♀. Habitat: <1500 m. Forests.

15 **PINK-FOOTED PUFFBACK** *Dryoscopus angolensis* L 15 cm. Note white throat of ♂. Habitat: 750-2500 m. Forests.

16 **BROWN-CROWNED TCHAGRA** *Tchagra australis* L 20 cm. Note white (not buff) eyebrow. Centr of crown is brown (not black). Habitat: <2000 m. Tall grassy places in more or less damp, bushed and wooded areas. Voice: dry, short castanet-like rattles '*rrra-rrra-rrra-*' and low, hoarse, repeated whistles like '*throw-throw-throw-*'.

17 **THREE-STREAKED TCHAGRA** *Tchagra jamesi* L 15 cm. Note narrow black crown-stripe betweer wide eyebrows. Mantle has no black edging. Habitat: <1250 m. Dry bushland.

18 **BLACK-CROWNED TCHAGRA** *Tchagra senegala* L 20 cm. Note all-black crown and buffish eyebrow. Habitat: <2000 m. Dry, bushed and wooded areas with tall grassy places. Voice: mid-high, loud, unhurried, human-like whistles interrupted by cackling, often sweeping, laughter.

19 **MARSH TCHAGRA** *Tchagra minuta* L 15 cm. Only ♀ has (buff) eyebrow. Note dark streak in mantle and buff edges of tail. Habitat: <2000 m. Tall grass and herbage near streams and swamps. Voice: high, sweeping, rapid '*wheetwheetwheetoh*' and slow, rasping croaks.

82

Plate 83

1 **GREY-GREEN BUSH-SHRIKE** *Malaconotus bocagei* L 15 cm. Habitat: 1000-2250 m. Undergrowth at forest edges and bushland.

2 **BLACK-FRONTED BUSH-SHRIKE** *Malaconotus nigrifrons* L 20 cm. Four colour forms (a,b, c and d shown. Habitat: 750-2500 m. Canopies and midstrata of forests. Voice: low, melodious '*pwop*' followed by miauling, swept-up '*twueet*'; together as '*pwop twueet*'.

3 **MANY-COLOURED BUSH-SHRIKE** *Malaconotus multicolor* L 20 cm. Three different colour forms (a, b and c) shown. Habitat: <1750 m. Forests.

4 **SULPHUR-BREASTED BUSH-SHRIKE** *Malaconotus sulfureopectus* L 20 cm. Two colour forms (a and b) shown. Habitat: <1500(&>) m. Dense canopies and midstrata of forest edges and dense parts of more or less wooded and bushed areas. Voice: very high, fluted '*tututututêeeeh*'.

5 **GREY-HEADED BUSH-SHRIKE** *Malaconotus blanchoti* L 25 cm. Note green (not black) wings with white bands. Throat is less orange than breast. Habitat: <1750(&>) m. Dense foliage of wood- and bushland. Voice: high, fluted, crescendoing '*fweeee-fweeee-fweeee-fwee*' and mid-high, repeated crescendo '*wheuuú*'.

6 **FIERY-BREASTED BUSH-SHRIKE** *Malaconotus cruentus* L 25 cm. No wing-bars visible in folded wing. Habitat: 500-750 m. Canopies and midstrata of forests.

7 **ULUGURU BUSH-SHRIKE** *Malaconotus alius* L 20 cm. Habitat: 1750-2000 m. Forest canopies. E (Tanzania)

8 **LAGDEN'S BUSH-SHRIKE** *Malaconotus lagdeni* L 20 cm. Note black, yellow and green wing pattern. Habitat: 2000-3000 m. Forests.

9 **FOUR-COLOURED BUSH-SHRIKE** *Malaconotus quadricolor* L 20 cm. Note yellow (not red or saffron) eyebrow and saffron-yellow (not green) underparts. Habitat: <750(&>) m. Forest undergrowth. Voice: mid-high, sweeping '*pup-wick-wick-wick*' or '*hooh-hooh youwêh*' ('-*wêh*' is second voice in duet).

10 **DOHERTY'S BUSH-SHRIKE** *Malaconotus doherteyi* L 20 cm. Note red forehead. Habitat: 1500-3500 m. Dense forest undergrowth and bamboo.

11 **GORGEOUS BUSH-SHRIKE** *Malaconotus viridis* L 20 cm. (Species level as by Britton.) Note saffron forehead and green (not yellow) underparts. Habitat: dense undergrowth of forest edges, often near streams. Voice: mid-high, fluid '*puwêe-puwêe-puwêe*' or low, fluid, fast '*pupupuwêe*' ('-*wee*' is second voice in duet).

12 **BLACK-HEADED BUSH-SHRIKE** *Laniarius erythrogaster* L 20 cm. Habitat: dense parts of bushland Voice: very high, pure, fluted '*fêe-fju-fee-ju*'.

13 **PAPYRUS BUSH-SHRIKE** *Laniarius mufumbiri* L 20 cm. Habitat: 1000-1750 m. Papyrus swamp.

14 **RED-NAPED BUSH-SHRIKE** *Laniarius ruficeps* L 15 cm. Habitat: <750 m. Ground and undergrowth of bush- and shrubland.

15 **LUEHDER'S BUSH-SHRIKE** *Laniarius luehderi* L 20 cm. Habitat: 500-2500 m. Dense undergrowth of forest edges, often near streams.

16 **TROPICAL BOUBOU** *Laniarius ferrugineus* L 25 cm. (Not all races depicted.) Race *sublacteus* (a) in SE Somalia, E Kenya and E Tanzania, type (b) of several other races such as *erlangeri* in Somalia of which an all-black form also exists, type (c) of several races in Uganda, C and W Kenya and E Tanzania. Habitat: <3000(and more). Forest undergrowth, wood- and bushland, gardens and parks. Voice: duet; sounds like pure, hollow, piping whistle '*puuu-wêe*'.

17 **SLATE-COLOURED BOUBOU** *Laniarius funebris* L 20 cm. Note silvery sooty appearance, deepest black in face. Habitat: <1500(&>) m. Thickets and undergrowth of dry, more or less wooded and bushed natural and cultivated habitats. Voice: duet; low, running down, fast (almost trilling) '*cierookookookôo*' answered with high '*sweep*', together sounding like '*cierookookôokoosweep*'.

18 **FUELLEBORN'S BOUBOU** *Laniarius fuelleborni* L 20 cm. Race *f. fuelleborni* (a) in Tanzania (deep slaty black), race *holomelas* (b) in Uganda (brownish-black, upperparts darker, especially face). Habitat: <3000 m. Forest undergrowth and bamboo. Voice: duet; high fluid '*whit-whit*' followed by descending trill, and low dry trill '*turrrr*' followed by high fluid '*whéet*'.

19 **SOOTY BOUBOU** *Laniarius leucorhynchus* L 20 cm. Note deep black appearance. Often fluffs out rump feathers. Habitat: 500-1500 m. Forest undergrowth. Voice: mid-high '*ooh-ooh-ooh*' like rubbing the rim of a glass.

20 **BULO BURTI BOUBOU** *Laniarius liberatus* L 20 cm. The only specimen of this newly discovered species was not killed and put in a museum, but preserved through photographs and blood samples before being released (hence Latin name *liberatus*). Habitat: <250 m. Riverine woodland. E (Somalia)

83

Plate 84

1 **RED-BACKED SHRIKE** *Lanius collurio* L 20 cm. Note black, black-and-white and white (not brown and white) tail feathers and grey (not chestnut) rump. Habitat: <3000 m. Wooded and bushed areas. NM

2 **RED-TAILED SHRIKE** *Lanius isabellinus* L 20 cm. Habitat: <2000 cm. Dry, more or less wooded, bushed and shrubbed habitats including farmland. Crossbred *collurio* x *isabellinus* (a) occasionally in SW and S Kenya and in N Tanzania. NM

3 **NUBIAN SHRIKE** *Lanius nubicus* L 20 cm. Habitat: wooded, natural and cultivated areas. NM

4 **WOODCHAT-SHRIKE** *Lanius senator* L 20 cm. Habitat: bushed areas. NM

5 **MAGPIE-SHRIKE** *Corvinella melanoleuca* L 15 cm (excluding tail streamers). Habitat: 750-2000 m. Bushed and wooded areas.

6 **YELLOW-BILLED SHRIKE** *Corvinella corvina* L 20 cm (excluding tail streamers). Habitat: <2250 m. Bushed and wooded areas.

7 **MACKINNON'S FISCAL** *Lanius mackinnoni* L 20 cm. Wings all black except for white shoulders. White in tail restricted to feather tips. Habitat: 500-2250 m. Forest edges and more or less wooded and bushed areas, including gardens.

8 **GREAT GREY SHRIKE** *Lanius excubitor* L 25 cm. Black eye-stripes may be joined (or almost joined) over bill. Outer tail-feathers all white (not partly black). Races from Ethiopia have far more white in wings. Habitat: dry, more or less wooded and bushed areas. (NM)

9 **SOMALI FISCAL** *Lanius somalicus* L 20 cm. Resembles Taita Fiscal but with white tips to secondaries and tertials. Habitat: 250-1000 m. Arid, open or sparsely bushed country.

10 **TAITA FISCAL** *Lanius dorsalis* L 20 cm. Resembles Somali Fiscal but no white in flight feathers. Habitat: <1500(&>) m. Dry, more or less wooded and bushed areas.

11 **SOUZA'S SHRIKE** *Lanius souzae* L 15 cm. Note wing and mantle barring. Habitat: miombo.

12 **EMIN'S SHRIKE** *Lanius gubernator* L 15 cm. Note chestnut (not grey) rump and brown-and-white (not black-and-white) tail feathers. Habitat: 500-1500 m. Open or lightly wooded and bushed areas.

13 **GREY-BACKED FISCAL** *Lanius excubitoroides* L 25 cm. Gregarious. Note black forehead and partly white outer tail-feathers. Habitat: wooded and bushed natural and cultivated areas, including gardens.

14 **LONG-TAILED FISCAL** *Lanius cabanisi* L 20 cm. Note plain black (not white-edged) mantle. Habitat: <1750 m. Wooded and bushed natural and cultivated areas.

15 **UHEHE FISCAL** *Lanius marwitzi* L 20 cm. (Species level as by Mackworth-Praed and Grant.) Note white eyebrow. Habitat: 1500-3000 m. E (Tanzania)

16 **LESSER GREY SHRIKE** *Lanius minor* L 20 cm. No white between black forehead and grey crown. All primaries partly white. Habitat: <3000(&>) m. More or less bushed natural and cultivated areas.

17 **COMMON FISCAL** *Lanius collaris* L 20 cm. Habitat: <1500-3500 m. More or less wooded and bushed country, including gardens; often on telephone lines. NM

84

Plate 85

1 **YELLOW-CRESTED HELMETSHRIKE** *Prionops alberti* L 20 cm. Habitat: mountainous areas.

2 **WHITE HELMETSHRIKE** *Prionops plumata* L 20 cm. (Not all races depicted.) Race *cristata* (a) in E Ethiopia, NW Kenya and C and NW Uganda. White in wing may be narrow or missing. Habitat: <2000 m. Miombo and other dry wooded and bushed areas.

3 **GREY-CRESTED HELMETSHRIKE** *Prionops poliolopha* L 25 cm. Habitat: 1000-2000 m. Woodland

4 **RETZ'S HELMETSHRIKE** *Prionops retzii* L 20 cm. Habitat: <1500(&>) m. Miombo and well-wooded streams.

5 **RED-BILLED HELMETSHRIKE** *Prionops caniceps* L 20 cm. Habitat: 500-1250 m. Tall trees at forest edges.

6 **CHESTNUT-FRONTED HELMETSHRIKE** *Prionops scopifrons* L 20 cm. Habitat: <500(&>) m. Moist woodland and mangroves.

7 **WHITE-RUMPED HELMETSHRIKE** *Eurocephalus rueppelli* L 25 cm. Habitat: <1500(&>) m. More or less wooded and bushed areas.

8 **STRESEMANN'S BUSH-CROW** *Zavattariornis stresemanni* L 30 cm. Habitat: bushland. E (Ethiopia

9 **PIAPIAC** *Ptilostomus afer* L 35 cm. Habitat: 500-1500 m. Lightly wooded grassland with palms and cattle or game.

10 **CHOUGH** *Pyrrhocorax pyrrhocorax* L 35 cm. Habitat: normally near bare rocky slopes of high mountains.

11 **BROWN-NECKED RAVEN** *Corvus ruficollis* L 45 cm. Note brown wings and mantle (but this colouring not always so distinct). Habitat: desert and semi-desert.

12 **PIED CROW** *Corvus albus* L 45 cm. Habitat: <2000(&>) m. Towns and villages, wooded grassland, areas near rivers, lakes and swamps.

13 **HOUSE CROW** *Corvus splendens* L 45 cm. Introduced from Asia. Imm less buffy-grey in neck and on mantle. Habitat: towns, villages and other settled areas at the coast and spreading from there.

14 **WHITE-NECKED RAVEN** *Corvus albicollis* L 55 cm. Habitat: 1000(&<)-3000 (&>) m. Rocky, open bushed and wooded areas, often near cliffs.

15 **THICK-BILLED RAVEN** *Corvus crassirostris* L 65 cm. Habitat: rocky areas. [E] (Ethiopia)

16 **FAN-TAILED RAVEN** *Corvus rhipidurus* L 45 cm. Note short tail. May be as brown as Brown-necked Raven. Habitat: 250-1500(&>) m. Dry rocky areas.

17 **AFRICAN ROOK** *Corvus capensis* L 45 cm. Note slender long bill. Habitat: 1200(&<)-2500 m. Grassland with some trees.

85

Plate 86

1 **NARROW-TAILED STARLING** *Poeoptera lugubris* L 20 cm. Note small size (as sparrow), lengthened middle tail-feathers and strong purple-blue gloss. The ♀ has rufous inner flight-feather webs (not visible in folded wing). Habitat: 500-1750 m. Forests. AM

2 **STUHLMANN'S STARLING** *Poeoptera stuhlmanni* L 15 cm. Note small size (as sparrow) and blue gloss. Rufous inner flight-feather webs of ♀ not visible in folded wing. Habitat: 1500-2750 m. Forests.

3 **KENRICK'S STARLING** *Poeoptera kenricki* L 15 cm. Note small size (as sparrow). No gloss. Rufous inner flight-feather webs of ♀ not visible in folded wing. Habitat: 750-2500 m.

4 **BRISTLE-CROWNED STARLING** *Onychognathus salvadorii* L 40 cm. Habitat: 250-1500 m. Cliffs and ravines in arid and dry areas.

5 **SLENDER-BILLED STARLING** *Onychognathus tenuirostris* L 25 cm. Note greenish tail gloss and (in ♀) scaly feathering. Habitat: 1250-4500 m. Forests, moorland and cultivation. Voice: mid-high, somewhat rasping, rapid '*pju pjêe-pjêepji*'.

6 **RED-WINGED STARLING** *Onychognathus morio* L 30 cm. The ♀ has short stripes on throat. Habitat: 500-1500 m. Any more or less wooded areas near rocks or buildings including town centres.

7 **CHESTNUT-WINGED STARLING** *Onychognathus fulgidus* L 30 cm. Note greenish gloss of ♂ head and finely striped ♀ head. Only red-winged starling in its area except Waller's Starling which is smaller and has all-purple (not green-headed) gloss. Habitat: 500-1500 m. Forests.

8 **SOMALI CHESTNUT-WINGED STARLING** *Onychognathus blythii* L 20 cm. Note long tail of ♂ and plain (not striped or scaled) head of ♀. Habitat: rocky ravines in wooded and bushed areas.

9 **SOCOTRA CHESTNUT-WINGED STARLING** *Onychognathus frater* L 30 cm. Habitat: no information available. E (Socotra)

10 **WALLER'S STARLING** *Onychognathus walleri* L 20 cm. Note small size and short bill. Habitat: 750-3000 m. Forest. Voice: very high whistling '*fju-fjêe-fjêe-fjie*'.

11 **WHITE-BILLED STARLING** *Onychognathus albirostris* L 25 cm. Habitat: cliffs and ravines in montane moor- and grassland. [E] (Ethiopia)

12 **BLACK-BELLIED GLOSSY STARLING** *Lamprotornis corruscus* L 20 cm. Note unspotted wings and yellow eye. Habitat: <1500(&>) m. Forest edges and woodland. On Pemba also in mangroves. Voice: high '*pjêe-peep-peep-pûppip*'.

13 **BRONZE-TAILED GLOSSY STARLING** *Lamprotornis chalcurus* L 20 cm. Note purple (not greenish) middle tail-feathers. Purple of underparts restricted to lower flanks and belly. Imm brownish black with green gloss above. Habitat: 500-1250 m. Bushed areas.

14 **GREATER BLUE-EARED GLOSSY STARLING** *Lamprotornis chalybeus* L 25 cm. Note greenish (not purple) middle tail-feathers. Underparts extensively purple. Imm brownish-black with slight green gloss above. Habitat: <3000 m. More or less wooded and bushed natural and cultivated areas including gardens and parks. Voice: mid-high, twittering, short chatters connected by miauling '*wèèhèh*'.

15 **LESSER BLUE-EARED GLOSSY STARLING** *Lamprotornis chloropterus* L 20 cm. Note green (not blue-green) chest and purplish blue (not pure purple) underparts. Imm has pale brownish-rufous underparts (useful feature for identifying birds in flocks). Habitat: <1750 m. Wooded and bushed habitats including gardens. Voice: high, reed warbler-like, unhurried '*chat chit chûrrah chah*'.

16 **SHARP-TAILED GLOSSY STARLING** *Lamprotornis acuticaudus* L 20 cm. Note tail shape and red eye. Habitat: miombo. Voice: very high, sweeping, shrieking '*chreek-chreek-chreek*'.

17 **RUEPPELL'S LONG-TAILED STARLING** *Lamprotornis purpuropterus* L 35 cm. Habitat: <2000 m. More or less wooded and bushed areas, normally near settlement.

18 **SPLENDID GLOSSY STARLING** *Lamprotornis splendidus* L 30 cm. Note purple chin and dark bar over secondaries and tertials. Habitat: 500-2000 m. Forests, cultivation and gardens. Keeps to trees. Voice: mid-high, miauling '*kiauw-kjêw*' (like Grey-backed Shrike). AM

19 **PURPLE GLOSSY STARLING** *Lamprotornis purpureus* L 25 cm. Green gloss only on wings. Habitat: more or less wooded and bushed natural and cultivated habitats, including gardens.

20 **PURPLE-HEADED GLOSSY STARLING** *Lamprotornis purpureiceps* L 20 cm. Note dark eye and unspotted wings. Habitat: 500-2000 m. Forests, cultivation and gardens. Voice: high '*pjeep pjeep -*' (every second one '*jeep*').

86

Plate 87

1 **AFRICAN DRONGO** *Dicrurus adsimilis* L 25 cm. Race *coracinus* (a) in S Uganda and W Kenya. Habitat: <2250 m. Forest edges, dry woodland, wooded grassland, farm- and pastureland with scattered trees. (Race *coracinus* keeps to forests.)

2 **SQUARE-TAILED DRONGO** *Dicrurus ludwigii* L 20 cm. Note short bill and sharply bent outwards tail feathers. Habitat: <2000 m. Forests.

3 **YELLOW-BILLED OXPECKER** *Buphagus africanus* L 20 cm. Habitat: <3000 m. Areas with game and cattle.

4 **RED-BILLED OXPECKER** *Buphagus erythrorhynchus* L 20 cm. Habitat: <3000 m. Areas with game and cattle.

5 **CHESTNUT-BELLIED STARLING** *Spreo pulcher* L 20 cm. Habitat: wooded and bushed areas ofte near settlement.

6 **SHELLEY'S STARLING** *Spreo shelleyi* L 15 cm. Note uniformly dark rufous underparts and small black wing-spots. Habitat: <1500 m. Dry wooded and bushed areas. AM

7 **HILDEBRANDT'S STARLING** *Spreo hildebrandti* L 20 cm. Rufous belly darker than breast. Note distinct large black wing spots and greenish hind-collar. Habitat: 500-1750(&>) m. More or less bushed and wooded areas.

8 **SUPERB STARLING** *Spreo superbus* L 20 cm. Note white chestband. Habitat: <2250(&>) m. Towns, villages and open settlement. Also in any grassy wooded and bushed area.

9 **FISCHER'S STARLING** *Spreo fischeri* L 20 cm. Habitat: <1250 m. Dry bush and bushed grassland.

10 **WHITE-CROWNED STARLING** *Spreo albicapillus* L 25 cm. Habitat: 250-1000 m. Dry bushland.

11 **MAGPIE-STARLING** *Speculipastor bicolor* L 20 cm. Note orange eye and white wing-panel. Habitat: <1250 m. Wooded and bushed areas. AM

12 **WHITE-WINGED STARLING** *Neocichla gutturalis* L 20 cm. Habitat: miombo canopies.

13 **SHARPE'S STARLING** *Cinnyricinclus sharpii* L 15 cm. Note buff belly and under tail-coverts, and pale eye. Habitat: 1500(&<)-3000 m. Forest canopies.

14 **ABBOTT'S STARLING** *Cinnyricinclus femoralis* L 15 cm. No white in wing. Habitat: 1750-2500 m. Forest canopies.

15 **VIOLET-BACKED STARLING** *Cinnyricinclus leucogaster* L 15 cm. Note yellow gape of ♀. Habitat: <3000 m. Forest edges and woodland. (AM)

16 **GOLDEN-BREASTED STARLING** *Cosmopsarus regius* L 35 cm. Looks very dark in the field. Habitat: <1250 m. More or less wooded and bushed areas.

17 **ASHY STARLING** *Cosmopsarus unicolor* L 30 cm. Habitat: 1000-2000 m. More or less wooded and bushed areas. E (Tanzania)

18 **WATTLED STARLING** *Creatophora cinerea* L 20 cm. Irregular visitor in very large flocks. Habitat: <3000 m. Short grassy places in wood- and bushland. AM

19 **COMMON STARLING** *Sturnus vulgaris* L 20 cm. Habitat in Europe is 'wooded grassland' (like orchards) near towns and villages. NM

87

Plate 88

1 **GREY-HEADED SPARROW** *Passer griseus* L 15 cm. (Not all races depicted, for example the most warm-coloured race *diffuses* from coastal Tanzania that is often regarded as a full species, the Southern Grey-headed Sparrow.) Race *g. griseus* (a) in C and N Tanzania, W Kenya, most of Uganda, Ethiopia and NW Somalia, race *swainsonii* (b) in N Kenya, Ethiopia and N Somalia, race *gongonensis* (c) in Kenya, S Ethiopia and S Somalia. Habitat: <3000 m. Bushed and wooded areas, including cultivation, gardens and towns and villages.

2 **HOUSE SPARROW** *Passer domesticus* L 15 cm. Note chestnut crown and nape of ♂. Introduced from India in some coastal towns and now spreading inland from there; might have reached Nairobi.

3 **RUFOUS SPARROW** *Passer motitensis* L 14 cm. Race *rufocinctus* (a) in Kenya and Tanzania, race *shelleyi* (b) in Ethiopia, Somalia and (uncommon in) Uganda. Note grey crown and chestnut rump. Habitat: 1250(&<)-2250(&>) m. More or less wooded and bushed natural and cultivated areas including gardens.

4 **SOCOTRA SPARROW** *Passer insularis* L 15 cm. (Species level as by Mackworth-Praed and Grant.) Note grey rufous-edged mantle. The ♀ has no clear eyebrow. Habitat: no information available. E (Socotra)

5 **SOMALI SPARROW** *Passer castanopterus* L 13 cm. Habitat: 250-1000 m. Dry open areas.

6 **SUDAN GOLDEN SPARROW** *Passer luteus* L 11 cm. Habitat: open areas with some bush, scrub and grass cover. Also near settlement. (Note that bill of ♂ is pale white when n-br.)

7 **ARABIAN GOLDEN SPARROW** *Passer euchlorus* L 11 cm. Habitat: wooded and bushed areas with some grass cover.

8 **CHESTNUT SPARROW** *Passer eminibey* L 12 cm. Habitat: <2000 m. Dry wooded areas near papyrus swamp and settlement.

9 **YELLOW-THROATED PETRONIA** *Petronia superciliaris* L 15 cm. Note striped mantle and wide pale eyebrow. Yellow throat-patches normally concealed. Habitat: <1500 m. Miombo and other more or less wooded and bushed natural and cultivated areas.

10 **YELLOW-SPOTTED PETRONIA** *Petronia pyrgita* L 13 cm. Note white chin and greyish buff (not grey) mantle. Habitat: 500-1500(&>) m. More or less wooded and bushed natural and cultivated areas.

11 **BUSH PETRONIA** *Petronia dentata* L 13 cm. The ♂ is faint rufous around cheek. Habitat: <1500 m. Forest edges and woodland, often near water.

12 **PALE PETRONIA** *Petronia brachydactyla* L 13 cm. Very similar to Yellow-spotted Petronia but not in same area. Habitat: <500 m. Arid areas (including open seashore) with no or sparse grass cover. NM

13 **SPECKLE-FRONTED WEAVER** *Sporopipes frontalis* L 13 cm. Habitat: 250-2000 m. Bushed (and wooded) areas, often near water.

14 **WHITE-BROWED SPARROW-WEAVER** *Plocepasser mahali* L 15 cm. Note white rump. Habitat: 250-1500(&>) m. Dry wooded areas, often near settlement.

15 **CHESTNUT-CROWNED SPARROW-WEAVER** *Plocepasser superciliosus* L 15 cm. Habitat: 500-2000 m. Dry wooded and bushed areas.

16 **DONALDSON-SMITH'S SPARROW-WEAVER** *Plocepasser donaldsoni* L 15 cm. Note heavy bill. Habitat: 250-1500 m. Dry rocky areas with some grass and scattered trees.

17 **GREY-HEADED SOCIAL WEAVER** *Pseudonigrita arnaudi* L 13 cm. Note white cap. Habitat: 500-1500(&>) m. Wooded and bushed areas with some grass cover.

18 **BLACK-CAPPED SOCIAL WEAVER** *Pseudonigrita cabanisi* L 13 cm. Habitat: <1500 m. Dry wooded and bushed areas.

19 **RUFOUS-TAILED WEAVER** *Histurgops ruficauda* L 20 cm. Habitat: 1000-2000 m. More or less wooded areas in dry hilly country. E (Tanzania)

20 **WHITE-BILLED BUFFALO-WEAVER** *Bubalornis albirostris* L 25 cm. Habitat: 250-1250 m. Wooded and bushed areas.

21 **RED-BILLED BUFFALO-WEAVER** *Bubalornis niger* L 25 cm. Habitat: <1500 m. Open more or less wooded and bushed areas.

22 **WHITE-HEADED BUFFALO-WEAVER** *Dinemellia dinemelli* L 25 cm. Note red rump. Habitat: <1500 m. Wooded and bushed areas.

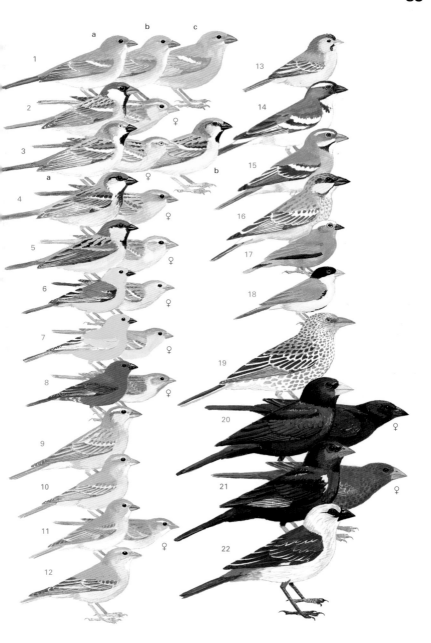

88

Plate 89

1 **BLACK-HEADED WEAVER** *Ploceus cucullatus* L 20 cm. (Not all races depicted.) Social (breeds in colonies). Layards' Black-headed Weaver (a) formerly a separate species, now included in this species as a group of races with regularly spotted mantle. Habitat: <2000(&>) m. More or less wooded and bushed areas, including farmland and gardens.

2 **VIEILLOT'S BLACK WEAVER** *Ploceus nigerrimus* L 20 cm. Social. Note sooty (not glossy) black colouring. The ♀ is 'sparrow-like' (not black). Habitat: 500-2000 m. Forest edges and other more or less wooded areas.

3 **SPEKE'S WEAVER** *Ploceus spekei* L 15 cm. Social. Combines black face mask and heavy mantle streaking. Habitat: 1000-2250 m. Wooded and bushed areas, including cultivation and gardens.

4 **FOX'S WEAVER** *Ploceus spekeoides* L 15 cm. Social. Note almost completely dark mantle and wings. Habitat: wet wooded and bushed habitats. E (Uganda)

5 **ORANGE WEAVER** *Ploceus aurantius* L 13 cm. Social. Combines 'spectacles' and yellow-edged black wing feathers. Habitat: forest edges, swamps and reedbeds.

6 **TAVETA GOLDEN WEAVER** *Ploceus castaneiceps* L 14 cm. Social. Note saffron edge of 'disappeared' mask. Habitat: 250-1500 m. Reedbeds, papyrus and shrubbery along streams and swamps.

7 **PALM GOLDEN WEAVER** *Ploceus bojeri* L 15 cm. Social. Note red (not pale) eye, saffron head and edge around yellow throat. Habitat: <1250(&>) m. Bushed and wooded areas including cultivation and gardens.

8 **LARGE GOLDEN WEAVER** *Ploceus xanthops* L 20 cm. Not social. Combines white eye, yellow face and plain yellow upperparts. Habitat: 750-2500 m. Gardens and moist bushed areas, often near water.

9 **EASTERN GOLDEN WEAVER** *Ploceus subaureus* L 15 cm. Very social. Combines pale eye, saffron face and plain upperparts. Habitat: <1500(&>) m. Tall grassy wooded and bushed areas including gardens

10 **NORTHERN BROWN-THROATED WEAVER** *Ploceus castanops* L 14 cm. Social. Note heavy bill, small rufous mask and plain mantle. Habitat: 750-2000 m. Breeds in papyrus and reedbeds, but wanders to forest edges and other wooded areas when not breeding.

11 **SOUTHERN BROWN-THROATED WEAVER** *Ploceus xanthopterus* L 15 cm. Social. Combines dark eye with small rufous mask. Habitat: around 1750 m. Papyrus, reedbeds and shrubbery over water.

12 **YELLOW-BACKED WEAVER** *Ploceus melanocephalus* L 15 cm. Social. Note yellow nape. Habitat: 500-1750 m. Tall grass, reeds, papyrus, shrubbery and bush near water.

13 **JUBA WEAVER** *Ploceus dichrocephalus* L 15 cm. Social. Note mottled transition from head to rest of body. Habitat: arid areas normally near settlement.

14 **NORTHERN MASKED WEAVER** *Ploceus taeniopterus* L 15 cm. Very social. Note saffron rim round small black mask. Habitat: reedbeds and nearby bushes.

15 **GOLDEN-BACKED WEAVER** *Ploceus jacksoni* L 15 cm. Very social. Note contrasting yellow mantle. Habitat: 500-2000 m. Wooded and bushed areas near swamps and water.

16 **LESSER MASKED WEAVER** *Ploceus intermedius* L 14 cm. Less social. Note yellow (not olive-green) neck and pale yellow (not brown) eye. Demarcation between black and saffron-rufous above eye not sharp. Habitat: <1500(&>) m. Wooded and bushed areas often near water.

17 **VITELLINE MASKED WEAVER** *Ploceus velatus* L 14 cm. Less social. Note greenish (not yellow) neck. Demarcation between black and saffron-rufous on crown normally rather sharp and before eye. Habitat: <2000 m. Wooded and bushed natural and cultivated areas.

18 **TANZANIAN MASKED WEAVER** *Ploceus reichardi* L 14 cm. Social. Note extensive rufous-saffron colouring. Habitat: swampy areas. E (Tanzania)

19 **HEUGLIN'S MASKED WEAVER** *Ploceus heuglini* L 14 cm. Less social. Note pale yellow eye. Habitat: <1500 m. Dry woodland.

20 **RUEPPELL'S WEAVER** *Ploceus galbula* L 14 cm. Very social. Rufous mask reaches cheek behind eye. Note faintly streaked mantle. Habitat: more or less wooded and bushed areas.

21 **CHESTNUT WEAVER** *Ploceus rubiginosus* L 15 cm. Social. Habitat: <1500(&>) m. Dry wooded and bushed areas. (AM)

22 **LITTLE WEAVER** *Ploceus luteolus* L 12 cm. Very social. Note small size, short bill, faint mantle striping and yellow (not saffron) colouring. Habitat: <250-1500 m. Dry, more or less wooded and bushed areas.

23 **SLENDER-BILLED WEAVER** *Ploceus pelzelni* L 12 cm. Less social. Note small size, slender bill, (almost) plain mantle and yellow (not saffron) colouring. Habitat: 500-1750 m. Papyrus, tall grass and shrubbery at swamps, forest edges and cultivation.

24 **COMPACT WEAVER** *Ploceus superciliosus* L 13 cm. Social. Note dark mantle, nape and (in ♀) crown Habitat: 500-1750 m. Forests, swamps and more or less wooded and bushed areas.

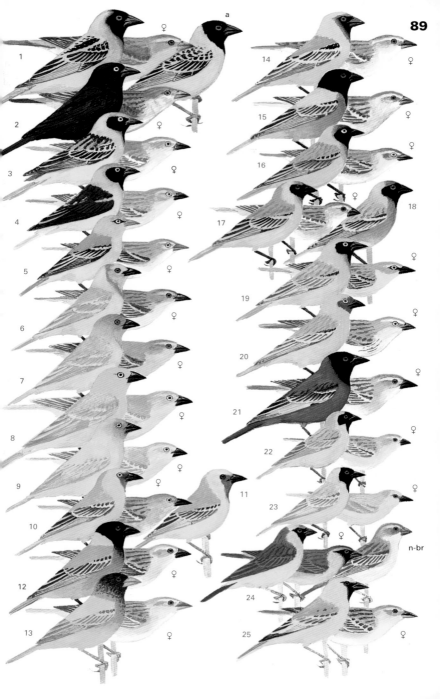

89

25 KILOMBERA WEAVER *Ploceus burnieri* L 15 cm. Social. Note sharply demarcated mask. Less saffron around mask then Northern Masked Weaver. Habitat: 250 m. Riverside swamp. E (Tanzania)

Note: the ♂ of 89.1, 9, 11-22 and 24 also have a n-br plumage resembling the ♀ plumage. There are no n-br plumages for the species on plate 90 except for the races 90.9a and b.

Plate 90

1 WEYNS'S WEAVER *Ploceus weynsi* L 15 cm. Less social. Note brown-black mantle and rufous flanks. Habitat: 1000-1500 m. Forest edges and moist bush.

2 CLARKE'S WEAVER *Ploceus golandi* L 13 cm. Breeding habits as yet unknown. Habitat: <250 m. Sokoke Forest. E (Kenya)

3 DARK-BACKED WEAVER *Ploceus bicolor* L 15 cm. Not social. Race *kersteni* (a) in E Somalia, E Kenya and E & S Tanzania, race *stictifrons* (b) in SE Tanzania, race *mentalis* (c) in W Kenya and Uganda, race *kigomaensis* (d) in W Tanzania. Habitat: 750-2500 m. Forests and moist woodland. Voice: high, sweeping '*weep*' followed by delightful, masterly, toy trumpet-like, whistling '*pwee pwee-pwee-pweeup-pwee-pwee*' like out-of-tune songs.

4 SPECTACLED WEAVER *Ploceus ocularis* L 15 cm. Not social. Note olive-green back. Habitat: <2250 m. Forest edges and more or less wooded and bushed areas, including gardens and parks.

5 BLACK-NECKED WEAVER *Ploceus nigricollis* L 15 cm. Not social. Habitat: <1500 m. Dry wood- and bushland often in river valleys.

6 BLACK-BILLED WEAVER *Ploceus melanogaster* L 14 cm. Not social. Habitat: 1000-1500 (&>) m. Dense forest undergrowth.

7 STRANGE WEAVER *Ploceus alienus* L 14 cm. Combines rufous bib with black (not dark brown) head and olive-green mantle. Habitat: 1500-2750 m. Forest edges and bamboo.

8 BROWN-CAPPED WEAVER *Ploceus insignis* L 14 cm. Not social. Habitat: 1000-3000 m. Forests and bamboo.

9 BAGLAFECHT WEAVER *Ploceus baglafecht* L 15 cm. (Not all races depicted.) Not social. Race *reichenowi* (a) in C and W Kenya, N Tanzania and S Ethiopia, race *emini* (b) (Emin's Weaver) in NW Uganda, C and SE Ethiopia, race *b. baglafecht* (c) in W Ethiopia, race *stuhlmanni* (d) (Stuhlmann's Weaver) in C and S Uganda. Habitat: 1500-3000 m. Bamboo, forest edges and woodland, gardens and parks. Race *emini* in more swampy habitats.

10 NICOLL'S WEAVER *Ploceus nicolli* L 14 cm. Not social. Note yellow forehead and rufous bib of ♂. Brown (not black) head merges in darker mantle. Habitat: 1250-2250 m. Forests. E (Tanzania)

11 OLIVE-HEADED WEAVER *Ploceus olivaceiceps* L 14 cm. Not social. Habitat: 1000-1500 m. Miombo.

12 YELLOW-MANTLED WEAVER *Ploceus tricolor* L 15 cm. Not social. Habitat: 500-2000 m. Forest canopies.

13 MAXWELL'S BLACK WEAVER *Ploceus albinucha* L 13 cm. Not social. Note glossy (not sooty) black colouring. The ♀ is black too (not sparrow-like). Habitat: 500-1000 m. Forest canopies.

14 BERTRAM'S WEAVER *Ploceus bertrandi* L 15 cm. Not social. Note black nape-patch of ♂ and all-black head of ♀. Habitat: 750-2000 m. Forest edges, wood- and bushland and cultivation, often along rivers.

15 RED-BELLIED MALIMBE *Malimbus erythrogaster* L 20 cm. Habitat: <1500 m. Forest canopies.

16 RED-COLLARED MALIMBE *Malimbus rubricollis* L 20 cm. Habitat: 500-1750 m. Forest canopies.

17 CRESTED MALIMBE *Malimbus malimbicus* L 20 cm. Habitat: 750-1500 m. Forests and dense thicket.

18 BLUE-BILLED MALIMBE *Malimbus nitens* L 15 cm. Habitat: 500-750 m. Forest undergrowth, often along streams.

19 PARASITIC WEAVER *Anomalospiza imberbis* L 12 cm. Gregarious. Note very short bill. Habitat: <2000 m. Moist, open and bushed, natural and cultivated areas.

20 RED-HEADED MALIMBE *Anaplectes rubriceps* L 15 cm. (Sc name as by Britton.) Not social. Race *leuconotus* (a) in N Tanzania, Uganda, Kenya, Ethiopia and NW Somalia, race *rubriceps* (b) in most of Tanzania, race *jubaensis* (c) in S Somalia and E Kenya. Habitat: <2000 m. More or less wooded and bushed areas, including gardens.

21 GROSBEAK-WEAVER *Amblyospiza albifrons* L 20 cm. Less social. Note white wingspot of ♂. White forehead spot may be small or missing. Habitat: <3000 m. Nests in reeds and papyrus.

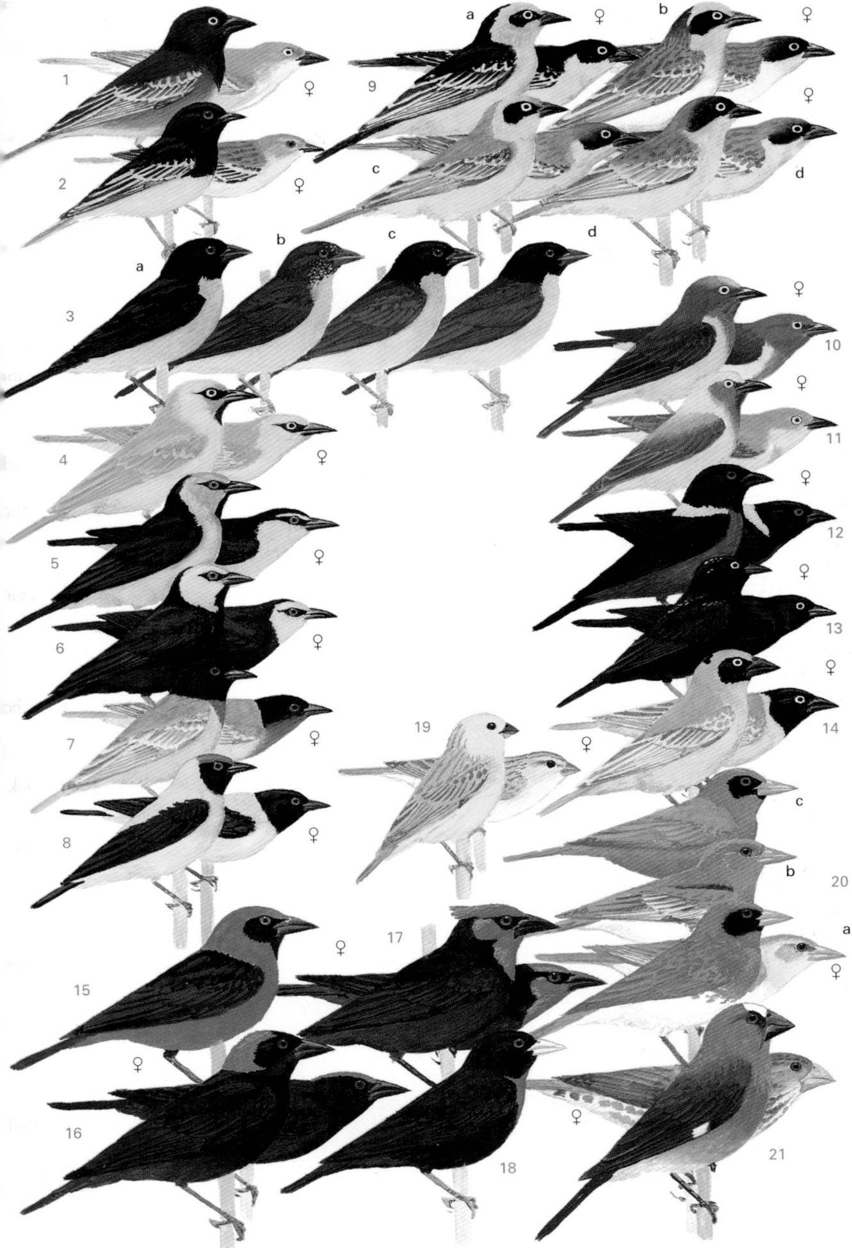
1
♀
2
♀
9
a
♀
b
♀
♀
c
d
3
a
b
c
d
10
♀
11
♀
4
♀
12
♀
5
♀
13
♀
6
♀
14
♀
7
♀
19
♀
8
♀
20
c
b
a
♀
15
♀
17
♀
16
18
♀
21

90

Plate 91

1 **LONG-TAILED WIDOWBIRD** *Euplectes progne* L 15 cm (excluding tail streamers).
Habitat: 1750-3000 m. Marshy open grassland.

2 **JACKSON'S WIDOWBIRD** *Euplectes jacksoni* L 14 cm (excluding tail streamers). Habitat: 1500-3000 m.
Open rough grassland.

3 **RED-COLLARED WIDOWBIRD** *Euplectes ardens* L 13 cm (excluding tail streamers). Race *suahelica*
(a) in SW Kenya and N Tanzania, race *tropicus* (b) in Tanzania, SW Uganda and SE Kenya, race *concolor*
(c) in NW Uganda. Note loose tail feathers. Habitat: 1000-2000 m. Tall grass and herbage in open and
bushed areas.

4 **YELLOW-MANTLED WIDOWBIRD** *Euplectes macrourus* L 14 cm (excluding tail streamers). Race
m. macrourus (a) in Uganda and Kenya (race *conradsi*, not depicted, very similar but with longer tail), race
macrocercus (b) in Ethiopia. Habitat: 1000-2000 m. Moist open grassland.

5 **MONTANE MARSH WIDOWBIRD** *Euplectes psammocromius* L 15 cm (excluding tail streamers).
Note pale upper wing-coverts and white bill. Habitat: 1750-3000 m. Grassland.

6 **MARSH WIDOWBIRD** *Euplectes hartlaubi* L 15 cm (excluding tail streamers). Note partly rufous,
partly white (not brown) upper wing-coverts. Habitat: 1000-2000 m. Swamp edges and moist grassland.

7 **WHITE-WINGED WIDOWBIRD** *Euplectes albonotatus* L 12 cm (excluding tail streamers). Habitat:
<2000 m. Bushed areas with tall grass.

8 **FAN-TAILED WIDOWBIRD** *Euplectes axillaris* L 14 cm (excluding tail streamers). Only very little
white in rufous and brown wing. Habitat: <1500(&>) m. Swamp edges, bush- and grassland.

9 **SOUTHERN RED BISHOP** *Euplectes orix* L 12 cm. Note red crown and buff-orange (not pure
orange) mantle. Tail just visible. Habitat: 1000 (&<)-1500 m. Tall grassland near water.

10 **NORTHERN RED BISHOP** *Euplectes franciscanus* L 10 cm. Note black (not red) crown and pure
orange mantle. Tail concealed between red tail coverts. Habitat: open and bushed tall grass areas.

11 **ZANZIBAR RED BISHOP** *Euplectes nigroventris* L 10 cm. Underparts black from chin to belly.
Habitat: <2000 m. Open and bushed grassland.

12 **BLACK-WINGED RED BISHOP** *Euplectes hordeaceus* L 14 cm. Note red chest. Habitat: <1750 m.
Forest edges and bushed tall grassland.

13 **BLACK BISHOP** *Euplectes gierowii* L 15 cm. Note yellow (not red) nape and black rump.
Habitat: 500-1750 m. Bushed tall grassland.

14 **YELLOW-CROWNED BISHOP** *Euplectes afer* L 11 cm. Note black neck-collar.
Habitat: 250-2000 m. Swamps and moist grassland.

15 **FIRE-FRONTED BISHOP** *Euplectes diadematus* L 10 cm. Note orange forehead-patch.
Habitat: <1000 m. Dry bushed areas, but also in rice fields. (AM)

16 **YELLOW BISHOP** *Euplectes capensis* L 15 cm. Habitat: <2500 m. Tall bushed grass- and farmland.

17 **RED-BILLED QUELEA** *Quelea quelea* L 13 cm. Very social. No mask in n-br plumage.
Habitat: 500(&<)-1500(-3000) m. Dry, bushed, natural and cultivated areas. (AM)

18 **RED-HEADED QUELEA** *Quelea erythrops* L 12 cm. Social. Note blackish chin and sharp
demarcation of red colouring. Habitat: <1500(&>) m. Marsh shrubbery and moist grassland. AM

19 **CARDINAL QUELEA** *Quelea cardinalis* L 11 cm. Very social. Chin not blackish and red colouring not
sharply demarcated. Habitat: 250-3000 m. Grass- and farmland. (AM)

Note: all species on this plate except 18 and 19 also have a n-br plumage, resembling the ♀ plumage.

91

Plate 92

1 **RED-FRONTED ANTPECKER** *Parmoptila rubifrons* L 9 cm. Habitat: midstrata and undergrowth of forest edges.

2 **BROAD-TAILED PARADISE WHYDAH** *Vidua obtusa* L 15 cm (excluding tail streamers). Habitat: miombo and other woodland.

3 **ACACIA PARADISE WHYDAH** *Vidua paradisaea* L 15 cm (excluding tail streamers). Parasitises mainly Green-winged Pytilia. Habitat: more or less wooded and bushed, natural and cultivated areas.

4 **GREY-HEADED OLIVEBACK** *Nesocharis capistrata* L 12 cm. Habitat: 500-1250 m. Undergrowth of forest edges and wet, wooded and bushed areas.

5 **WHITE-COLLARED OLIVEBACK** *Nesocharis ansorgei* L 10 cm. Habitat: 1000-2000 m. Wet, wooded and bushed areas with thick grass and shrubbery.

6 **GREY-CROWNED BLACKFINCH** *Nigrita canicapilla* L 13 cm. Note white wing-bar. Habitat: 1500-3500 m. Woodland, often near water.

7 **PALE-FRONTED BLACKFINCH** *Nigrita luteifrons* L 10 cm. Note plain upper wing. Habitat: 500-1000 m. Open forests.

8 **CHESTNUT-BREASTED BLACKFINCH** *Nigrita bicolor* L 10 cm. Habitat: 500-750 m. Forests.

9 **WHITE-BREASTED BLACKFINCH** *Nigrita fusconota* L 10 cm. Habitat: 500-2000 m. Forests.

10 **GREEN-WINGED PYTILIA** *Pytilia melba* L 13 cm. Note yellow-green breast and dark barring of underparts. Habitat: <1500(&>) m. Groundstrata of wooded and bushed, natural and cultivated areas.

11 **ORANGE-WINGED PYTILIA** *Pytilia afra* L 13 cm. Note yellow edges of flight feathers and moss-green barring of underparts. Habitat: <2000 m. Groundstrata of bushed and wooded areas, including gardens.

12 **RED-WINGED PYTILIA** *Pytilia phoenicoptera* L 13 cm. Race *lineata* (a) in Ethiopia, race *p. phoenicoptera* (b) in N Uganda. Habitat: 500-1250 m. Tall grass of bushed and wooded areas.

13 **BROWN TWINSPOT** *Clytospiza monteiri* L 13 cm. Habitat: 1000-1500 m. Tall grass and shrubbery in forest glades and moist bushland.

14 **DUSKY TWINSPOT** *Euschistospiza cinereovinacea* L 12 cm. Habitat: 1750-2500 m. Tall grassy places in forest glades.

15 **PETERS'S TWINSPOT** *Hypargos niveoguttatus* L 13 cm. Habitat: <1000(&>) m. Tall grassy places in forests, wood- and bushland; often near water.

16 **GREEN TWINSPOT** *Mandingoa nitidula* L 9 cm. Habitat: <2250 m. Groundstrata of forest edges and moist thickets.

Note: the ♂ of all whydah and indigobird species (92.2 and 3) also have n-br plumages that are indistinguishable from the ♀ plumage.

92

Plate 93

1 **BLACK-BELLIED SEEDCRACKER** *Pyrenestes ostrinus* L 15 cm. Note black (not blue and red) bill, rufous-brown (not black) The ♀ is red and brown (not white-spotted black) underneath. Habitat: 500-1500 m. Tall grass, herbage and shubbery in forest glades, forest edges and gardens.

2 **LESSER SEEDCRACKER** *Pyrenestes minor* L 13 cm. Note brown (not red) nape. Habitat: 250-1000 m. Dense undergrowth of forest edges, often near water.

3 **BLACK-BELLIED FIREFINCH** *Lagonosticta rara* L 13 cm. Mantle uniformly plum-coloured with head and breast. Habitat: 750-1750 m. Tall grass and herbage in wooded and bushed areas.

4 **BLACK-FACED FIREFINCH** *Lagonosticta vinacea* L 12 cm. (Previous scientific name was *larvata*.) Habitat: 1000-1750 m. Ground of bamboo and woodland, often near streams.

5 **RED-BILLED FIREFINCH** *Lagonosticta senegala* L 9 cm. Very similar to Bar-breasted Firefinch but upperparts reddish (not plain uniform brown) and white spots on breast (not on chest). Habitat: <2250 m. Open, natural and cultivated areas, often near water. Enters houses.

6 **BAR-BREASTED FIREFINCH** *Lagonosticta rufopicta* L 10 cm. Very similar to Red-billed Firefinch but upperparts uniformly brown not tinged red. White spots on chest (not on breast), forming irregular bars. Rump and upper tail-coverts more crimson-red than breast and head. Habitat: 500-1500 m. Herbaceous places in wooded and bushed habitats, often near water.

7 **AFRICAN FIREFINCH** *Lagonosticta rubricata* L 12 cm. Note greyish brown crown and nape, brown (not red) mantle and red lower mandible. Habitat: <2000(&>) m. Tall grass, herbage and shrubbery in bushed, moist habitats.

8 **JAMESON'S FIREFINCH** *Lagonosticta rhodopareia* L 12 cm. Note bluish black bill. Belly centre and under tail-coverts black. Habitat: <1500 m. Tall grass, herbage and shrubbery in bushed and wooded areas normally away from settlement.

9 **RED-HEADED BLUEBILL** *Spermophaga ruficapilla* L 15 cm. Note black tail and blue and red bill. The ♀ has white-spotted underparts. Habitat: 500-2250 m. Undergrowth of damp forests.

10 **GRANT'S BLUEBILL** *Spermophaga poliogenys* L 14 cm. As Red-headed Bluebill but with black nape. Habitat: 500-1000 m. Forest undergrowth.

11 **RED-FACED CRIMSONWING** *Cryptospiza reichenovii* L 12 cm. Rather dark with red cheek. Habitat: 1500-2500 m. Dense forest undergrowth, often near streams.

12 **ABYSSINIAN CRIMSONWING** *Cryptospiza salvadorii* L 12 cm. Rather pale. Red restricted to scapulars and wings. Habitat: 1500-3000 m. Forest edges and bamboo.

13 **SHELLEY'S CRIMSONWING** *Cryptospiza shelleyi* L 13 cm. Note red bill of ♂ and black and red bill of ♀. Habitat: 1500-2750 m. Dense undergrowth of forest edges.

14 **DUSKY CRIMSONWING** *Cryptospiza jacksoni* L 12 cm. Habitat: 1500-2750 m. Dense forest undergrowth.

15 **VILLAGE INDIGOBIRD** *Vidua chalybeata* L 12 cm. Race *amauropterix* (a) in E Kenya and E Tanzania, race *centralis* (b) in Uganda, Kenya and Tanzania. Ethiopia and Somalia may have other races. Parasitizes mainly Red-billed Firefinch. Note combination of bill and foot colour and general bluish gloss. Habitat: <2000 m. More or less wooded and bushed areas, including gardens. Voice: nervous, loud *'tweet tweet tweet -'* in flight. Song a very high, hurried *'wheetohwheetohwheet'* with dry rattles, tics and very high twitters.

16 **VARIABLE INDIGOBIRD** *Vidua funerea* L 12 cm. Race *codringtoni* (a) (rare) in SE and C Tanzania, race *nigerrima* (b) from SE to NW Tanzania. Parasitises mainly African Firefinch. Note combination of bill and foot colour and general greenish (a) or purplish blue (b) gloss. Habitat: <1750 m. Forest edges, wood- and shrubland, often near water. Voice: high, hurried twitter with dry rattles.

17 **PURPLE INDIGOBIRD** *Vidua purpurascens* L 12 cm. Parasitises mainly Jameson's Firefinch. Note combination of white bill and feet and purple (not purplish blue) gloss. Habitat: <1500(&>) m. Open wood- and bushland. Voice: very high, rapid, fluted twitters.

Note: the ♂ of the indigobird species (93.15, 16 and 17) also have n-br plumages that are indistinguishable from the ♀ plumage.

93

Plate 94

1 **BLUE-CHEEKED CORDON-BLEU** *Uraeginthus angolensis* L 13 cm. Both ♀ and ♂ have more extensive blue underneath than ♀ of other cordon-bleus. Habitat: <1250 m. Bushed and wooded areas with thickets.

2 **RED-CHEEKED CORDON-BLEU** *Uraeginthus bengalus* L 13 cm. Habitat: <2500 (&>) m. Bushed and wooded habitats, often near settlement.

3 **BLUE-CAPPED CORDON-BLEU** *Uraeginthus cyanocephalus* L 13 cm. Note blue crown of ♂. Habitat: <1500 m. Dry bushed areas. (Introduced near Nairobi.)

4 **COMMON WAXBILL** *Estrilda astrild* L 10 cm. Note black centre of belly and under tail-coverts. Habitat: <3000 m. Tall grass and shrubbery in wooded and bushed areas, often near water or settlement.

5 **BLACK-RUMPED WAXBILL** *Estrilda troglodytes* L 9 cm. Note black rump and black-and-white tail. Habitat: 750-1500 m. Dry, natural and cultivated areas with scattered scrub, often along streams. Also a swamp edges.

6 **CRIMSON-RUMPED WAXBILL** *Estrilda rhodopyga* L 10 cm. Note red rump and red-and-brown tail. Habitat: <1500(&>) m. Tall grass and shrubbery in wooded and bushed areas.

7 **FAWN-BREASTED WAXBILL** *Estrilda paludicola* L 12 cm. Note red (not black-and-red) bill and pa white flanks. Habitat: 1000-2000 m. Swampy, open wooded and bushed areas with tall grass.

8 **BLACK-FACED WAXBILL** *Estrilda erythronotos* L 13 cm. Note black chin. Habitat: <1750 m. Open, more or less wooded and bushed, natural and cultivated areas with thickets.

9 **BLACK-CHEEKED WAXBILL** *Estrilda charmosyna* L 13 cm. Note pale (not black) chin. Generally paler than Black-faced Waxbill. Habitat: dry, rocky bush- and shrubland.

10 **BLACK-TAILED LAVENDER-WAXBILL** *Estrilda perreini* L 12 cm. Habitat: <2250 m. Tall grass an undergrowth near forest edges, bamboo and miombo.

11 **BLACK-CROWNED WAXBILL** *Estrilda nonnula* L 10 cm. Note creamy white (not grey-and-red) flanks and underparts. Habitat: 750-2250 m. Moist tall grass near forest edges, wood- and bushland, cultivation and gardens.

12 **BLACK-HEADED WAXBILL** *Estrilda atricapilla* L 10 cm. Note red flanks and greyish-brown underparts. Habitat: 2000-3500 m. Open forests and bamboo.

13 **YELLOW-BELLIED WAXBILL** *Estrilda melanotis* L 9 cm. Note yellow (not creamy white) flanks, short tail and black-and-red (not all-red) bill. Habitat: 750-3000 m. Tall grassy places in forest glades and other wooded areas.

14 **PURPLE GRENADIER** *Uraeginthus ianthinogaster* L 14 cm. Habitat: <2500 m. Ground of more or le wooded and bushed areas with thickets, including gardens and parks.

15 **STRAW-TAILED WHYDAH** *Vidua fischeri* L 10 cm (excluding tail streamers). Parasitises mainly Purple Grenadier. Habitat: <1750 m. Dry, more or less bushed areas. (Note that bill colour of ♀ should be as red as ♂.)

16 **PIN-TAILED WHYDAH** *Vidua macroura* L 12 cm (excluding tail streamers). Parasitises mainly estrilda waxbills. Habitat: <2500(&>) m. Forest edges and wooded and bushed, natural and cultivated areas, including gardens.

17 **STEEL-BLUE WHYDAH** *Vidua hypocherina* L 10 cm (excluding tail streamers). Supposed to parasitise Black-faced and Black-cheeked Waxbills. Habitat: <1500 m. Dry, more or less bushed areas.

Note: the ♂ of the whydah species (94.15, 16 and 17) also have n-br plumages that are indistinguishable from the ♀ plumage.

94

Plate 95

1 **ZEBRA WAXBILL** *Amandava subflava* L 9 cm. Habitat: <2250 m. Open, moist tall grassland, normally near water.

2 **LOCUSTFINCH** *Ortygospiza locustella* L 8 cm. Note spotted upperparts. Habitat: 1500-2000 m. Moist grassland.

3 **AFRICAN QUAILFINCH** *Ortygospiza atricollis* L 8 cm. Habitat: <3000 m. Wet grassland, occasionally in dry areas.

4 **BLACK-FACED QUAILFINCH** *Ortygospiza gabonensis* L 8 cm. Habitat: 750-1500 m. Wet grassland.

5 **BRONZE MANNIKIN** *Lonchura cucullata* L 9 cm. Note bronze-brown (not black) nape, mantle and unbarred wings. Habitat: <2000 m. Places with long grass in wooded and bushed habitats including gardens and parks.

6 **BICOLOURED MANNIKIN** *Lonchura bicolor* L 10 cm. Race *nigriceps* (a) (Rufous-backed Mannikin) in most of Tanzania, Somalia and E,C and SW Kenya, race *poensis* (b) in NW Tanzania, Uganda, SW and N Kenya and Ethiopia. Note barred flight feathers. Habitat: <2000 m. Forest edges and more or less wooded and bushed areas, including gardens.

7 **PIED MANNIKIN** *Lonchura fringilloides* L 13 cm. Note black patchy barring on breast sides. Habitat: <1000 m. Open forests, moist shrubby woodland and gardens.

8 **AFRICAN SILVERBILL** *Lonchura cantans* L 10 cm. Note creamy colouring and faintly barred upperparts. Habitat: 250-1500(&>) m. Dry open areas often near settlement.

9 **GREY-HEADED SILVERBILL** *Lonchura griseicapilla* L 12 cm. Note white rump. Habitat: <2000 m. Dry, more or less wooded and bushed areas.

10 **CUT-THROAT** *Amadina fasciata* L 12 cm. Habitat: <1500 m. Dry, more or less wooded and bushed natural and cultivated areas.

11 **JAVA SPARROW** *Padda oryzivora* L 13 cm. (English and scientific names as by Clement et al.) Introduced on Zanzibar, Pemba and in other places.

12 **CINNAMON-BREASTED ROCK BUNTING** *Emberiza tahapisi* L 14 cm. Note buff-brown upper- and underparts. Conspicuous rufous wing-panel. Habitat: 250-3000 m. Dry wooded and bushed areas with rocky slopes. Often at roadsides.

13 **SOUTHERN ROCK BUNTING** *Emberiza capensis* L 15 cm. Note unstreaked underparts. Habitat: rocky slopes with rough grass.

14 **HOUSE BUNTING** *Emberiza striolata* L 13 cm. Only bunting with streaked breast. Habitat: arid stony areas.

15 **GOLDEN-BREASTED BUNTING** *Emberiza flaviventris* L 15 cm. Note extensive white in wing. Mantle streaked chestnut-brown (not black and chestnut). Habitat: <2250 m. On the ground in more or less wooded areas.

16 **SOMALI GOLDEN-BREASTED BUNTING** *Emberiza poliopleura* L 14 cm. Note white underparts. Mantle streaked cream, rufous and black. Habitat: <1250 m. Dry open bushed and wooded areas.

17 **BROWN-RUMPED BUNTING** *Emberiza forbesi* L 15 cm. Note brown upperparts faintly streaked darker and without white. Habitat: 1000-2000 m. Dry, open, bushed and wooded areas.

18 **CABINIS'S BUNTING** *Emberiza cabanisi* L 15 cm. Race *c. cabanisi* (a) in Uganda, race *orientalis* (b) in Tanzania. Habitat: 250-2000 m. On the ground in open wood- and bushland, often near water.

19 **SOCOTRA MOUNTAIN BUNTING** *Emberiza socotrana* L 15 cm. Very much like Southern Rock Bunting, which is not present on Socotra Island. Habitat: >1500 m. E (Socotra)

20 **ORTOLAN BUNTING** *Emberiza hortulana* L 15 cm. Note pale eye-ring and olive-yellow head and rump. Habitat: short-grassed areas with some trees and bush. NM

21 **CRETZSCHMAR'S BUNTING** *Emberiza caesia* L 15 cm. Note pale eye-ring and rusty colouring. Habitat: dry wooded and bushed areas, often near settlement. NM

22 **CINEREOUS BUNTING** *Emberiza cineracea* L 15 cm. Note narrow eye-ring, pale yellow-olive head and grey (not pinkish) bill. Habitat: dry open areas, especially near coast. NM

95

Plate 96

1 **YELLOW-CROWNED CANARY** *Serinus canicollis* L 13 cm. Note unstreaked head of ♂ and black-and-yellow wing. Habitat: 1500-4500 m. Forest edges, wood- and bushland, bamboo, moorland and garden

2 **BLACK-HEADED SISKIN** *Serinus nigriceps* L 12 cm. Habitat: >1500 m. Grass- and moorland with giant heath patches. [E] (Ethiopia)

3 **AFRICAN CITRIL** *Serinus citrinelloides* L 12 cm. Only one race shown; other races may have grey (n black) faces. Habitat: 1000-3500 m. Forest edges, bamboo and wooded and bushed areas, including cultivation and gardens.

4 **PAPYRUS SERIN** *Serinus koliensis* L 12 cm. Very difficult to distinguish from other serins except by habitat. Habitat: 750-1750 m. Papyrus.

5 **YELLOW-FRONTED SERIN** *Serinus mozambicus* L 12 cm. Note black malar stripe and yellow underparts including lower belly and under tail-coverts. Habitat: <2500 m. More or less wooded and bushed natural and cultivated areas, including gardens. Voice: high, rapid, fluted variations of '*pipêeuh-wêeh*'.

6 **WHITE-BELLIED SERIN** *Serinus dorsostriatus* L 13 cm. Note dark (not black) malar stripe. Belly centre and under tail-coverts white. Habitat: 250-1500(&>) m. Dry, more or less wooded and bushed mainly natural habitats.

7 **WHITE-THROATED SERIN** *Serinus xanthopygius* L 11 cm. (Species level as by Short.) Note yello rump and white chin. Habitat: >750 m. Dry, open and bushed areas.

8 **YELLOW-RUMPED SERIN** *Serinus atrogularis* L 10 cm. Note yellow rump and dark-mottled throa Habitat: <2000 m. Wooded and bushed areas. Voice: mid-high, rapid, warbled medley of fluted notes, trills and rolls.

9 **REICHENOW'S SERIN** *Serinus reichenowi* L 11 cm. Note yellow rump, striped chest and faint mala stripe. Habitat: wooded and bushed areas.

10 **ANKOBER SERIN** *Serinus ankoberensis* L 11 cm. (Species discovered in 1976.) Overall ground colour almost white. Habitat: 3000 m. Steep cliffs with some shrub. E (Ethiopia)

11 **WHITE-RUMPED SERIN** *Serinus leucopygius* L 10 cm. Note white rump and pale colouring. Habitat: 500-1000 m. Wooded and bushed, natural and cultivated areas including gardens.

12 **YELLOW-THROATED SERIN** *Serinus flavigula* L 11 cm. Note yellow rump and throat. Habitat: wooded and bushed areas with some rough grass. E (Ethiopia)

13 **SALVADORI'S SERIN** *Serinus xantholaemus* L 14 cm. (Species discovered in 1980.) Note yellow rump. Yellow throat divided by black line. Habitat: dry rocky areas with some trees and shrub.

14 **BRIMSTONE SERIN** *Serinus sulphuratus* L 15 cm. Note complicated face pattern. Habitat: <2500 n Moist, open, wooded and bushed areas including suburban gardens. Voice: very high, rather short warbl medleys of up-and-down flutes, trills and rolls.

15 **GROSBEAK-SERIN** *Serinus donaldsoni* L 15 cm. Race *buchanani* (a) in N Kenya, Ethiopia and Somalia, race *d. donaldsoni* (b) in C and S Kenya, S Somalia and Tanzania. Note heavy bill. Habitat: <1500(&>) m. Dry wooded and bushed areas.

16 **STREAKY-HEADED SERIN** *Serinus gularis* L 14 cm. Forehead and crown striped black and white. Underparts unstreaked. Habitat: 1000-2000 m. Dry woodland, miombo and gardens.

17 **STRIPE-BREASTED SERIN** *Serinus reichardi* L 14 cm. Chest loosely streaked black. Habitat: 500-1500 m. Miombo. E (Ethiopia)

18 **BROWN-RUMPED SERIN** *Serinus tristriatus* L 13 cm. Note narrow white eyebrow. Habitat: >1500 m. Forest edges.

19 **BLACK-EARED SERIN** *Serinus mennelli* L 14 cm. Note dark cheek, white wing-bars and striped breast. Habitat: 1000-1500 m. Miombo.

20 **THICK-BILLED SERIN** *Serinus burtoni* L 15 cm. Race *tanganjicae* (a) in Uganda and W Kenya, ♀ of race *melanochrous* (b). Races *albifrons* and *b. burtoni* (neither depicted) with white forehead. Note dark colouring, pale eyebrow, chin streaks, wing-bars and yellow-edged flight feathers. Habitat: 1500(&<)-3000 m. Undergrowth of montane forest and bamboo.

21 **STREAKY SERIN** *Serinus striolatus* L 15 cm. Note complicated face pattern. Greenish edges of flig feathers not always distinct. Habitat: 1250-4500 m. Including forest edges, woodland, gardens and par

22 **ORIOLE-FINCH** *Linurgus olivaceus* L 13 cm. Habitat: 1500-3000 m. Undergrowth at forest edges.

23 **WARSANGLI LINNET** *Acanthis johannis* L 13 cm. Habitat: >1750 m. Dry, stony and rocky areas wi some trees and scrub. E (Somalia)

24 **GOLDEN-WINGED GROSBEAK** *Rhynchostruthus socotranus* L 15 cm. Race *s. socotranus* (a) on Socotra Island, race *louisae* (b) in N Somalia. Habitat: dry wooded areas.

96

DISTRIBUTION MAPS

The first and most important step when trying to identify an unknown species is by comparing it with the plates. Confirmation of an identification is possible when the bird is seen in its described habitat.

Following is a distribution map for each of the species described and illustrated in the book. For a technical explanation of the maps see pp. 9 and 10 under 'Occurrence'. There are 1488 maps in all, each referenced to its species by the plate number and species number (e.g. species number 4 on plate 20 is 20.4). These maps have their own restrictions, but if you more or less know what your position is with the help of a larger scale map opposite, the information about range and status provided here can support or weaken your identification.

Look for instance at map 90.9 which gives the range of a typical highland species with its many races (including Reichenow's Weaver which might be one of the five most common birds in Nairobi); according to the distribution map it is highly unlikely if not impossible to see it in coastal areas, in Mombassa for instance.

To take another example, when you see a plain sparrow-like bird and you think it is a petronia, the maps can help you to decide that it is a Yellow-spotted Petronia (88.10) rather than a Pale Petronia (88.12) if the bird is in Kenya; or that it is probably Black-bellied Bustard (27.6) and not Hartlaub's Bustard (27.9) that you see in Nairobi National Park because the darker shading on the map indicates that the first species is more common in the Kenyan Highlands.

The larger annotated map gives some information about the positioning of the localities mentioned in the text and about the basic structure of the eastern African landscape. Eastern Africa is in many aspects a very interesting part of the world. One of the most breathtaking views that you can expect to see in your life is that of the rift valley from the Ngong Hills near Nairobi. This valley, with branches east and west of Uganda, is 50–100 km wide and splits near Djibouti, to one side via the Red Sea into the Dead Sea of Jordan, and to the other side north and around Socotra Island into the Indian Ocean. The valley is actually a system of fissures in the earth's crust caused by upwelling magma from deep within the earth's mantle, which forces eastern Africa up and apart. Via 'leaks' in the earth's crust this magma formed the now sleeping volcanoes Mount Kenya, Mount Elgon and Mount Kilimanjaro. The fissures are still widening very slowly and after many millions of years the Ngong Hills will be at the edge of a sea, separating eastern Africa from the rest of the continent.

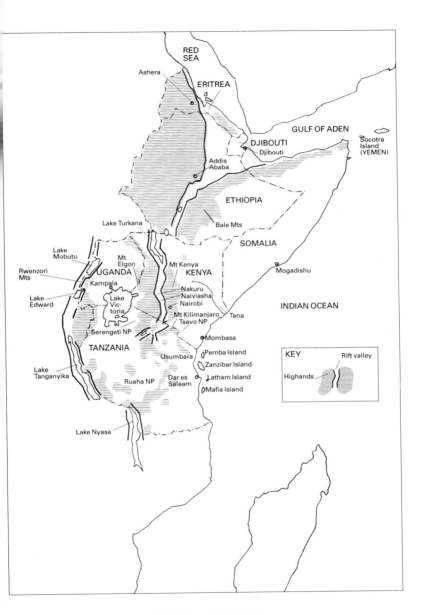

EASTERN AFRICA

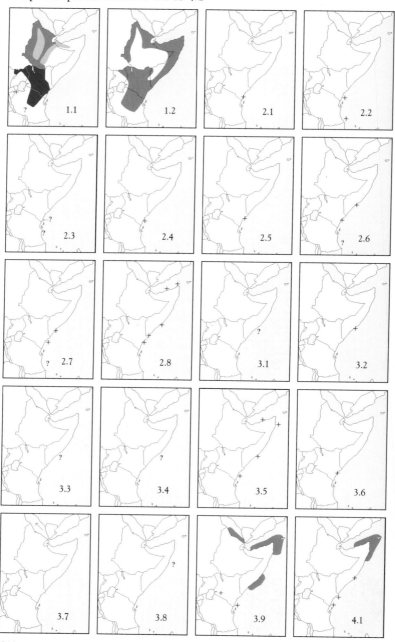

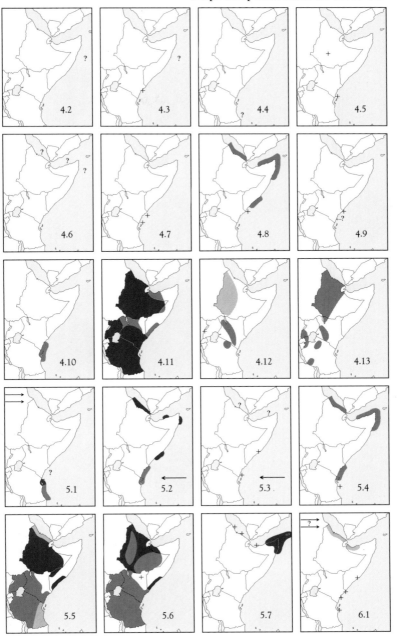

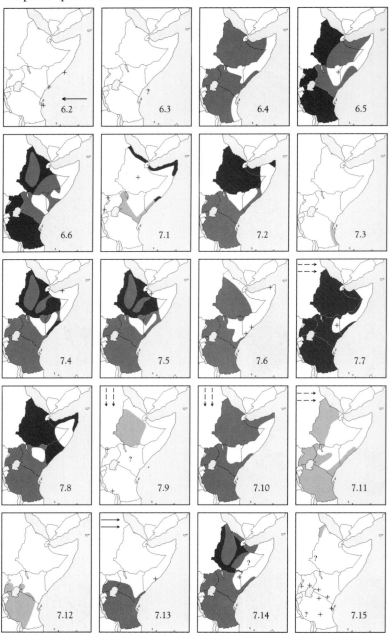

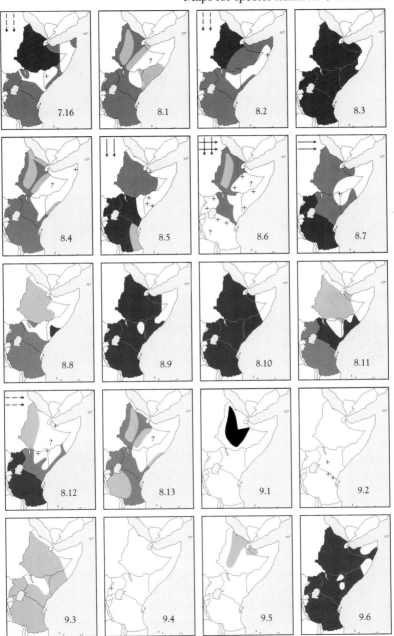

Maps for species numbers 9.7 to 10.14

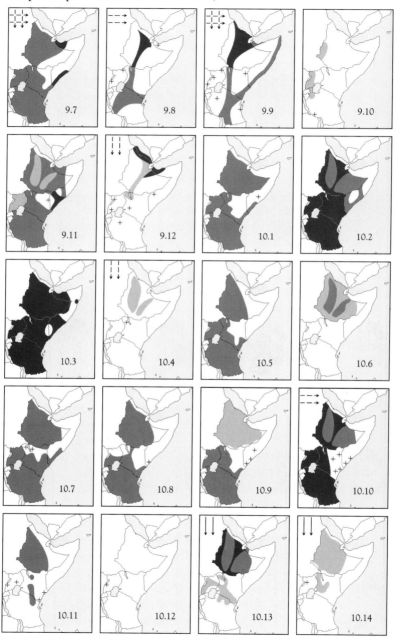

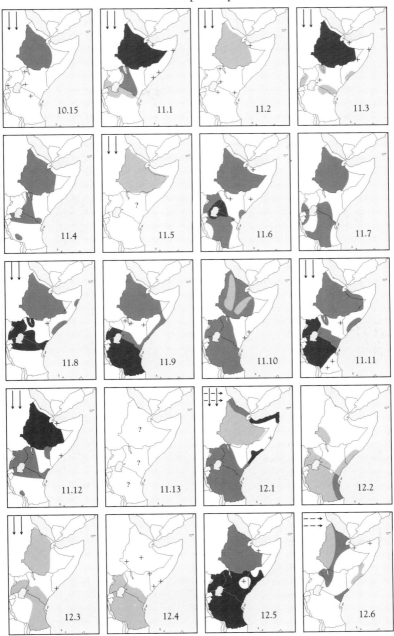

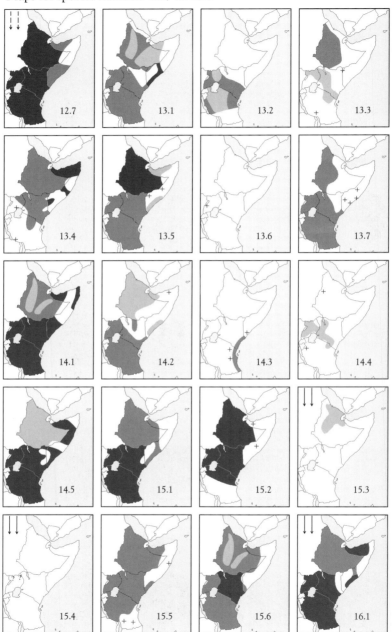

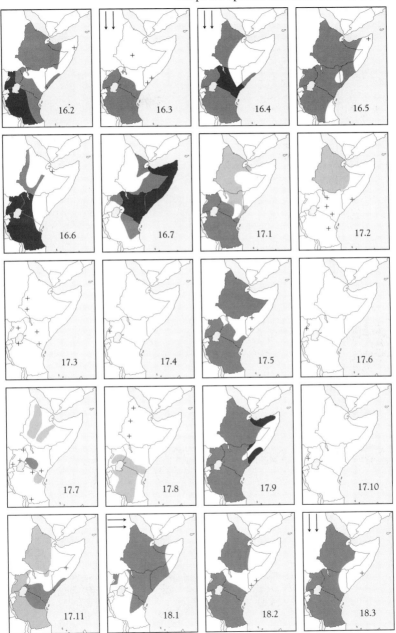

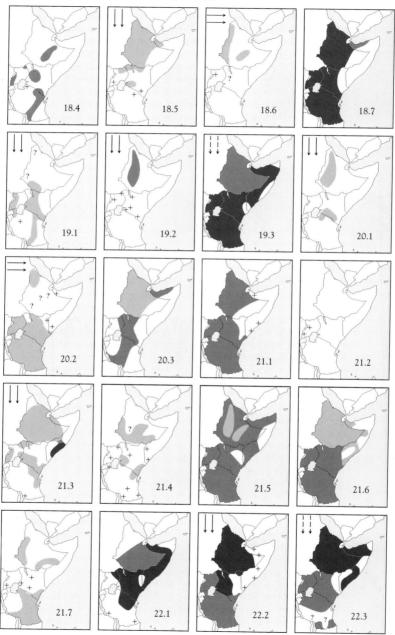

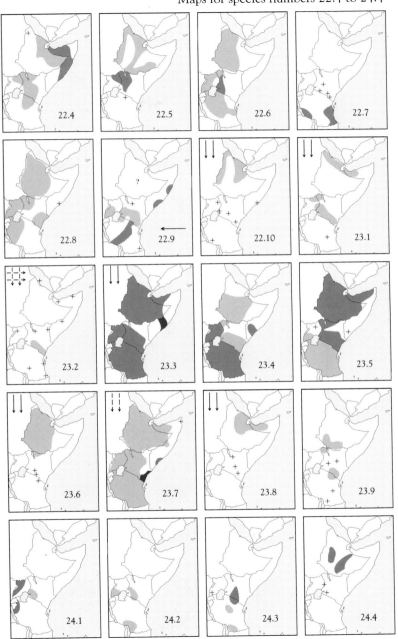

Maps for species numbers 24.5 to 25.2

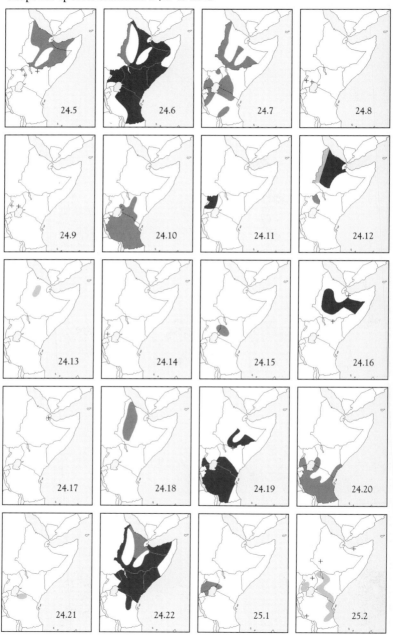

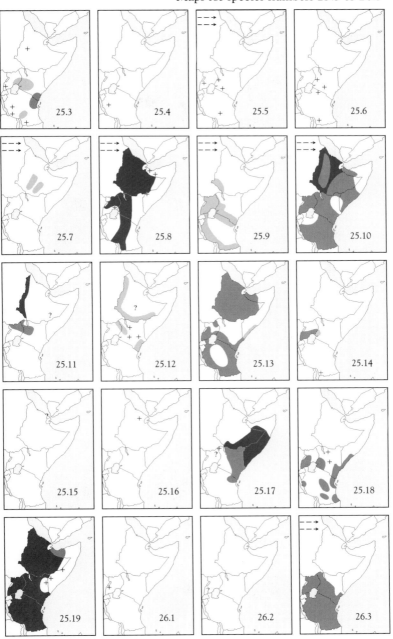

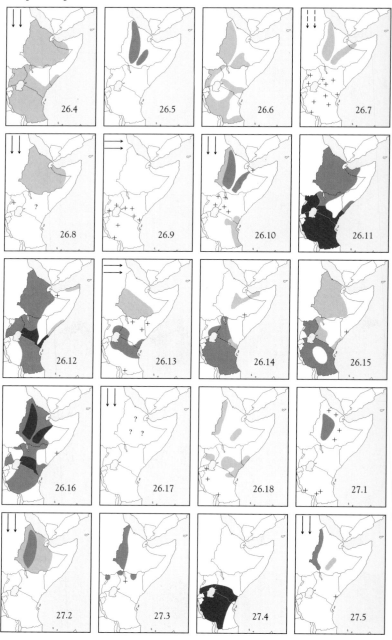

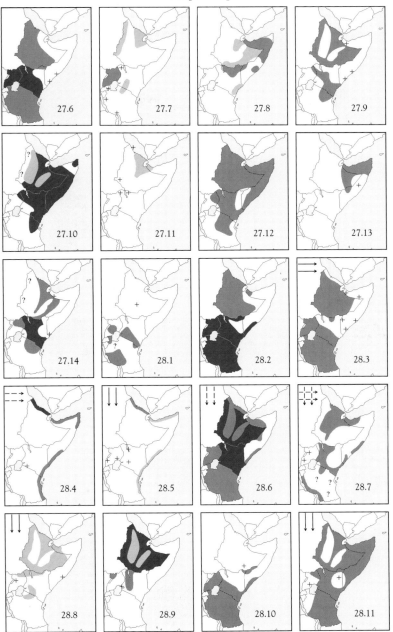

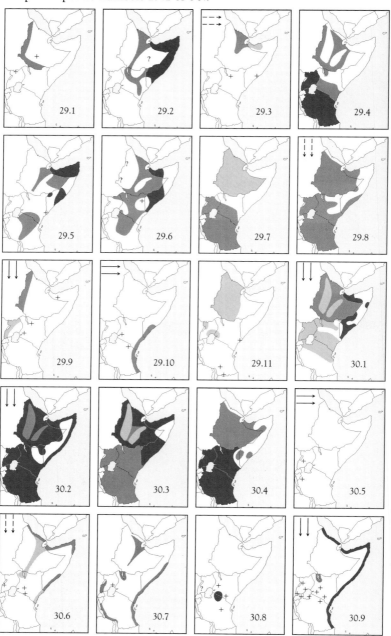

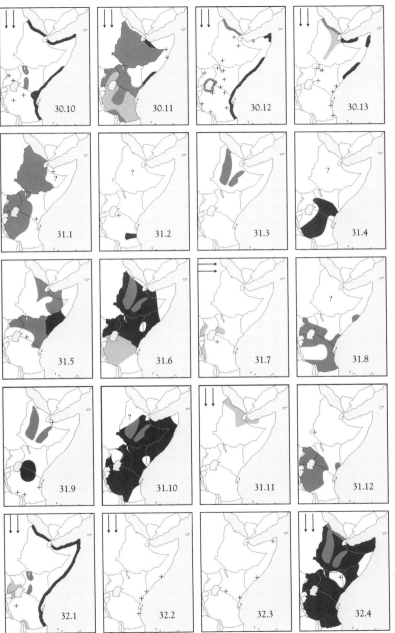

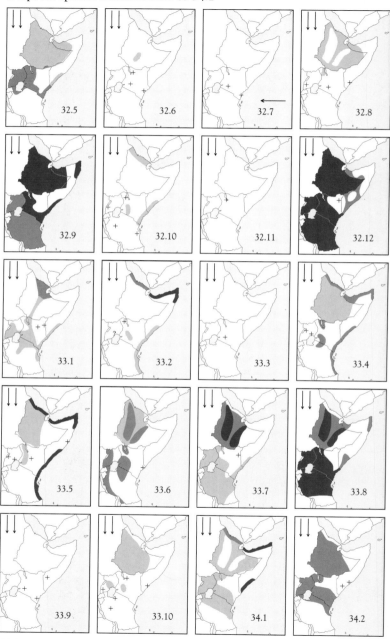

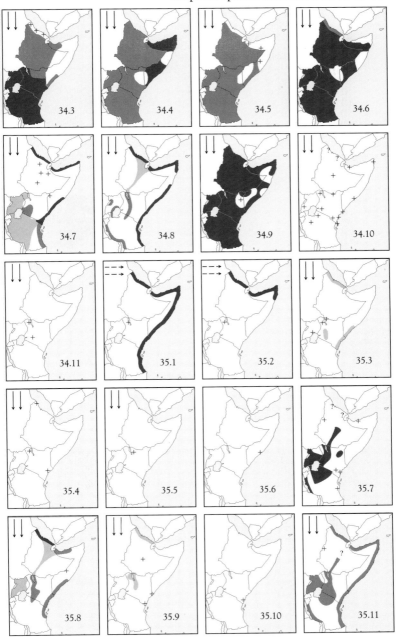

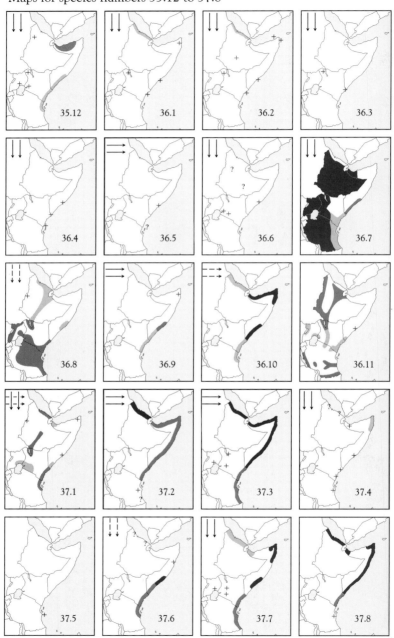

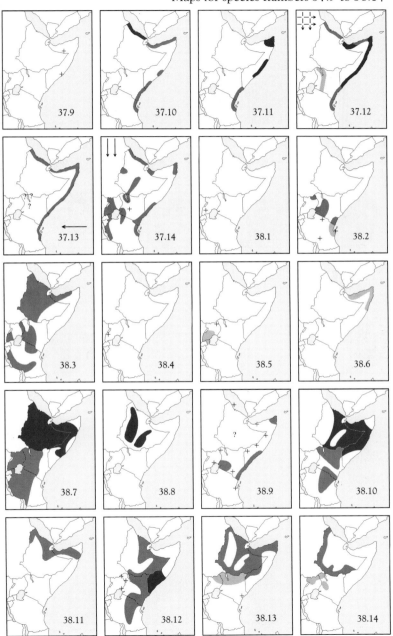

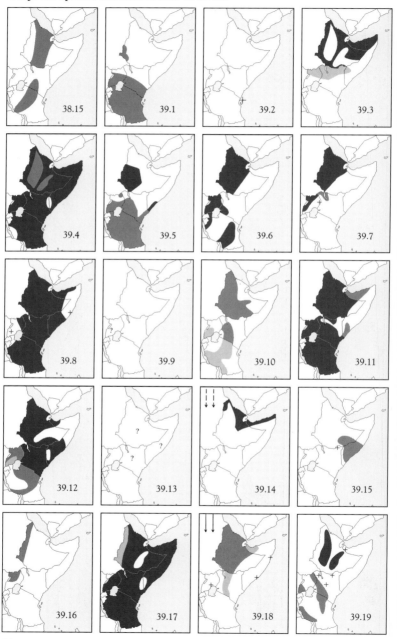

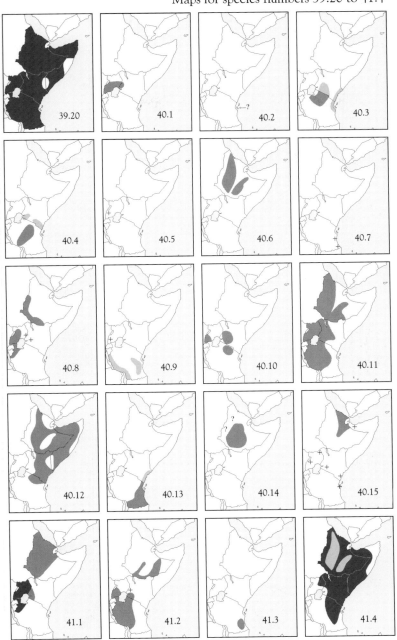

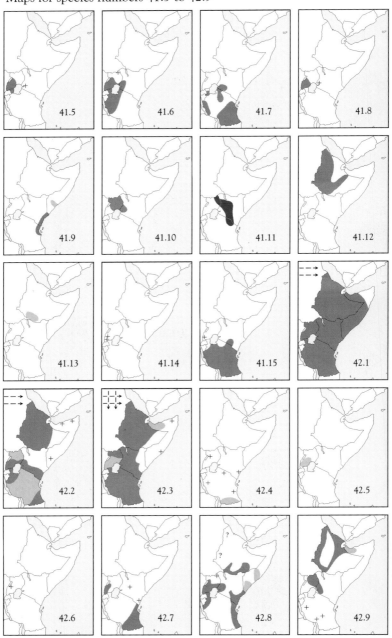

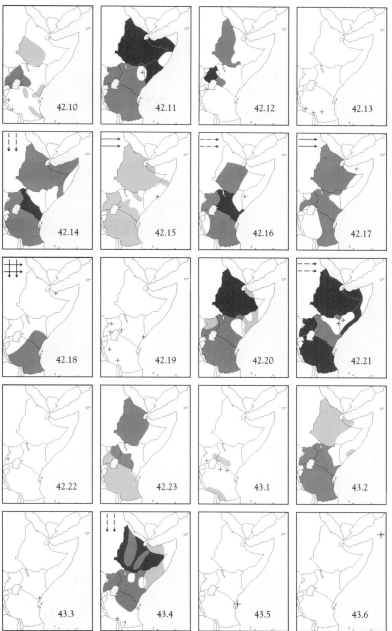

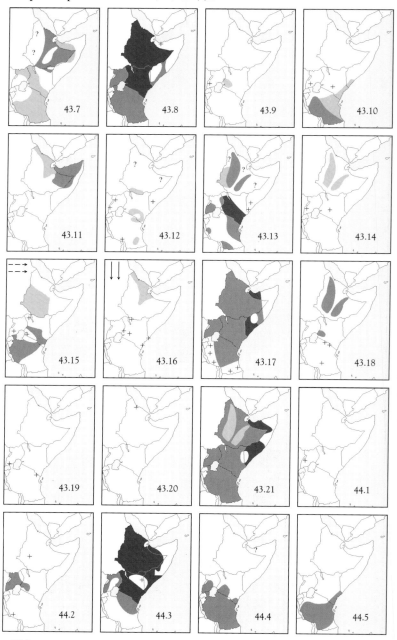

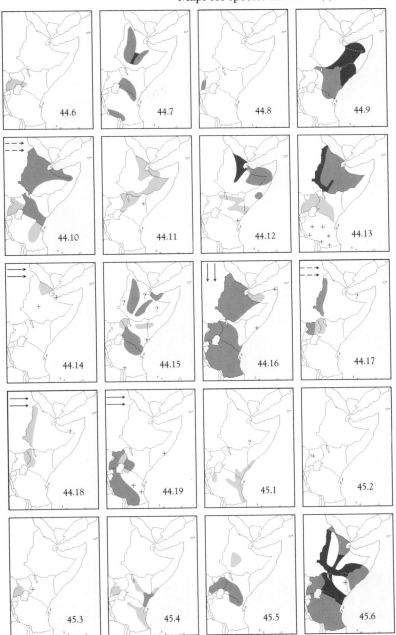

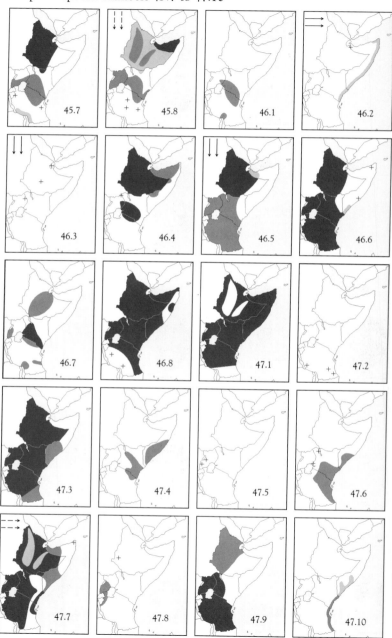

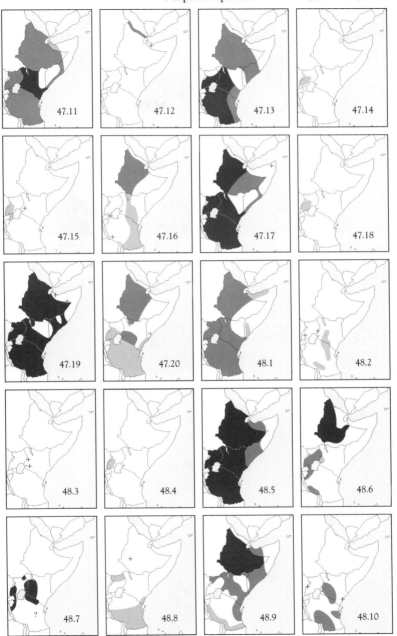

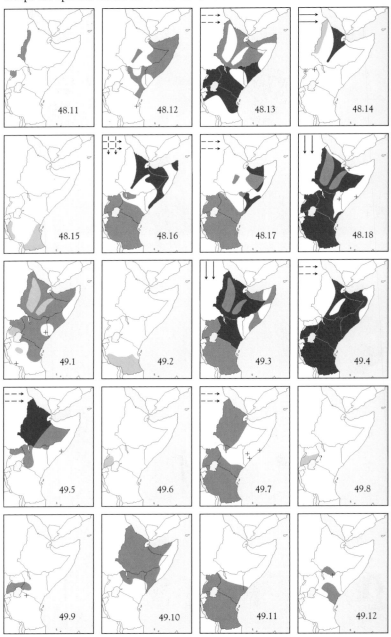

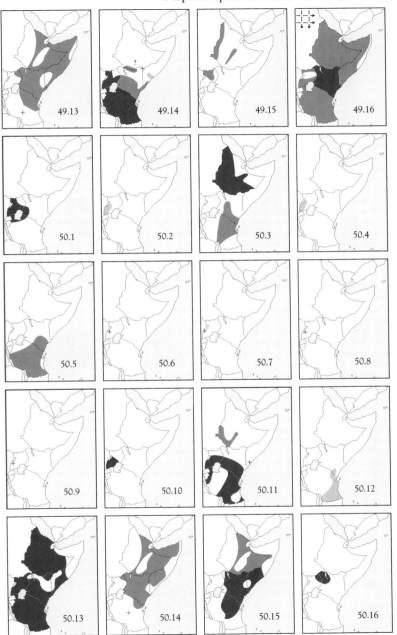

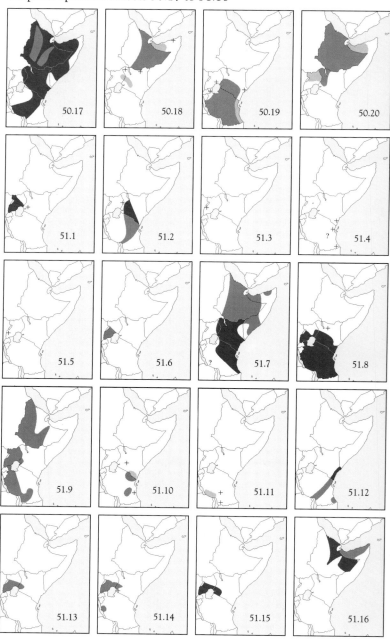

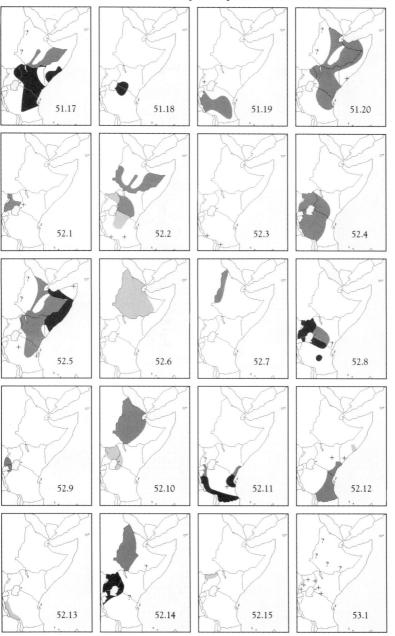

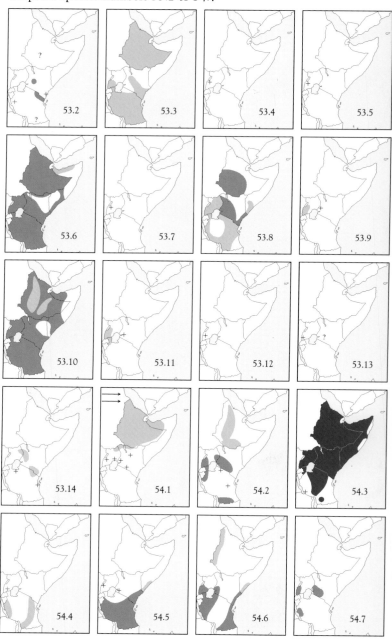

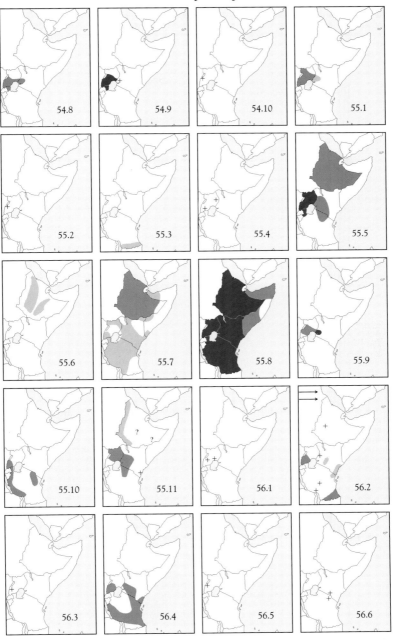

Maps for species numbers 56.7 to 57.4

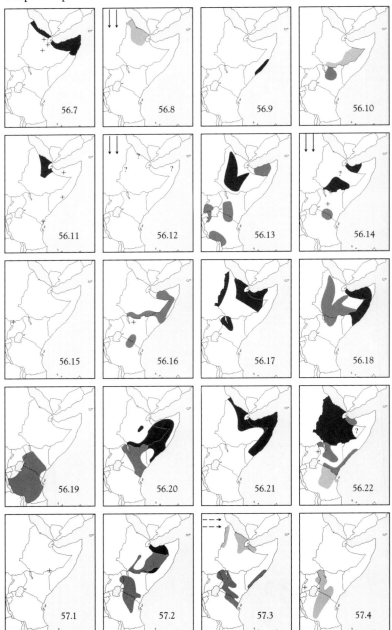

244

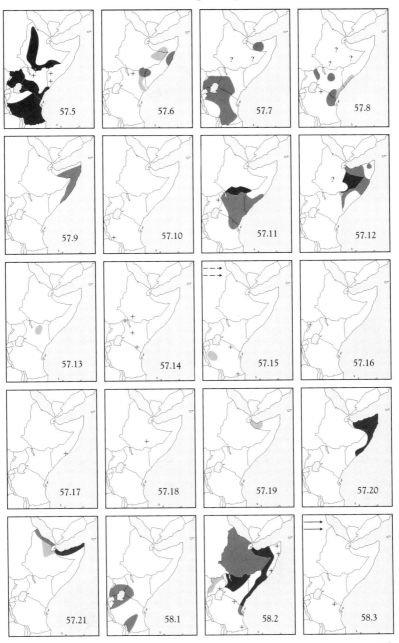

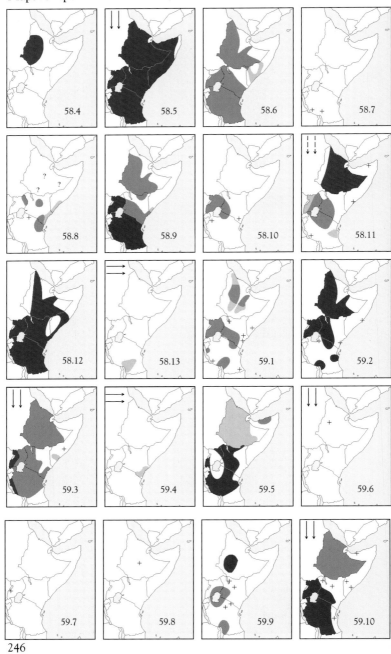

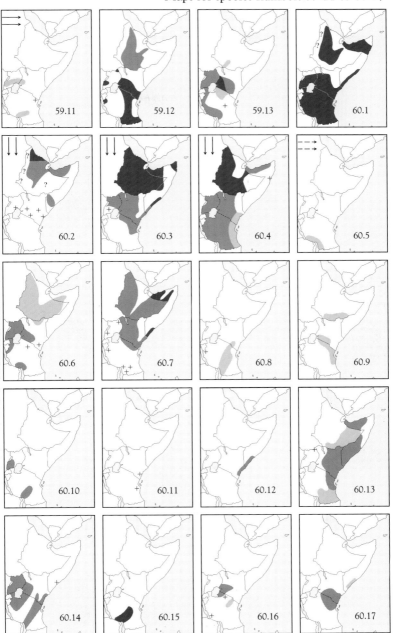

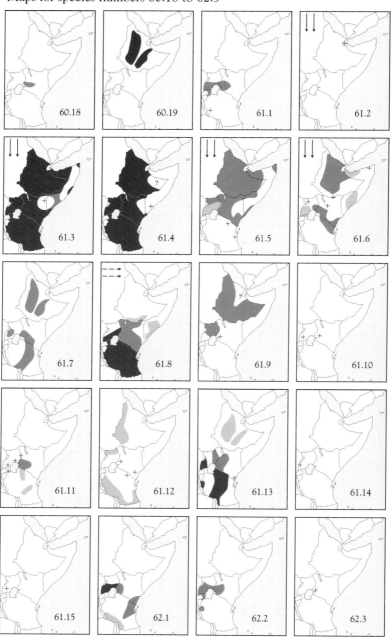

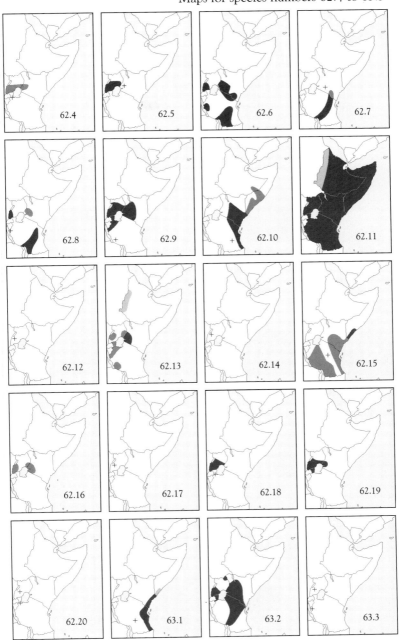

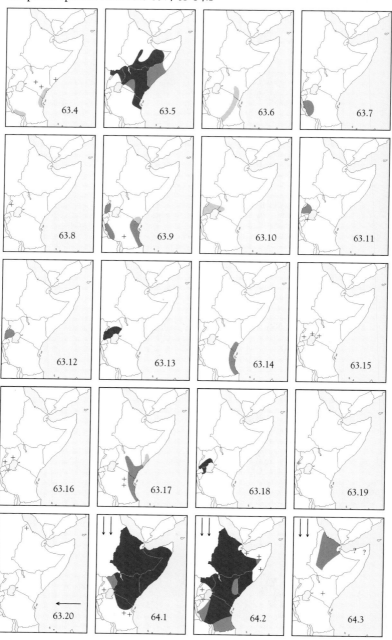

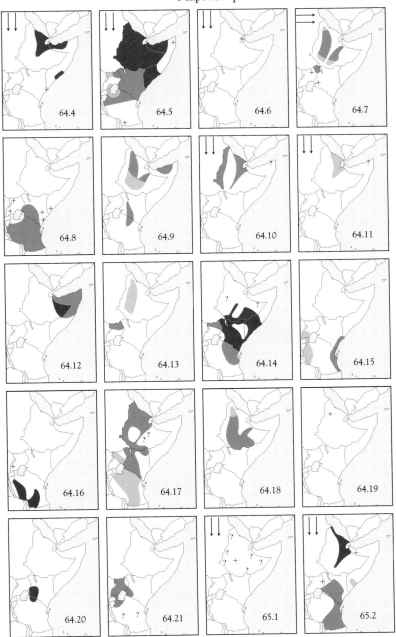

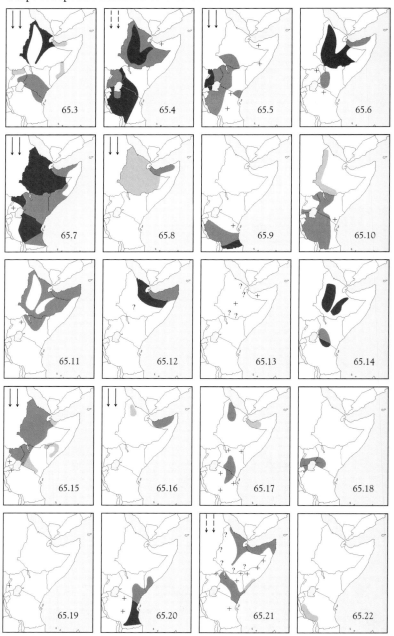

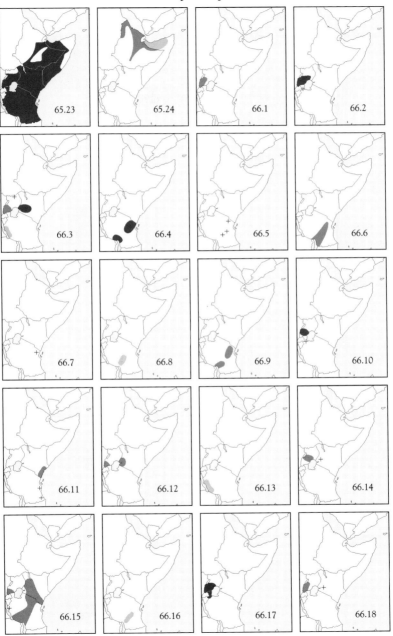

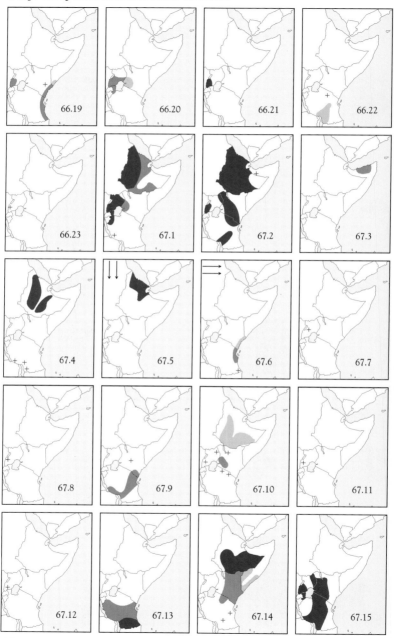

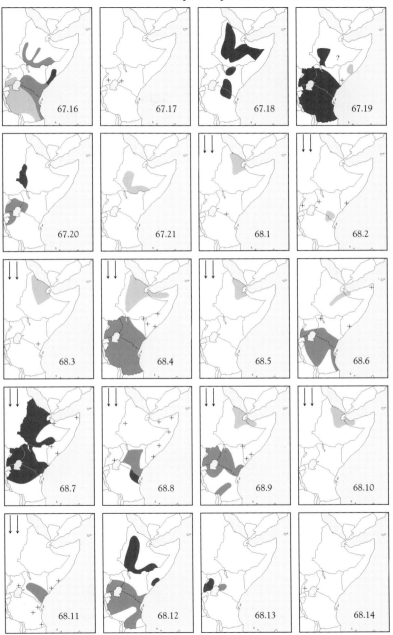

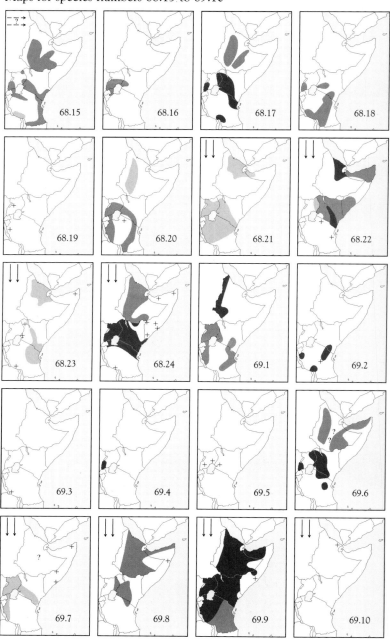

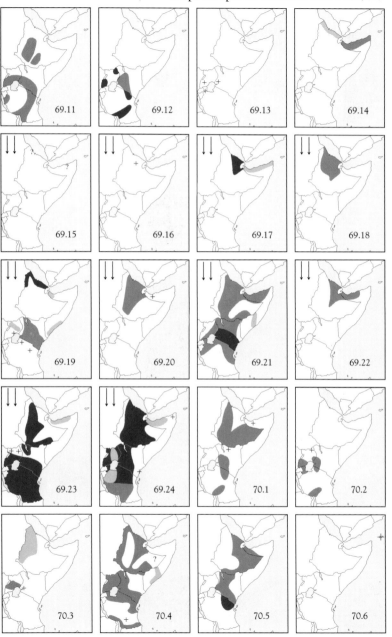

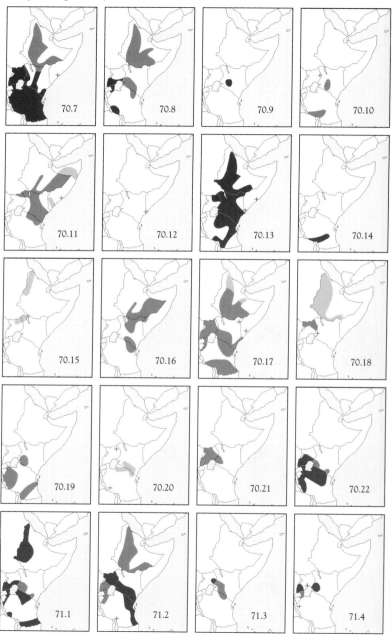

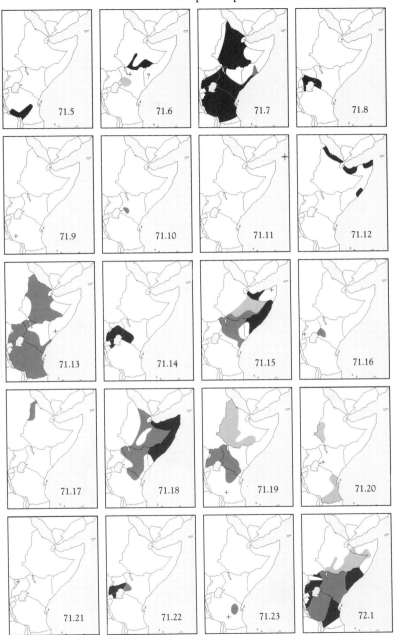

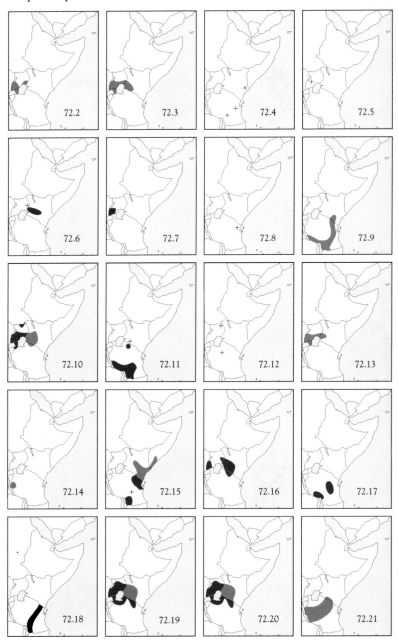

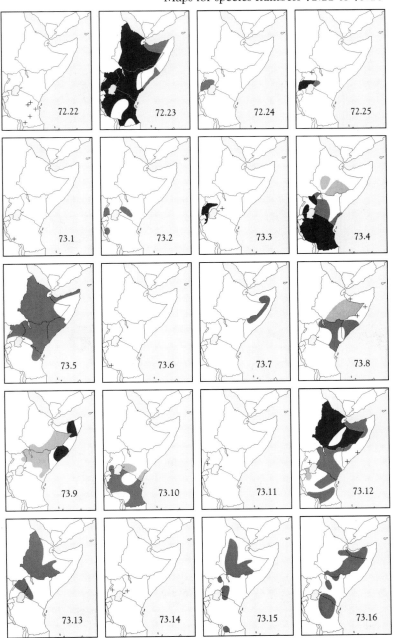

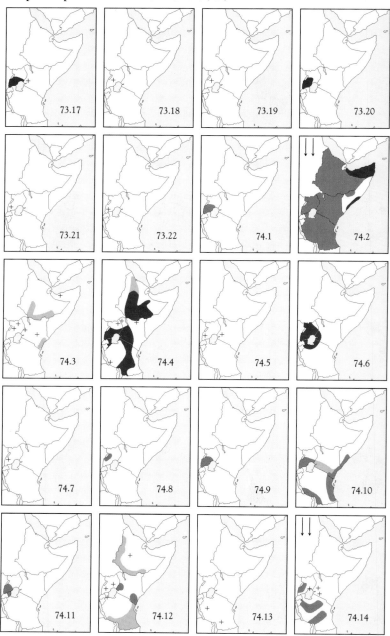

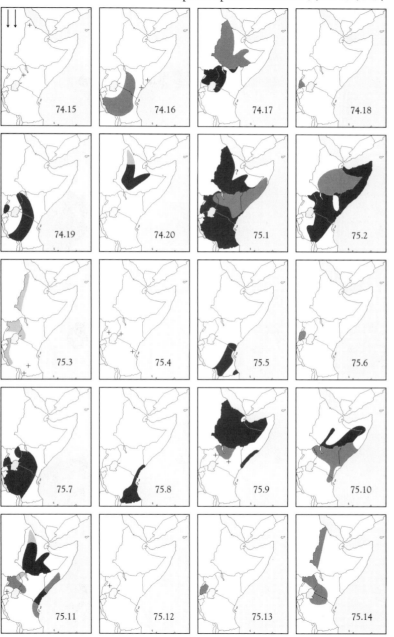

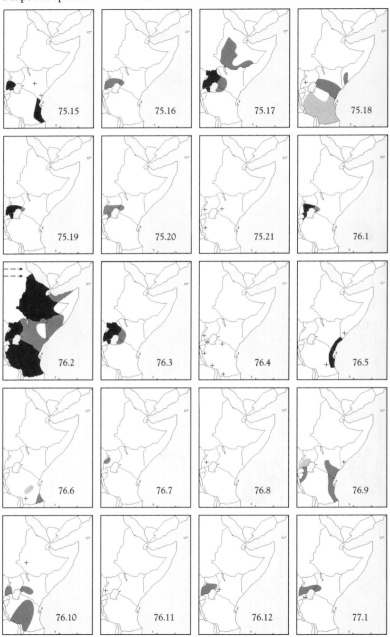

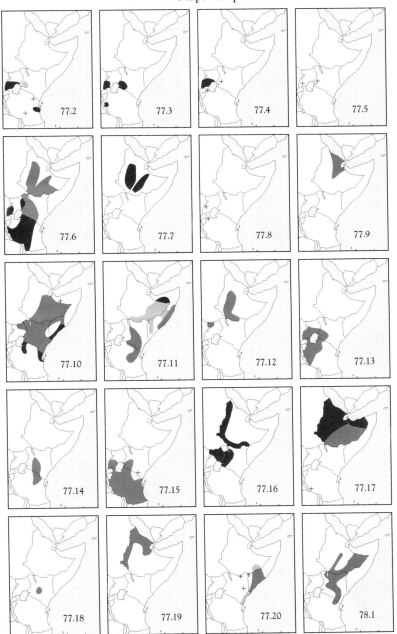

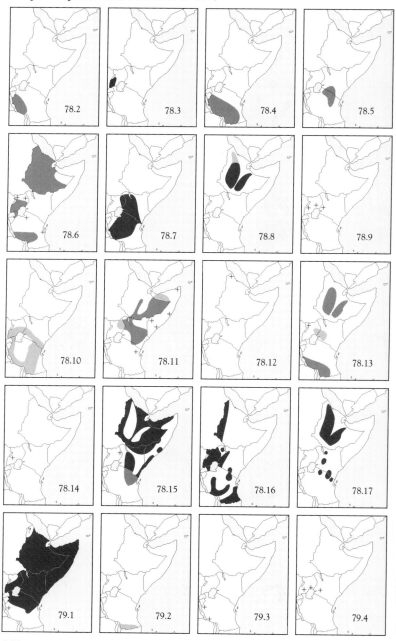

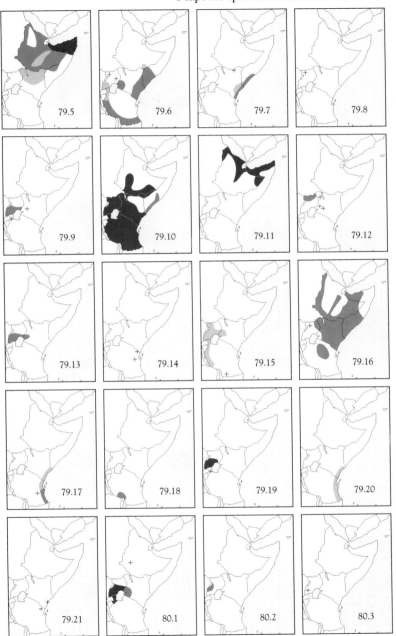

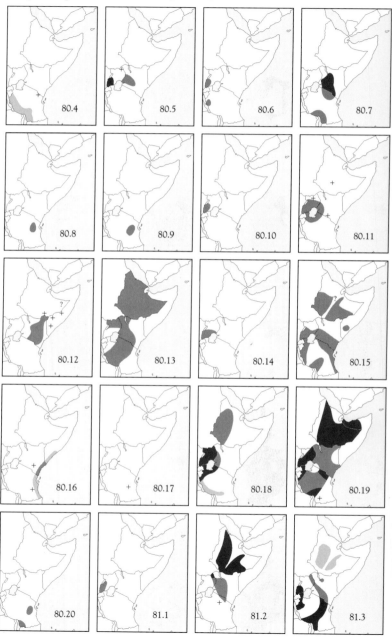

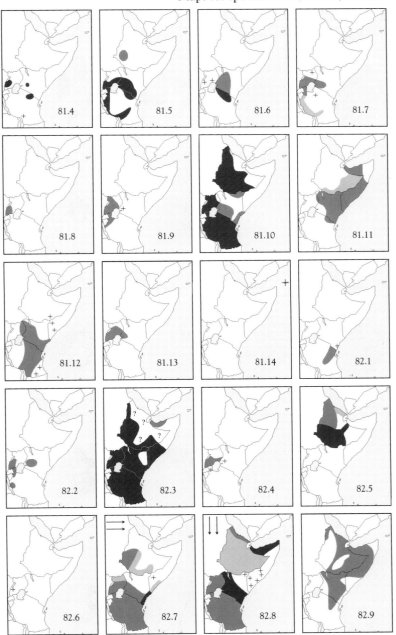

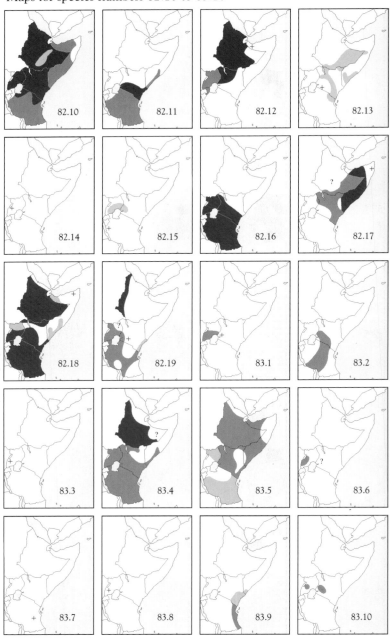

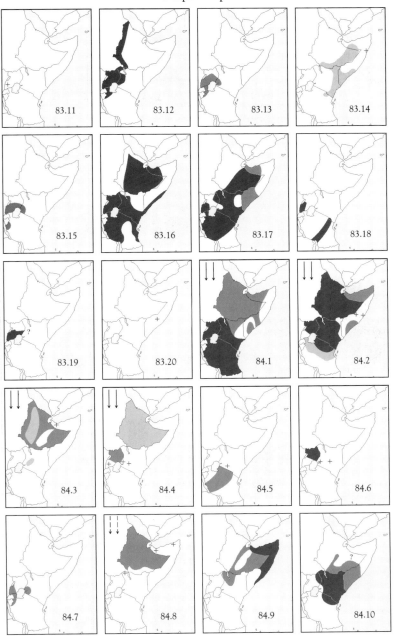

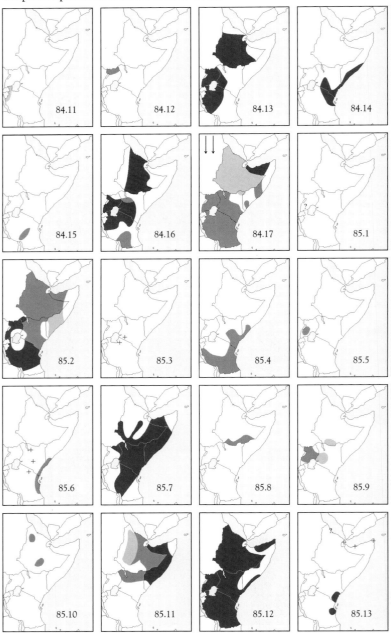

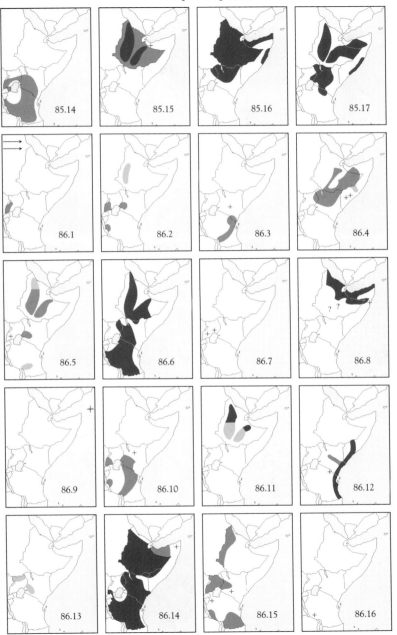

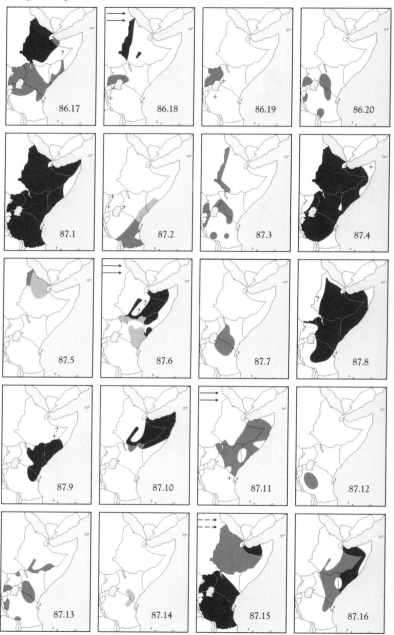

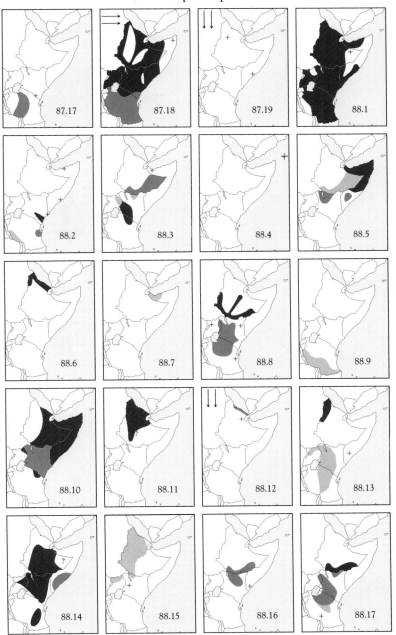

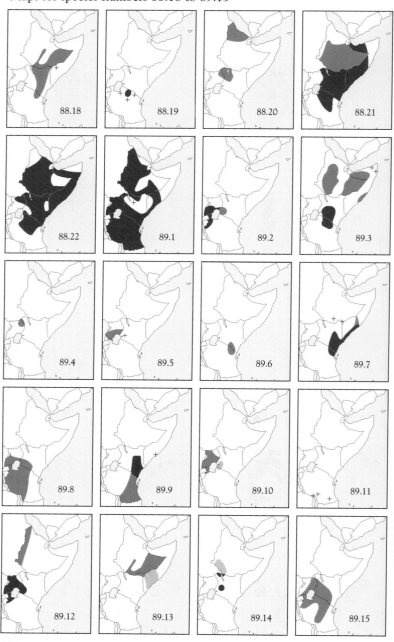

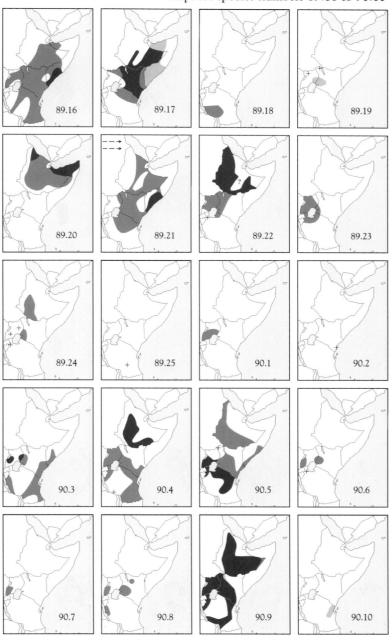

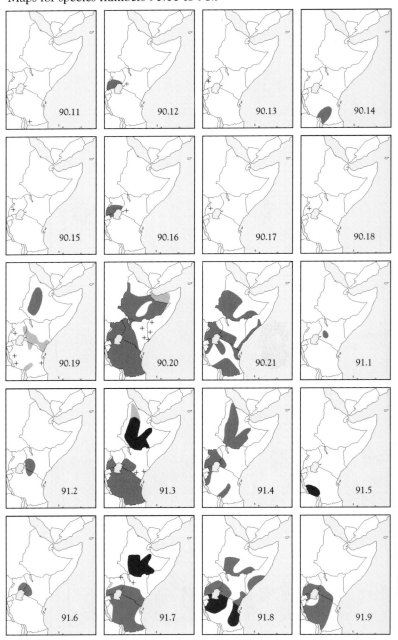

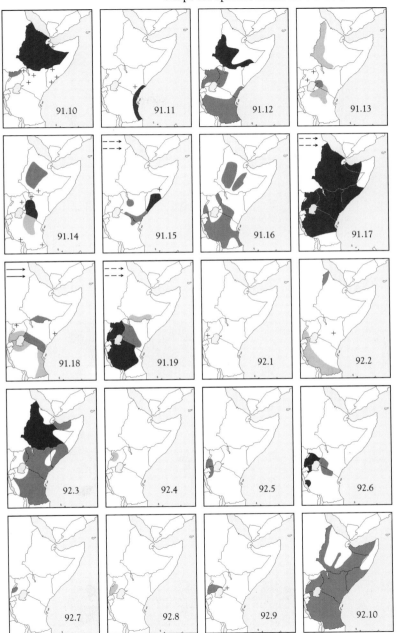

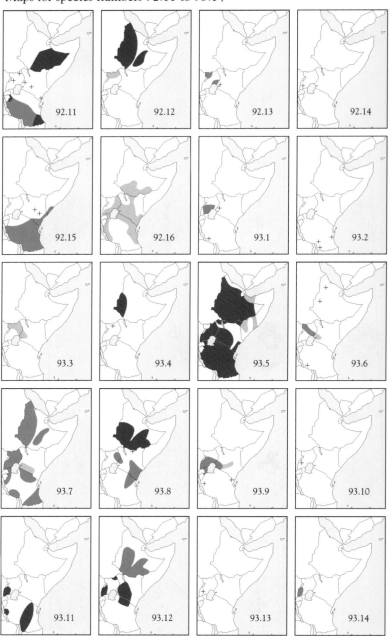

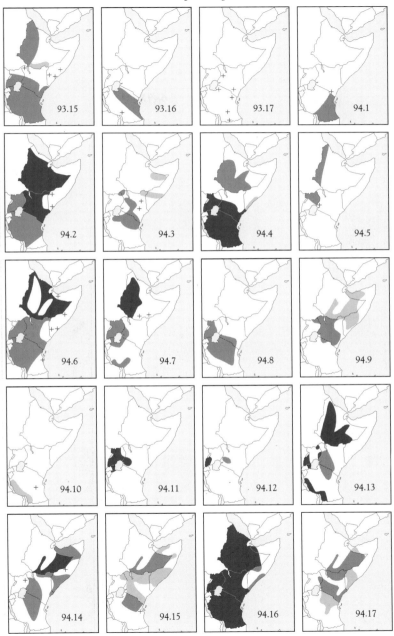

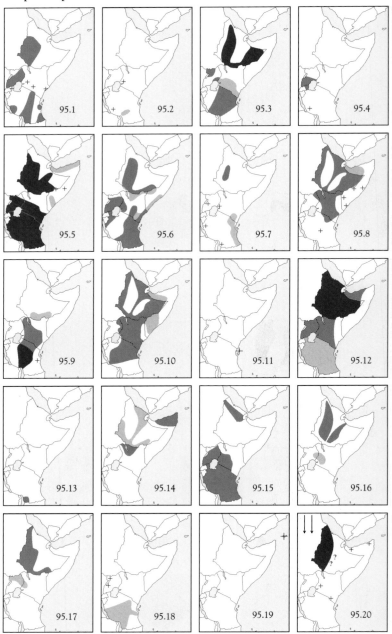

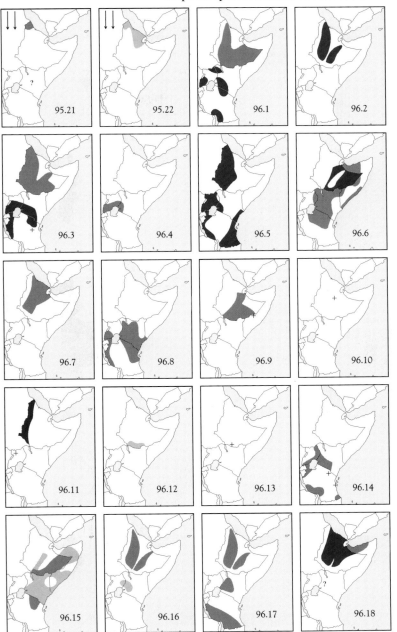

Maps for species numbers 96.19 to 96.24

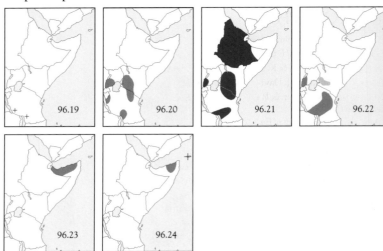

BIBLIOGRAPHY and list of further reading

J. S. Ash & J. E. Miskell, *Birds of Somalia* (Nairobi, EANHS, 1983).

P. L. Britton (ed.), *Birds of East Africa* (Nairobi, EANHS, 1980).

L. H. Brown, E. K. Urban & K. Newman, *The Birds of Africa* (vol. I) (London, 1982).

P. Clement , A. Harris & J. Davis, *Finches and Sparrows* (London, 1993).

P. J. Ginn, W. G. Mcilleron & P. Le S. Milstein, *The Complete Book of Southern African Birds* (Cape Town, 1989).

C. A. W. Guggisberg, *Birds of East Africa* (Nairobi, 1980 [vol. I], 1986 [vol. II]).

B. P. Hall & R. E. Moreau, *An Atlas of Speciation in African Passerine Birds* (London, 1970).

P. Harrison, *Seabirds* (Beckenham, 1985).

P. Hayman, J. Marchant & T. Prater, *Shorebirds* (Boston, 1986).

C. Hilary Fry, S. Keith & E. K. Urban, *The Birds of Africa* (vol. III) (London, 1988).

L. Johnsson, *Birds of Europe* (London, 1992).

S. Keith, E. K. Urban & C. Hilary Fry, *The Birds of Africa* (vol. IV) (London, 1992).

A. Lewis, & D. Pomeroy, *A Bird Atlas of Kenya* (Rotterdam,1989).

G. L. Maclean, *Roberts' Birds of Southern Africa* (Cape Town,1984).

C. W. Mackworth-Praed, & C. H. B. Grant, *African Handbook of Birds* (London, 1981 [series I vol. I], 1980 [series I vol. II]).

K. Newman, *Birds of Southern Africa* (Johannesburg, 1988).

W. Serle, G. J. Morel & W. Hartwig, *A Field Guide to the Birds of West Africa* (London, 1986).

L. L. Short, J. F. M. Horne & C. Muringo-Gichuki, *An Annotated Check-list of the Birds of East Africa* (Los Angeles, 1990).

E. K. Urban, C. Hilary Fry & S. Keith, *The Birds of Africa* (vol. II) (London, 1986).

E. K. Urban & L. H. Brown, *A Checklist of the Birds of Ethiopia* (Addis Ababa, 1971).

K. H. Voous, *List of Recent Holarctic Bird Species* (London, 1977).

J. G. Williams & N. Arlott, *A Field Guide to the Birds of East Africa* (London, 1981).

Journals in which the main information about birds in Eastern Africa is published:

Alauda, Société d'Etudes Ornithologiques, Paris.

Scopus, Ornithological Sub-Committee of the East Africa National History Society, Nairobi.

Le Gerfaut, Institut Royal des Sciences Naturelles de Belgique, Brussels.

The Ibis, British Ornithologists Union, London.

Recorded bird sounds of African birds can be found on the following discs and tapes:

AIT, *Birds of Kenya* (featuring 30 species). Cassette for sale in Nairobi book shops.

C. Chappuis, *Illustration Sonore de Problèmes Bioacoustiques posés par les Oiseaux de la Zone Ethiopienne*. Alauda Supplement sonore (11 LP records featuring 460 species).

S. Keith. *Birds of the African Rain Forests* (2 cassettes featuring 92 species).

G. Gibbon, *Southern African Bird Sounds* (6 cassettes featuring 920 species).

The African Bird Club was established in 1994 to provide a worldwide focus for African ornithology. The club publishes a twice-yearly bulletin with articles on identification of difficult groups, bird inventories of certain areas, reports on recent sightings, reviews on new publications etc. It features colour illustrations and photographs. Further details can be obtained from the Membership Secretary, African Bird Club, c/o Birdlife International, Wellbrook Court, Girton Road, Cambridge CB3 ONA, U. K.

Index of scientific names

Numbers refer to the relevant plate, followed by the number of the bird on that plate.

287

288

Index of common names

Numbers refer to the relevant plate, followed by the number of the bird on that plate.